ARCTIC HELL-SHIP

William Barr

ARCTIC
HELL-SHIP

THE VOYAGE OF HMS *ENTERPRISE* 1850–1855

THE UNIVERSITY
OF ALBERTA PRESS

Published by

The University of Alberta Press
Ring House 2
Edmonton, Alberta, Canada T6G 2E1

William Barr copyright © 2007
ISBN 978-0-88864-472-5

Library and Archives Canada Cataloguing in Publication

Barr, William, 1940–
    Arctic Hell-ship : the voyage of HMS Enterprise, 1850–55 / William Barr.

ISBN-13: 978-0-88864-472-5
ISBN-10: 0-88864-472-8

    1. Collinson, Richard, Sir, 1811–1883. 2. Franklin, John, Sir, 1786–1847.
3. Enterprise (Ship). 4. Arctic regions—Discovery and exploration—British.
5. Canada, Northern—Discovery and exploration—British. 6. Northwest
Passage—Discovery and exploration—British. I. Title.

G665 1850.B37 2007   910.9163'27   C2006-906917-4

The University of Alberta Press is committed to protecting our natural environment. As part of our efforts,
this book is printed on Enviro Paper: it contains 100% post-consumer recycled fibres and is acid- and
chlorine-free.

The University of Alberta Press gratefully acknowledges the support received for its publishing program from
The Canada Council for the Arts. The University of Alberta Press also gratefully acknowledges the financial
support of the Government of Canada through the Book Publishing Industry Development Program (BPIDP)
and from the Alberta Foundation for the Arts for its publishing activities.

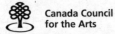

Canada Council   Conseil des Arts
for the Arts   du Canada

Contents

Maps and Illustrations

FOREWORD

The SEARCH FOR SIR JOHN FRANKLIN'S EXPEDITION was not only one of the most important events in the history of nineteenth-century arctic America, but it also captured the attention of many persons in the western world and beyond. Although it was primarily a British endeavour, men and women of several nations donated their energies and their treasure—and occasionally their own lives—to save the lives of Franklin and his crew.

To date, about 1,500 books and articles have been published about the Franklin expedition and the Franklin search, and the number continues to grow. At the core of this substantial body of literature are the narratives of the searchers themselves. For the most part, these accounts resonate with good will, a unity of spirit, and a sense of urgency about the noble task before them.

It is understandable that within this high-minded and generous effort most accounts omit references to awkward or embarrassing events. Although the search was largely carried out by highly competent persons in often difficult circumstances, it is inevitable that in any effort involving so many ships and men some things would go wrong. Yet there are few allusions to such unpleasant events as blunders, cowardice, poor judgement, drunkenness, or abusive behaviour; rather, when things go wrong in the narratives, the blame is often put on a hostile environment or simple bad luck.

Professor William Barr's history of HMS *Enterprise*'s voyage of 1850 to 1855 is an exception. Through careful research and analysis, Professor Barr has looked beyond the sanitized official accounts of the expedition. By drawing on the journals and documentary records of the *Enterprise*'s officers, he has dispassionately revealed one aspect of the Franklin search that has rarely been addressed: the frictions that can arise among isolated men who must cope, in close quarters, with boredom and monotony.

Most of the commanding officers in the Royal Navy's arctic service dealt with these problems well, keeping their men occupied, relatively free of boredom, and hence tolerably happy during the long winters. But aboard HMS *Enterprise*, add a captain who was a suspicious, arbitrary, vindictive martinet to the monotony and the boredom—and you have a toxic brew. The captain of the *Enterprise*, Richard Collinson, punished his officers mercilessly, yet kept the enlisted men relatively happy by, one assumes, cleverly playing one group against the other.

On the other hand, despite Collinson's devious behaviour and evident timidity when in the vicinity of pack ice, he was, without doubt, a skilful northern mariner. The great polar explorer Roald Amundsen, who, in a far smaller vessel achieved the first traverse of the Northwest Passage 50 years after the *Enterprise*'s voyage, considered Collinson to have proved himself one of the most able arctic navigators by not only taking his heavy ship through uncharted, reef-strewn waters all the way to Cambridge Bay on Victoria Island, but, most important, also bringing her home safely—and Collinson did this after he had placed most of his officers under arrest. Nevertheless, it is a testimony to the discipline and endurance of the *Enterprise*'s officers that they did not mutiny. Had they done so, our perceptions of the Franklin search might be very different.

Professor Barr has produced a valuable and engrossing account. •

—— JOHN R. BOCKSTOCE

PREFACE

On 21 AUGUST 1854 HMS *Enterprise*, Captain Richard Collinson, emerged from Bering Strait, having spent three winters in what is now Canada's Western Arctic and on the north coast of Alaska, searching for the missing Franklin expedition. At Port Clarence, on the Alaskan coast just east of Bering Strait, she encountered HMS *Rattlesnake*, Commander Henry Trollope; the latter ship had wintered there specifically to render assistance to *Enterprise* if required.

In his official report to the British Admiralty, Trollope's only observations on the state of *Enterprise*'s complement were that, while three men had died, "Captain Collinson himself, and the remaining officers and crew, 59 in number, are in good health" and that "his crew are looking in most admirable health."[1] While Trollope's remarks about the physical health of those aboard *Enterprise* were generally accurate, it is clear that he was deliberately (and in an official communiqué, wisely) refraining from any comment on morale on board, and particularly on that of the officers.

Philip Sharpe, Mate on board *Rattlesnake*, had no such compunctions in describing the situation on board *Enterprise* in his journal. Although he heard that *Enterprise* was approaching, since he would soon be going on watch he declined the chance to go aboard her, but was regaled with some disturbing details by his fellow officers when they returned:

About 1 they came back, with oh! such Sad accounts. Every executive officer was under arrest. The master had been under arrest for 2 years and 8 months. Fancy that, in such a climate. The 1st Lieut. had been suspended from duty for 14 months. The 2nd Lieut. had been lately placed under close arrest; & the 3rd had been under arrest for some time. The only officers free were the surgeon & the Assistant Surgeon, & those Capt. Collinson dare not arrest. The Commanding officer was an ice mate, a nobody. Not a soul had been out of the ship for 15 months, among the officers. Things had gone so far that all are determined to go to the utmost, lose their commissions, everything, to try Capt. Collinson by a Court Martial, for lying, drunkenness, tyranny & oppression & cowardice. Now there must be some truth in all this, as the Enterprise's officers are all known & picked men, a first rate set. It is well known that the clerk in charge so long ago as 1851 was driven mad & committed suicide from the Captain's treatment.... Oh! The accounts are horrible; we thought our own plight was bad enough, but it is nothing compared to this. Collinson's associates consisted entirely of the Ice Mates & his men, whom he actually had in his cabin; and things have gone to such a pass that the other day his steward went into his cabin, bolted the door & began abusing him, saying how disgraceful it was to him & how degrading to his position as Captain, to make companions of his crew & have them in his cabin. For this the steward got put in irons...; in the dinner hour [I] went on board the Enterprise & saw the gun room fellows,[2] all a very nice set, and worked up to the highest pitch of desperation by the captain's treatment. Took letters for them; had a chat with each. Skead, the master, looks wasted to nothing after his long imprisonment; and Adams [Assistant Surgeon] looked very ill. The latter was on the point of throwing up his commission that day; & applying to go south with us, when he was dissuaded by the others, who intend to stick to Captn. Collinson, as they say "to the last drop of their blood & have justice done themselves." Never was there an expedition set sail under such auspicious auspices, had such golden opportunities which were thrown away; and made such signal failures. I had an opportunity of seeing this beau idéal of a captain, whose aspect is nearly as forbidding as our man's [Captain Trollope's]. He is a lean, spare, withered looking man, with a vinegar countenance & wears spectacles. He has not <u>one</u> good look about him.[3]

Collinson had searched the coasts of Banks and Victoria islands, penetrating as far east as Cambridge Bay. Apart from a few small pieces of wood, he found no trace of the missing expedition. Several authors have hailed Collinson's voyage as a masterly piece of seamanship; his was the first ship to penetrate the treacherous, uncharted waters of Dolphin and Union Strait, Coronation Gulf, and Dease Strait, to reach Cambridge Bay, and to extricate his ship again safely. But this is to ignore a very intriguing aspect of the voyage, namely the bizarre situation described by Mr. Sharpe, whereby, when *Enterprise* emerged from the Arctic, all four executive offices were under arrest. Francis Skead, the Second Master, had been under arrest for three years by the time the ship reached England, including two-and-a-half arctic winterings. In every case where the officer's "offence" can be identified, that offence can only be described objectively as trivial. The atmosphere on board the ship must have been unbelievably tense and unpleasant, especially in the gunroom, but this unpleasant atmosphere must also have permeated the warrant officers' mess and the crew's quarters. There is clear evidence that ship's discipline was also adversely affected. To give Collinson his due, one must recognize that since he had deprived himself of the skills and experience of his executive officers, his achievement in reaching Cambridge Bay and in extricating his ship from the Arctic safely is all the more impressive. Collinson requested that his officers be court-martialled; they wanted him court-martialled. In the end, no courts-martial occurred.

I have presented the first detailed account of the voyage since Collinson's own narrative, published in 1889, augmenting that account from unpublished journals and official correspondence. But this book also covers in detail the frictions between Collinson and his officers, revealing that the offences with which Collinson charged his men were extremely trivial. The two themes are pursued in parallel. Thus the book is a detailed study (the first since publication of Collinson's own narrative in 1889) both of one of the Royal Navy's numerous searches for the missing Franklin expedition and of the ramifications that could develop from the strict discipline on board the Royal Navy's ships in the 19th century under the peculiar conditions of Arctic service and under an insecure and intolerant captain.

Collinson's account of the expedition was published posthumously by his brother in 1889.[4] Conspicuous by its absence from that account is any mention of Collinson's problems with his officers. This published account is based on two manuscript journals held in the archives of the National Maritime Museum, Greenwich, London, one a rough draft[5] and the other a fair copy,[6] but they, too, contain no reference to the disputes between captain and officers. But it is clear, for example from the fact that there are extended periods when there are no daily entries in these journals, that Collinson had edited his original shipboard journal quite severely, removing any reference to his embarrassing personnel problems, in order to produce a publishable manuscript.

He did not, however, do the same with official documents; these he was unable to sanitize in this fashion. These include his Letter Book, his In-Letter Book, his Order Book, his Night Order Book, and the various copies of the ship's log. All of these documents have survived, either in the archives of the National Maritime Museum at Greenwich or in the Karpeles Manuscript Library, a private depository in Santa Barbara, California.

There are two other particularly important sources for the events on board HMS *Enterprise*. The ship's Second Master, Francis Skead, kept a very detailed journal up until the moment of his arrest on 10 March 1852 during the first arctic wintering. As one might expect, Skead's journal dwells at length on his treatment by his captain. This journal now resides in the archives of the Scott Polar Research Institute, Cambridge, England. The other is the journal of Richard Shingleton, the gun-room steward; unfortunately, only the second volume of this journal has survived, and is held at the Vancouver Maritime Museum; there is also a microfilm copy at Library and Archives Canada in Ottawa. The entries in this second volume begin on 11 September 1852, that is, early in the 1852 navigation season. Given his position on board, and the fact that all journals had to be submitted to the captain at the end of the voyage, Shingleton very wisely kept his head down and made no reference in his journal to the bizarre situation of so many officers being under arrest, although he was naturally well aware of the situation. His journal is nevertheless a valuable source on daily events and activities on board HMS *Enterprise*.

I hope that my account of the expedition, based on these various sources, provides a more balanced view of the voyage of HMS *Enterprise* than the one that has prevailed thus far. ●

ACKNOWLEDGEMENTS

I WAS ABLE TO WRITE THIS BOOK only because I was given free access to manuscript documents in a number of widely scattered repositories. I am particularly indebted to Mr. David Karpeles of Santa Barbara, California, owner of the Karpeles Manuscript Libraries, for allowing me to transcribe the documents pertaining to the cruise of HMS *Enterprise* in his possession. Similarly, I am indebted to Mr. Robert Headland, Archivist at the Scott Polar Research Institute, Cambridge, and to the staffs of the Public Record Office, Kew, and the Archives of the National Maritime Museum, Greenwich. In connection with my visits to the latter repository, I am extremely grateful to Dr. Glyndwr Williams and his wife Dr. Sarah Palmer, for their generous hospitality over the years. I am also grateful to Dr. James Delgado, Director of the Vancouver Maritime Museum, for providing access to Richard Shingleton's journal, and to Dr. John Batts of the University of Ottawa for generously providing me with his transcript of that journal, based on a copy at Library and Archives Canada. I also wish to thank Dr. Alan Pearsall, formerly Curator of the National Maritime Museum, Greenwich, London, for his interpretation of some of Collinson's orders to his officers. Finally, I am indebted to Mr. Cameron Treleaven, owner of Aquila Books of Calgary, for providing me with a copy of Collinson's Memorial to the House of Commons Committee responsible for allocating the award for discovering the Northwest Passage, and also for providing the photos of Captain Collinson, which Mr. Clive Coy obligingly scanned for me.

The travel that my visits to these widely scattered repositories involved was made possible by various Sabbatical Leave Research Grants and grants from the President's SHERC Fund, University of Saskatchewan.

Thanks are also due to Michael Luski, Mary Mahoney-Robson, Peter Midgley, Alan Brownoff and Linda Cameron at The University of Alberta Press—all of whom helped to turn the manuscript into a book. Thanks are also due to Leslie Robertson, who did the copyediting.

I am enormously indebted to Howard Irving, Samuel and Nancy Liebermann, Sandy and Cécile Mactaggart, J. Douglas and Katherine Matheson, Douglas and Margaret Matheson, Ross and Linda McBain, Stanley and Lorraine Milner, Max and Marjorie Ward, and Donald and Marion Wheaton, all of Edmonton, Alberta, for their very generous financial contributions towards publication of my book. And I also owe a debt of gratitude to John Bockstoce for contributing an excellent Foreword, as well as a generous donation towards the cost of publishing Edward Adams's paintings. In connection with the latter I am also very grateful to Ms. Lucy Martin, Picture Library Manager at the Scott Polar Research Institute for making those paintings available and to Dr. Julian Dowdeswell, Director of that institution for assisting in the arrangements for the reproduction of the paintings. ●

THE TASK AND THE MAN

On 19 MAY 1845 Captain Sir John Franklin had put to sea from Greenhithe on the River Thames in command of two bark-rigged bomb vessels, HMS *Erebus* and *Terror*. Their combined crews totalled 134 officers and men, and their objective was to sail through the Northwest Passage from Baffin Bay to Bering Strait; from there they were ordered to proceed to the Sandwich Islands (Hawaii) and to return home via Cape Horn.[1] More specifically, Franklin's instructions were to proceed west through Lancaster Sound and Barrow Strait to Cape Walker, the northeasternmost point of Russell Island (just north of Prince of Wales Island). From there he was to steer southwestwards towards Bering Strait on as straight a course as ice and/or unknown land would permit.

These instructions, in hindsight, may appear to have been ludicrously over-optimistic, but on the face of it, the task that Franklin was being ordered to tackle did not appear especially daunting. Captain William Edward Parry had penetrated as far west along Parry Channel as the southwest corner of Melville Island in HMS

Hecla and *Griper* in 1819–20 and had wintered at Winter Harbour.[2] In 1821 Franklin had led a party that explored the mainland coast by canoe from the mouth of the Coppermine River to Kent Peninsula.[3] Then in the summer of 1826 he had explored the coast westward from the mouth of the Mackenzie River to Return Reef (just west of Prudhoe Bay) while Dr. John Richardson had simultaneously coasted eastwards from the mouth of the Mackenzie to the mouth of the Coppermine.[4] In 1829–33 a private expedition under Sir John Ross, on board *Victory*, had pushed south along Prince Regent Inlet to Felix Harbour on Boothia Isthmus, where his ship had wintered.[5] From there, in the spring of 1830, his nephew, James Clark Ross, had sledged west across the isthmus and had explored the north coast of King William Island as far as Victory Point.

Less than a decade later another expedition would reach almost the same point from the west. In the summer of 1839, Peter Dease and Thomas Simpson of the Hudson's Bay Company, travelling by boat, headed east along the mainland coast from the mouth of the Coppermine.[6] Running through Simpson Strait, they explored the south coast of King William Island and turned back at the mouth of the Castor and Pollux River on the west coast of Boothia Peninsula. At Cape John Herschel they were within 100 km of Victory Point, the most westerly point reached by James Clark Ross.

In the light of the extent of the areas already mapped by these various expeditions, Franklin's task appeared relatively simple. But it is one thing to travel across sea ice and tundra with sledges, as James Ross had done, or to sail the coastal waters by boat or canoe during the brief weeks of open water in summer as Franklin, Richardson, Dease, and Simpson had done, and quite another matter to challenge the ice and to navigate these same uncharted waters, studded with shoals and reefs, in ocean-going ships.

Erebus and *Terror* were well chosen for the task they were about to tackle. As bomb vessels they were built to carry large mortars capable of hurling large-calibre shells on a high trajectory into coastal towns under siege. The mortars were mounted on massive wooden beds amidships and, since there was no mechanism for absorbing the recoil, the ships as a whole were unusually strongly built. They were thus ideal for withstanding the massive pressures they might encounter if nipped in arctic ice. They were provided with additional ice sheathing, and their bows were plated with sheets of iron. They were also the first naval vessels to be provided with steam power for arctic work: railway engines, with only minimal modifications, were mounted athwartships in the holds, a drive shaft extending aft from one of the driving wheels to a two-bladed propeller.[7] The ships were provisioned for three years; in other words, Franklin was realistically prepared to winter up to three times if impeded by ice.

Erebus and *Terror* made rendezvous with a supply vessel near Godhavn (Qeqertarssuaq) in West Greenland to take on a final consignment of stores; four men were invalided home at this point, making the expedition's complement 129 men; then the ships continued north on 12 July. On 26 July they encountered the whalers *Enterprise* (Captain Robert Martin) of Peterhead and *Prince of Wales* (Captain Dannett) in Melville Bay. When last seen by Captain Martin, *Erebus* and *Terror* were moored to an iceberg. He and his men were the last Europeans to see any member of Franklin's expedition alive.[8]

In light of the ships' provisioning, there was no particular concern felt in Britain when there was no word from Franklin in 1846, but by 1847 some concern was starting to develop and plans for the first search expeditions were laid. In 1848, under the auspices of the British Admiralty, Sir John Richardson and Dr. John Rae travelled west via the fur-trade route, descended the Mackenzie River, and searched the coast east to the mouth of the Coppermine by boat.[9] After wintering at Fort Confidence on Great Bear Lake, Rae resumed his search in 1849, intending to search the coast of Victoria Island by boat, but ice prevented him from crossing Dolphin and Union Strait.[10] Returning to this area again in the spring of 1851, he searched long stretches of the southwest coast of Victoria Island by dog sledge and then, in the summer of 1851, much of the southeast and east coasts of Victoria Island by boat.[11]

Also in 1848, HMS *Plover* (Captain Thomas Moore) was dispatched to Bering Strait; she wintered at Bukhta Provideniya on the Siberian side of the strait, the first of many winterings she would spend in the area, ready to render assistance to *Erebus* and *Terror*, or to survivors of the Franklin expedition, if they should emerge from the Arctic.[12] Meanwhile, HMS *Herald*, under Captain Henry Kellett, engaged in surveying the Pacific coast of Central America, was dispatched northwards from Panama in the summer of 1848 to rendezvous with *Plover* in Kotzebue Sound, but failed to meet her and returned south.[13]

In that same year, an expedition was dispatched to attempt to follow the same route outlined in Franklin's instructions. Two ships, HMS *Enterprise* and *Investigator* (Captain Sir James Clark Ross and Captain Edward J. Bird, respectively) sailed from the Thames in May 1848. They wintered at Port Leopold on northeastern Somerset Island, and in the spring of 1849 sledging parties from the ships explored extensive sections of the coasts of Somerset and adjacent islands but found no traces of the missing expedition.[14] The expedition returned to England late in 1849.

In the summer of 1849, *Herald* under Captain Henry Kellett had again headed north through Bering Strait; having met *Plover* in Kotzebue Sound, Kellett pushed north to Wainwright Inlet but was blocked there by ice.[15] However, a party from *Plover*, travelling in two boats under the command of Lieutenants William Pullen and William Hooper, by taking advantage of shore leads, coasted round Point Barrow and east along the Alaskan coast to the mouth of the Mackenzie.[16] Hooper wintered at Fort Franklin on Great Bear Lake and Pullen at Fort Simpson. In the following summer (1850), they descended the Mackenzie to its mouth and started eastwards, planning to search the coasts of Banks Island and the southwest coast of Victoria Island. They were brought to a halt by close ice at Cape Bathurst, however, and were forced to turn back.

The year 1850 saw a great flurry of activity in the eastern Arctic, involving both private and naval search expeditions, and also including an American component. Four naval vessels, *Resolute* (Captain Horatio Austin), *Assistance* (Captain Erasmus Ommanney), *Intrepid* (Captain Bertie Cator), and *Pioneer* (Captain Sherard Osborn) sailed from England in May.[17] Lady Franklin dispatched a search vessel of her own, *Prince Albert*, under the command of Captain Charles Forsyth.[18] Another private expedition, financed by the Hudson's Bay Company, was organized and led by the arctic veteran Sir John Ross; it sailed aboard *Felix*, with a 12-ton yacht, *Mary*, as tender.[19] Yet another expedition sailed from Britain, bound for Lancaster Sound, that summer; the whaling captain William Penny, with instructions from the Admiralty, led an expedition consisting of *Lady Franklin* and *Sophia*.[20] And finally, the American contribution, consisting of the ships *Advance* (Captain E. J. De Haven) and *Rescue* (Captain Samuel P. Griffin), sailed from New York, northward bound, in May 1850.[21]

Finally, also in 1850, the British Admiralty dispatched to Bering Strait via Cape Horn the expedition that is the subject of this book, namely HMS *Enterprise* (Captain Richard Collinson) and HMS *Investigator* (Captain Robert M'Clure). These were almost identical bark-rigged vessels of 560 tons, each manned by around 60 officers and men.

Richard Collinson had no previous arctic experience, but several aspects of his earlier career probably worked to his advantage when the Lords of the Admiralty were choosing a person to command the expedition to search for Franklin from the west. He was born in 1811 at Gateshead, County Durham (now Tyne and Wear), third son of the Reverend John Collinson, Rector of Gateshead. Both he and his brothers attended the Reverend James Birkett's school at Ovingham on the River Tyne, about 19 km west of Newcastle. In 1823, at the age of 12, he entered as a midshipman on board HMS *Cambridge*, Captain Maling, at Chatham. She was bound for the Pacific Station on the west coast of South America. Here he made a very positive impression on his captain, who, on the ship's return to England some three-and-a-half years later, wrote to Collinson's father, describing Midshipman Collinson as follows:

> As excellent a good fellow as you could wish him to be. He has his first fault to commit with me; on not one single occasion has he given me an opportunity of finding fault with him. A better-disposed lad, or one more likely to do credit to his profession, never trod the deck of a ship. If he continues through life as I have found him, his parents will have reason to be proud of him.[22]

HMS *Cambridge* returned to Sheerness in June 1827. By November Collinson had joined HMS *Gloucester*, but he had set his sights on joining HMS *Chanticleer*, fitting out at Portsmouth for a scientific voyage to the southern hemisphere to carry out pendulum and magnetic observations at a number of sites under the command of Captain Henry Foster. The latter had considerable arctic experience, having been with Captain Douglas Clavering on the coast of East Greenland in HMS *Griper* in 1823, and with Parry in HMS *Hecla* in search of the Northwest Passage in 1824-5 and on his attempt at the North Pole from Svalbard in HMS *Hecla* in 1827.

With Midshipman Collinson on board, *Chanticleer* sailed from Portsmouth on 27 April 1828 and carried out the first set of pendulum observations at Montevideo between 15 August and 5 October. Collinson was particularly involved with magnetic observations. Subsequent sets of observations were made at Isla de los Estados (Staten Island), Deception Island (whose sheltered harbour inside the caldera is named Port Foster and the site of the observatory, Pendulum Cove), St. Martin's Cove, near Cape Horn, Cape Town, St. Helena, Ascension, Fernando Noronha, off the Brazilian coast, Maranham on mainland Brazil, Para (now Belém) at the mouth of the Amazon, Trinidad, and Porto Bello in Panama. Here, unfortunately, Captain Foster was drowned in a canoe accident in the Chagres River; Lieutenant Horatio Austin (who would later command the Navy's Arctic Squadron despatched to search for Franklin in 1850) then assumed command and took *Chanticleer* home to Britain, while Collinson was made Acting-lieutenant. *Chanticleer* reached Falmouth on 17 May 1831.

Due to his talent as a surveyor, Collinson had attracted the notice of the Admiralty's hydrographer, Sir Francis Beaufort. He was also invited to join the surveying vessel HMS *Aetna* by her captain, Edward Belcher, for a cruise to West Africa and the coasts of Spain and Portugal. Belcher would later command the Navy's Arctic Squadron searching for Franklin in 1852–54. This cruise lasted from November 1831 until May 1833. Initially Collinson got along well with Belcher, but they had a falling-out towards the end of the cruise. It was some consolation to Collinson that he became close friends with Midshipman Henry Kellett, with whom he would cross paths in the Far East and again during his own arctic expedition, and who would command HMS *Resolute* and HMS *Intrepid* during the Franklin search of 1852–54.

In September 1833 Collinson joined his first steam vessel, *Salamander*, again under Horatio Austin, but soon afterwards, along with his captain, transferred to the new paddle-steamer HMS *Medea*, serving aboard her, mainly in the Eastern Mediterranean, until 1835. Having made a name for himself as a marine surveyor, at this point he was made Lieutenant. In December 1835 he joined HMS *Sulphur* (Captain Frederick Beechey) as Third Lieutenant and Assistant Surveyor. Along with her consort, HMS *Starling*, *Sulphur* was to survey the west coast of the Americas from Cape Horn to Mt. St. Elias at about 60°N. Beechey was in poor health and was invalided home in the summer of 1836; he was replaced by Edward Belcher, who joined the ship at Panama in March 1837. In the interim, Lieutenant Kellett had taken command and Collinson had been named First Lieutenant and Assistant Surveyor; he retained these positions under Belcher. By the autumn of 1837, the expedition was surveying the coast in the area of Mt. St. Elias, having visited Sitka (in Russian America) on the way north. A detailed survey was made of San Francisco Bay, a survey in which Collinson was fully involved. Thereafter, however, Collinson fell foul of Belcher, who demanded of the Admiral on the Pacific station that he be court-martialled. In light of this, he was transferred to the flagship when *Sulphur* returned home in the autumn of 1838, and himself got back to England in November 1839.

Here, apparently, influential friends such as Captain Horatio Austin and Captain Francis Beaufort must have gone to bat for him, since no court-martial occurred, and by the end of the year he had been offered the position of Surveying Officer to the Fleet attached to the Chinese War Expedition that was about to sail. On 18 February 1840, Collinson joined HMS *Blenheim* at Portsmouth, bound for China.

The main British force had occupied the island of Chusan (Zhoushan Dao), just south of Shanghai, in June; Collinson, in *Blenheim*, arrived there in July. Early in 1841 he travelled south to join the force preparing to attack Canton. He joined his friend Lieutenant Henry Kellett on board HMS *Starling*, and together they surveyed a passage from Macao north to Canton, bypassing the Canton River. When the main attack started on 24 May, it was Collinson who piloted the main force up the Canton River. Canton was captured, trade was reopened, and Hong Kong was ceded to Britain. Among the promotions that followed, Lieutenants Kellett and Collinson were made Commanders.

In August 1841 the British force turned its attention farther north, first attacking the seaport of Amoy (now Xiamen). Collinson now had his own vessel, a small pilot boat, *Bentinck*, originally from the Hooghly River in Bengal. In her he sounded the approach channel under the guns of Chinese batteries, allowing the warships to close and the transports to land their troops to capture the port. Then, in September, Chusan (Zhoushan Dao), which had earlier been evacuated by the British and reoccupied by the Chinese and heavily fortified, was successfully attacked. Copies of Collinson's earlier surveys were of critical importance to this operation. Thereafter, in October, the town of Ningpo (Ningbo) was successfully attacked; once again Collinson played a major role in sounding and surveying the river up to the town in *Bentinck*.

There was something of a lull over the winter, but in March 1842 Collinson, in *Bentinck*, was called upon to survey the river estuary from Chapu (Zhapu) up to Hangchou (Hangzhou). On the basis of his survey, the decision was made to capture Chapu; this was achieved in May, and once again Collinson's contribution in sounding and surveying the approaches to the port was vital. In a special dispatch Admiral Sir W. Parker commended both Kellett and Collinson for their efforts, stressing how critical their surveys had been to the successes he had been able to achieve.

The next objective was the important seaport of Shanghai. In June, Collinson in *Bentinck* (now renamed *Plover*) sounded and buoyed the channel up to Woosung (Woosong); that town was then captured, followed by Shanghai. Thereafter, the fleet was able to advance up the Yangtze Kiang (Chiang Jiang), preceded by the two surveying vessels, *Plover*, Commander Collinson, and *Starling*, Commander Kellett, which sounded and buoyed the channels and bars of this impressive river, still over eight kilometers wide at Chin-kiang-fu (Zhenjiang) some 100 km from the river mouth. This city, controlling not only the Chiang Jiang, but also the Grand Canal that crosses the river here, was captured after heavy fighting.

Thereafter Collinson in *Plover* and Kellett in *Starling* led the way upriver, sounding and buoying the channel, to Nanking (Nanjing), some 65 km further upstream. The main force reached that city on 8 August, and the Chinese defenders capitulated on the 20th without any serious fighting. A peace treaty was signed on the 29th.

For their contributions Collinson and Kellett were promoted to Post-Captain and made Companions of the Bath, the promotion to take effect from December 1842. Their work was not finished, however. Until mid-November they were engaged in completing a proper survey of the Chiang Jiang from Nanjing to the sea. Collinson then spent the spring and summer of 1843 in Hong Kong, working up the charts from all his surveys. Thereafter, Sir Francis Beaufort ordered him to complete a survey of the entire coast from Hong Kong north to Chusan (Zhoushan Dao), including the Pescadores (P'eng-hu Lieh-tao), but not Formosa (Taiwan). For this massive task he was also given a schooner, *Young Hebe*, commanded by Lieutenant Bate. Serving as Assistant Master under Bate was Mr. Francis Skead, who was examined by Collinson at the Pescadores on 5 August 1844 and thereby gained his Certificate as Second Master. He was further examined by Admiral Parker on 1 February 1845 and was appointed Acting Second Master in H. M. Troop Ship *Sapphire*.[23] The massive task of surveying this long and intricate coastline took *Plover* and *Young Hebe* until the summer of 1846. Collinson then sailed for home in his small survey vessel *Plover*, with Skead as Second Master.

Plover reached Spithead on 24 September and Woolwich by 5 October 1846. There, very ironically in light of later events, Collinson wrote a very laudatory letter of reference for Skead to Captain Houston Stewart:

Sir,

I take the liberty of bringing to your notice, Mr. Francis Skead (Second Master) who is about to be paid off from Her Majesty's Ship under my command, in hopes that an appointment may be shortly provided for him. He is an able and promising young Officer and wishes at once practically to make himself acquainted with the Channel Pilotage.

He has served under my eye nearly 5 years, and has rendered himself exceedingly useful in our Surveying operations on the Coast of China.[24]

As we will see, Collinson's opinion of Skead would later change drastically.

Collinson was kept busy for several months completing his charts and reports from his six years on the China coast, but thereafter he enjoyed a fairly lengthy break, which he spent mainly at his home in the village of Boldon, between Newcastle and Sunderland. The only interruption was when he served briefly in 1847 on a committee to examine the suitability of Holyhead harbour to be upgraded to a national harbour of refuge. Then, in 1849, he was called upon by the Admiralty to command the expedition, consisting of HMS *Enterprise* and *Investigator*, which was to search for the missing Franklin expedition via Bering Strait.

While Collinson had no previous arctic experience, he had seen service in the Antarctic, having been at Deception Island in the South Shetland Islands with Captain Henry Foster in *Chanticleer* in 1829. In the waters of Bransfield Strait, en route to Deception Island, he had probably encountered sea ice and certainly would have encountered icebergs. Moreover, he had proved himself in the Far East and elsewhere to be a diligent and very competent surveyor, and since exploration was a major secondary objective of all the Franklin search expeditions, this experience must have stood him in very good stead when it came to his appointment to command the expedition dispatched to search for the missing Franklin expedition via Bering Strait. ●

2
FROM THE THAMES
TO BERING STRAIT

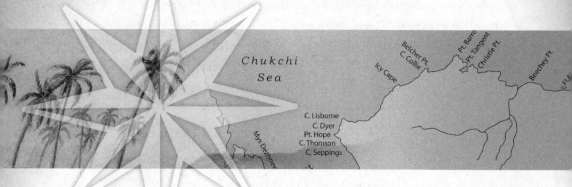

Collinson received his letter
of appointment to command the expedition on 14 December 1849, and on the same
day he travelled to Woolwich where he found the two ships being coppered to
protect them from teredos on their passage through the tropics.[1] He hoisted his
pennant on board HMS *Enterprise* while a party of riggers started setting up the
lower rigging and a gang of convicts cleared the stone ballast from the holds. On 18
December Commander Robert M'Clure took command of HMS *Investigator*.

Collinson, meanwhile, was involved in a steady stream of correspondence concerning the myriad of details associated with a protracted arctic voyage. On the 18th
he wrote to Captain William Baillie Hamilton, Second Secretary at the Admiralty,
to request that *Enterprise* and *Investigator* each be supplied with one of the inflatable rubber boats invented by Lieutenant Peter Halkett, R.N.; Halkett had already
agreed to superintend their construction.[2]

The Halkett boat was an inflatable boat made of rubber-coated cloth with a canvas
cover. It came in two sizes, the smaller one measuring about 2.7 by 1.2 m when inflated

and designed to carry two men. When deflated it could be folded up into a bundle readily carried by one man. It came equipped with paddles and with bellows for inflating it.[3]

Initially, Collinson discovered that he had been assigned a steam launch, with two engineers to run it; he felt it was too small, however, and when his request to have it lengthened was refused, he asked to be provided instead with a decked pinnace, the engineers to be replaced with a blacksmith and an able seaman.[4] Also on the 18th he wrote to the Senior Officer at Woolwich to say that *Enterprise* would be ready to embark her complement of Marines by the 25th.[5] That complement comprised a sergeant, two other NCOs, and seven privates.

On the 23rd he wrote to the Comptroller General to request that he be supplied with the same amounts of coal, firewood, candles, etc. as had been supplied for Captain James Clark Ross's arctic voyage in the same ship in 1848–49;[6] also on that date he wrote to the Secretary to the Admiralty to be allowed to purchase 50 pairs of fur boots that had been approved by the previous expedition.[7]

On the 26th he wrote to Captain Austin, in charge of the Woolwich Dockyard, for three of the workers who had volunteered for the expedition to be discharged from the dockyard.[8] Also on that date he wrote to Hamilton to request that two ice mates be allocated to each ship rather than the one ice mate that had been assigned.[9] Ice mates, usually whaling ship captains with considerable experience of ship-handling in ice, were assigned to all the Royal Navy's searches for the missing Franklin expedition. They were, of course, not naval officers.

On New Year's Day the ships hauled out into the river, but Collinson's stream of correspondence on last-minute details continued. On that date he wrote to Baillie Hamilton concerning a proposal from a Mr. George Shepperd to supply a hydrogen balloon 23 feet in diameter, designed to send up a lookout, to provide a wide over-view of the landscape.[10] A few days later Collinson was sufficiently impressed by a demonstration by Mr. Shepperd of his message-carrying balloons to request permission to order 50 balloons and the necessary apparatus to produce hydrogen using sulphuric acid and zinc, the entire cost amounting to £66 10/–.[11] Over the next few days the topics of his correspondence with Baillie Hamilton ranged from howit-zers, blue lights, rockets, Bickford's fuse, and muskets in one letter, to mustard and cress seeds (for growing on board as antiscorbutics) in another, and in a third the procuring of pile-driving machines for breaking ice (allegedly used successfully on the Neva River in Russia), which could be fitted under the bowsprit. Collinson requested one for each ship, but there is no indication that they were provided.[12]

On 10 January 1850, the two ships were towed downriver to Greenhithe, where their compasses were adjusted, and next day steam tugs passed them towlines (*Africa* towing *Enterprise*) and started towing them down the river, to loud cheers from crowds on the banks and to gun salutes from the naval vessels they passed.[13] The tugs towed them through the Downs on the 13th and cast off when abeam of Deal. They proceeded down Channel with a fair wind, but by the time they were off Portland it had increased to a strong gale, and the two ships hove-to so that they would not run past Plymouth during the night, since they were to call there to pick up their canned meats, which were expected to arrive from Ireland. Daylight on 15 January found them off the Stack, and by 2 PM they had dropped anchor off Devon-port in Plymouth Sound.

Here, as always, there was a flurry of last-minute preparations, and the last of the ships' complements came aboard. HMS *Enterprise* carried a complement of 71 officers and men (including the squad of Royal Marines). First Lieutenant was Lt. George Phayre; Second Lieutenant was Lt. John Barnard, who had been Third Lieutenant on board *Investigator* during her 1848–49 voyage; Third Lieutenant was Lt. Charles Jago; the mates were R.T. Legg and Murray T. Parkes; Second Master was Francis Skead. He was responsible for navigation; for some reason it had been decided (probably to save money) that the ship did not merit the appointment of somebody in the higher rank of Master. The Surgeon was Robert Anderson, who had been on board *Investigator* in 1848–49, as had the Assistant Surgeon, Edward Adams. As Collinson had requested, *Enterprise* carried two ice mates, John Atkinson and George Arbuthnott, assigned to the expedition for their expertise in ice navigation. Arbuthnott, from Peterhead, had been captain and part-owner of the whaling bark *Superior*, which had been lost in the ice of Davis Strait in June 1849;[14] Atkinson very probably was also a whaler.

Johann Miertsching, a Moravian missionary who had acquired a command of Inuktitut during his years in Labrador, was recruited to act as Inuktitut interpreter and joined *Enterprise* on the 18th. He "found the crew busily taking on provisions, coal, etc. ; a good many of them were drunk, and one was seated in irons near the wheel."[15] Miertsching was given a warm welcome by Collinson, and also by Captain M'Clure, who had been dining with Collinson. The latter then made temporary arrangements for Miertsching to sleep in his own cabin for the night.

Also on the 18th, Mr. Gamble arrived from Dublin with the preserved meats, almost simultaneously with Collinson's sailing orders, dated 15 January. The latter read (in part) as follows:

1. Whereas the efforts that have been made during the last two years to relieve the "Erebus" and "Terror" have failed, and all access to the Parry Islands has been prevented by the accumulation of ice in the upper part of Barrow Straits: And whereas it is possible that the same severity of weather may not prevail at the same time in both the eastern and western entrances to the Arctic Sea, we have now determined, in a matter of such moment, to send an Expedition into the Polar Sea from the westward; and, having a full confidence in your zeal and skill, we have thought proper to appoint you to the command of Her Majesty's ship "Enterprize," and also to place under your orders Her Majesty's ship "Investigator"; both of which vessels having been duly fortified against collision with the ice, equipped for the polar climate by warm-air apparatus, and furnished with provisions for three years, as well as a large supply of extra stores, you are now required and directed, so soon as they are in all respects ready for sea, to proceed to make the best of your way to Cape Virgins,[16] in order to arrive at Behring's Straits in July.

2. At Cape Virgins, the Commander-in-Chief in the Pacific has been desired to have a steam-vessel waiting for you, and by her you will be towed through the Straits of Magellan, and the Wellington Channel, and on to Valparaiso.

3. At that port you will use the utmost despatch in watering and refreshing your crews, and in fully replenishing your bread and other provisions and stores; and having done so, you will again use your best exertions to press forward to the Sandwich Islands.[17]

4. There is only a bare possibility of your reaching those islands in time to meet Her Majesty's ship "Herald" under the command of Captain Henry Kellett; but if that should be the case, you will receive from him, not only every assistance, but much useful information touching your passage to the Strait, and your further proceedings to the northward. It is still more improbable that Her Majesty's ship "Plover" should be there; but wherever you may fall in with her, you are hereby directed to take her and Commander Moore under your orders.

5. At the Sandwich Islands you will find additional orders from us for your guidance, which we propose to forward from hence by the Panama mail of next March; but if none should arrive, or if they do not in any way modify these directions, you will enforce the greatest diligence in

re-victualling your two vessels, in procuring, if possible, the necessary
Esquimaux interpreters, and in making all requisite preparations for at
once proceeding to Behring's Straits, in order to reach the ice before the
1st of August.... We consider it essential that, after entering the ice,
there should be a depot, or point of succour, for any party to fall back
upon. For this purpose the "Plover" is to be secured in the most favourable quarter, as far in advance as can be found—such as Wainwright's
Inlet, or the Creek at Hope Point; but if they be unsafe, and none has
been discovered nearer to Barrow's Point, then at Chamisso Island, or
any part of Kotzebue Sound, which may afford the necessary shelter....

12. On detaching the "Plover" to take up her winter quarters, you will direct
    Commander Moore to remain there until you join him, or, failing your
    return to him, until the end of the summer of 1853; when, but not until
    it is absolutely necessary for securing the "Plover's" passage through
    the Aleutian group of Islands, he is to quit Behring's Straits, and make
    the best of his way to Valparaiso touching at the Sandwich Islands for
    refreshment), where he will receive further instructions relative to his
    return to England from the Commander-in-Chief....

14. In the event of your having to winter your ships on the continent or
    Esquimaux shores, you will probably meet with some of the wandering
    tribes, or with Indians. With these you will cultivate a friendly feeling,
    by making them presents of those articles to which they are apt to attach
    a value; but you will take care not to suffer yourself to be surprised by
    them, but use every precaution, and be constantly on your guard against
    any treacherous attack. You will also, by offering rewards, to be paid in
    such a manner as you may be able to arrange, endeavour to prevail on
    them to carry to any of the settlements of the Hudson's Bay Company an
    account of your situation and proceedings, with an urgent request that it
    may be forwarded to England with the utmost possible despatch.

15. In whatever place you may have to establish your winter quarters, you
    will devote every resource in your power to the preservation of the health,
    the comfort and the cheerfulness of the people committed to your care.

16. We leave it to your judgement and discretion as to the course to be
    pursued after passing Point Barrow, and on entering the ice; and you
    will be materially assisted in this respect by what you will learn from
    Captain Kellett, if he should be fallen in with at the Sandwich Islands,

as well as from the observations of Sir E. Parry and Captain Beechey contained in the memoranda, of which we send you copies.

17. We have desired that you shall be furnished, not only with a copy of the orders under which Commander Moore is now acting, but also with copies of all the orders which from time to time have been given to Captain Kellett.... You will further be supplied with all the printed voyages or travels in those northern regions; and the memoranda and instructions drawn up by Sir John Richardson, as to the manners and habits of the Esquimaux, and the best mode of dealing with that people (a copy of which is also sent), will afford a valuable addition to the information now supplied to you.

18. We deem it right to caution you against suffering the two vessels placed under your orders to separate, except in the event of accident or unavoidable necessity; and we desire that you will keep up the most unreserved communication with the Commander of the "Investigator," placing in him every proper confidence, and acquainting him with the general tenor of your orders, and with your views and intentions from time to time; so that the service may have the full benefit of your united efforts in the prosecution of such a service; and that in the event of any unavoidable separation, or of any accident to yourself, Commander M'Clure may have the advantage of knowing, up to the latest period, all your ideas and designs relative to the satisfactory completion of this undertaking.

19. We also recommend that a frequent exchange may take place as conveniently may be of the observations made in the two ships; that any information obtained by the one, be as quickly as possible communicated for the advantage and guidance of the other.

20. In case of any irreparable accident happening to the "Enterprize," you are hereby authorized to take command of the "Investigator," and to make such arrangements for the officers and crews as may be most consonant to the rules of the service, and most conducive to the objects of the Expedition.

21. In the event of Great Britain being involved in hostilities with any foreign power during your absence, you are to abstain from the smallest act of aggression towards any vessel belonging to such nation, it being the practice of all civilized countries to consider vessels engaged in service of this kind as exempt from the rules and operations of war.

22. In carrying out the foregoing orders, you will avail yourself of every practicable occasion of acquainting our Secretary with every step of your progress, as well as with your future intentions; and occasionally during your voyage, you will throw overboard one of the tin cylinders with which you have been supplied (headed up in any cask or barrel that you could manufacture or spare), containing an account of the date, position etc. On your reaching England, you will call on every person, in both vessels, to deliver up their logs, journals, charts and drawings, but which, they may be informed, shall be returned to them in due time.

23. With respect to your search proving fruitless, and your finally quitting the Polar Seas, as well as your securing your winter quarters towards the close of any one season, we cannot too strongly impress upon you the necessity of the utmost precaution and care being exercised in withdrawing in time, so as in no case to hazard the safety of the ships, and the lives of those entrusted to your care, by your being shut up in a position which might render a failure of provisions possible.

   We feel it unnecessary to give you more detailed instructions, which might possibly embarrass you in a service of this description; and we have therefore only to repeat our perfect reliance on your judgement and resolution, both in doing all that is possible to relieve the missing ships, and in withdrawing in time, when you come to the painful conclusion that your efforts are unavailing.

24. You will bear in mind that the object of the Expedition is to obtain intelligence, and to render assistance to Sir John Franklin and his companions, and not for the purposes of geographical or scientific research; and we conclude these orders with an earnest hope that Providence may crown your efforts with success, and that they may be the means of dispelling the gloom and uncertainty which now prevails respecting the missing Expedition.

Given under our hands, this 15th day of January 1850.

F. T. BARING.

J. W. D. DUNDAS.[18]

Next morning Collinson took Miertsching ashore to Devonport and bought him a seagoing outfit and various essential items; Miertsching was then left to his own devices for the day, until Collinson took him back to his ship at 6 PM.[19] It had been intended that Miertsching be stationed on board *Enterprise*, but since for the moment there was no cabin available for him, he was now transferred to *Investigator*, with the understanding that he would revert to *Enterprise* at Valparaiso.

At 6 AM on the 20th the ships put to sea, heading down Channel with a fair wind. But this fair wind soon deserted them, at 47° 2′N; 13° 57′W, to be followed by a series of southwesterly gales that greatly delayed them and put a severe strain on the rigging of both ships. Indeed, on the 24th *Investigator* had her fore topmast and her main topgallant mast carried away, while her upperworks "leaked excessively," as M'Clure informed Collinson by signal.[20] *Enterprise* proved to be a better sailer than *Investigator*, and the latter vessel was soon left astern. She came up with her consort again on 31 January, but they parted company again on 1 February (27 January according to Skead). They would not see each other again until they reached the Strait of Magellan.

With winds of varying strength and from various directions, *Enterprise* worked her way steadily south. At noon on 21 February a fresh northeast breeze sprang up which, it was hoped, was the start of the Northeast Trades. This hope was soon dashed, however, and by the 20th, at 13° 40′N; 27° 04′W, the ship was lying becalmed. Collinson deliberately passed some 130 miles west of the Cape Verde Islands, to avoid the light airs and calms commonly encountered there, but even so the ship was becalmed for another 24 hours before a steady northeast wind began to blow.[21] It lasted for only five days, however, before calms and light winds were again encountered. Thus practically no Northeast Trade Wind was encountered at all, a situation that was very frustrating for the captain and his officers, who knew that it was essential that they get into the Arctic Ocean before the summer was over.

Enterprise crossed the Equator on 5 March at 27 °W, and the Southeast Trades were encountered immediately. On the 28th she ran into an area of discoloured water with large amounts of weed, and large numbers of birds were sighted around the ship. On April 6 land was sighted near Cabo de los Desvelos; approaching the land here, the ship crossed the meridian of Cape Horn, entitling the crew to double pay. In light of this, Collinson ordered the main brace spliced, that is, a tot of rum was issued to each man, to the delight of the crew. By noon that day the ship was abeam of Puerto San Julian, standing south for Cabo Virgenes. She was only five miles north of that cape, at the eastern entrance to the Strait of Magellan, when a southwesterly gale blew up; it was not unexpected, since the barometer had been dropping steadily, reaching 28.87 inches at noon on the 7th, and since a menacing bank of black clouds lay over the land. Collinson shortened sail and hauled off to the north before heaving-to to ride out the gale. When the gale slackened on 8 April, Collinson made sail again, and on the morning of the 9th, rounding Cabo Virgenes and crossing the Sarmiento shoal, entered the strait. Beating westwards, the ship dropped anchor off Cabo Possession in the early hours of the 10th. At 5:00 the next morning, she got under way again and, with the last of the ebb and a WSW wind, beat up for Bahia Possession, where she anchored at noon.

Here she found HM Steamer *Gorgon* (Captain Paynter), which was to tow the expedition ships through the straits, and the yacht *Nancy Dawson*. The latter had been taken to the Arctic Ocean by her owner, Robert Shedden, the previous year, with a view to help search for the Franklin expedition. He had even rounded Point Barrow and had left a depot of provisions some 80 km farther east, before turning back.[22] Unfortunately, Shedden had died at Mazatlan on the way back south, and Captain Henry Kellett of HMS *Herald* had placed his master, James Hill, in command of *Nancy Dawson* for the voyage back to England. Collinson had a long chat with Hill and acquired some very useful information concerning the ice conditions that *Nancy Dawson* had encountered, as well as some charts.[23]

On 10 April Collinson took the opportunity to send a "report of progress" to the Admiralty:

Sir,

I have the honour to acquaint you that Her Majesty's ship under my command reached this place today, after a passage of 80 days from England; that I have not seen the "Investigator" since the 1st of February, and that it is my intention to proceed to-morrow through the Straits, leaving the "Gorgon" to follow with our consort when she arrives; and that should she not do so early, I shall make my way to the Sandwich islands direct, instead of complying with their Lordships' directions and calling at Valparaiso. The necessity of this deviation will, I trust, be a sufficient reason; as I look upon our arrival in Behring's Straits during the first week in August, to be essential to their lordships' orders.

The "Gorgon" will supply both vessels with the amount of provisions expended, since leaving England, nearly, and as Captain Paynter has made arrangements for the procuration of bullocks and vegetables, during our passage through the Straits, the object of refreshing the ship's companies will be attained.[24]

In accordance with this report, since *Investigator* had not yet arrived, Collinson ordered Captain Paynter to wait for her and to tow her through the straits when she did turn up; he, meanwhile, would sail *Enterprise* through the straits.[25] Over the next few days he probably regretted this decision; calms, light winds, and strong tides in the confined waters of the straits meant that at times the boats were towing ahead, and at others the ship was beating into the wind, sometimes even being swept back east by the tidal currents. *Enterprise* finally reached Punta Arenas on the afternoon of 13 April, anchoring off the penal settlement that had moved from Puerto del Hambre only two years earlier.

A work party was sent ashore for water; the boat was rowed up a stream on the east side of the settlement, and the casks were filled by a pump once the water was fresh; a total of eight tonnes was embarked. On seeing some cattle among the trees, Collinson was keen to get some fresh meat; the Governor was very reluctant to supply any cattle, however, since he had evidently had strict instructions to protect them. Once Collinson had left a letter with the Governor, to be forwarded to the British consul in Valparaiso, stressing the importance of his mission and explaining the situation, the Governor relented and allowed him to take four bullocks. Three were taken aboard alive, but the Chileans slaughtered and dressed the fourth one, taking a quantity of the meat for their trouble.

In the meantime, a fresh northeasterly wind was blowing, a fair wind, but as soon as *Enterprise* got under way just after noon on the 14th, the wind dropped. None-theless, Collinson got under way again, beating southwestwards through the strait, with the land on both sides becoming steadily more mountainous. In the early hours of the 15th, since they were making little progress beating into the wind, Collinson decided to drop anchor in Bahia San Nicholas, and took the opportunity of filling a further nine tonnes of water and catching a few fish with a seine net in the Rio De Gennes at the head of the bay. Skead, Adams, and other officers took the opportunity to stretch their legs, as Skead reported in his journal:

With a clear atmosphere we enjoyed the beautiful scenery around us. Lofty snow-covered peaks rearing their heads in all directions formed a picture at once stern and imposing.... The scenery hereabouts was as picturesque as it

had been stern and rugged in the morning when viewed from the outside.
The river wound its way to the sea through a dense woodland of beech &
other trees mingled with a rank vegetation altogether impenetrable in many
places. We had very little of the shore, yet it was sufficient to break the
monotony of the long voyage already stretched out to the length of 90 days,
& the short rambles along the beach & as far into the woodlands as we
could penetrate proved a real pleasure only to be enjoyed fully after so long
a confinement on ship board.[26]

The Assistant Surgeon, Edward Adams, an accomplished artist, produced a striking
water-colour of the *Nothofagus* (southern beech) forest, a painting now preserved
in the archives of the Scott Polar Research Institute in Cambridge (see illustration
p. 254).

Getting under way again next morning (16th), by noon they were rounding
Cabo Froward, which Skead describes as

...a remarkable monument, a worthy & magnificent terminus to the New
World.[27] A lofty peak covered with snow stands over the Cape with its
Southn. Face sloping somewhat steeply until within 400 or 500 feet of the
sea level when it rises again forming a saddle and then falls abruptly into
the sea.[28]

Enterprise reached Bahia Fortescue at daybreak on the 17th, but then the wind
dropped and she had to be towed into the bay by her boats. Here they encountered
an American bark and two schooners; the bark had been trying for 42 days to beat
westwards through to the Pacific, while one of the schooners had lost all her anchors
while trying to get through the First Narrows.[29]

In the afternoon *Gorgon* appeared, towing *Investigator*. The latter filled her water
casks and Collinson shared some of the newly acquired fresh beef with her. He
also informed M'Clure that, in light of the time factor, he had decided not to call
at Valparaiso, but to head straight for the Sandwich Islands. By means of a letter
entrusted to the American steamer *New World*, Collinson also informed William
Baillie Hamilton, the Second Secretary, of this change of plan.[30] Johann Miertsching,
the Moravian missionary who was to have come aboard *Enterprise* as Inuktitut interpreter, but who had travelled this far aboard *Investigator*, was now meant to transfer
to *Enterprise*, where a cabin had even been prepared for him. He, however, was

keen to stay on board *Investigator* as far as the Sandwich Islands, and in this he was supported by Captain M'Clure and his officers.[31] Collinson relented. He would later greatly regret this decision.

On the morning of the 18th a strong west wind was blowing and Captain Paynter thought he would be unable to tow both ships against it; hence it was decided to wait for the wind to drop. During the day, as the tide changed and the ships swung at their anchors, *Enterprise* fouled *Gorgon*. On board *Enterprise*, the lanyards to the bobstays had to be cut to avoid more serious damage; *Gorgon* suffered only minor damage to her bulwarks.[32] This incident was the cause of Skead's earliest mildly critical annotation in his own copy of Collinson's narrative, namely "Ho! A lubberly job," which he certainly intended as criticism of the captain.[33]

Skead was particularly impressed with the surroundings of Bahia Fortescue:

> Very fine scenery is met with hereabouts, & from the head of the bay which is formed by a thickly wooded valley surrounded by lofty peaks of bare rock a magnificent view of the mountains of Tierra del Fuego was obtained. The mountains which were covered with snow appeared to rear their heads & shoulders which were laden with stupendous glaciers, out of the very bosom of the sea.[34]

The three ships got under way at 3:30 AM on the 19th, with *Gorgon* towing both *Enterprise* and *Investigator*. Collinson ordered the topgallant yards and masts sent down to reduce the wind resistance, and *Gorgon* was able to tow the two ships at 6 knots. But once the Pacific swell began to be felt, this speed dropped. On the morning of the 20th off Cabo Pillar, the cables by which *Investigator* was towing astern of *Enterprise* both parted. Despite the heavy swell, they were replaced and the little convoy got under way again. But when they both parted again around noon, Collinson decided to leave *Investigator* to fend for herself for a couple of hours, while *Gorgon* towed only *Enterprise*. Then, at 1:30 he sent *Gorgon* back to pass a tow to *Investigator* and to bring her on. As fate would have it, the two ships of the expedition would never get together again.

On the 22nd *Gorgon* came up with *Enterprise* again in heavy seas. Captain Paynter reported that he had managed to take *Investigator* in tow, but that all the cables had parted (Collinson had been forced to reduce sail to treble-reefed topsails) and he had had to leave her. Since *Gorgon* was almost out of coal, on the 23rd Collinson ordered her to proceed to Valparaiso.

For the next three weeks, as she worked her way northwards, *Enterprise* encountered nothing but strong westerly winds and heavy seas; as a result, she was forced to pass to the east of Islas Juan Fernandez, whereas the shortest route to Hawaii would have taken her well west of those islands. It was not until 30 May at 10° 10'S; 105° 50'W that she picked up the Southeast Trades, which thereafter blew at a steady force 3 to 5. *Enterprise* crossed the Equator at midnight on 6 June at 120°W and picked up the Northeast Trades at 7°N; 131°W on the 12th. Since the wind freshened to force 7 for the last 500 miles to the Sandwich Islands (Hawaii), she made excellent time to that archipelago. The snow-covered peak of Mauna Kea[35] on the island of Hawaii was sighted on 22 June. Since its height was already known (13,796 feet)[36] Skead was able to calculate that the island was 92 miles away.

Running along the north coast of Maui, *Enterprise* swung south between that island and Oahu, rounded Diamond Head (see illustration p. 255), and dropped anchor off Honolulu at 9 PM on the 24th. Next morning a pilot came aboard to take the ship into the harbour. Since the wind was very light, this was achieved by using the fore and aft sails, with the boats towing and a gang of natives tracking the ship along the edge of a coral reef.[37] Reaching the busy harbour, *Enterprise* dropped anchor; as added security a kedge[38] was led out from the stern to the coral reef.

Skead and some companions took advantage of the opportunity for an excursion ashore, travelling by horseback to the viewpoint on the cliff top where King Kamehameha had driven a hostile army over the cliff, thus securing a victory and authority over the entire island. This is still a popular tourist attraction, and Skead's description, even now, is remarkably accurate:

> a few miles further on we reached the fatal cliff. A broad level plain stretches from the foot of the precipice to the sea shore upon which the heavy constant swell of the Pacific was rolling its foam. Several cottages & patches of cultivated ground lay scattered over the plain forming a pleasing contrast to the ugly spot on which we were standing. The edge of the precipice lay in a gap formed by nature about 100 feet deep from which the cliff falls 500 or 600 feet perpendicularly to the plain below.[39]

On the way back to Honolulu, Skead and his companions were involved in an accident that might have had serious consequences. As they approached a native horseman at full gallop, his horse reared and threw him. They soon discovered that he was helplessly drunk and also that he had a child strapped to his back, but fortunately neither was hurt.

Meanwhile, back in Honolulu, a drama of a different kind was being played out. The day after *Enterprise* arrived, two of her crew were found in bed with native women on shore; in accordance with the rather strict local laws (with which they were unfamiliar), they were arrested and imprisoned. One of their messmates asked to be able to see them. When he had received no reply after an hour, he called upon some of his shipmates, "who were in that state which seamen generally indulge in after a five months cruize. A rescue was proposed and in the fracas severe blows were exchanged, and one of the *Enterprize*'s men severely cut about the head,"[40] as Collinson reported in a letter to London. Three of the men were overpowered by the Hawaiian police and were also thrown in prison. Fines of $25 each were imposed.

At the time, Collinson wrote to the Admiralty's Accountant General about the matter.[41] Nine months later, by which time *Enterprise* was wintering at Hong Kong, Collinson wrote to General Miller, the British consul in Honolulu, concerning the fines the Hawaiian government had imposed on his obstreperous men:

> I take this opportunity of expressing my obligation for the manner in which you have placed the circumstances which occurred before the King, and only regret that the attempt which was made by one of the crew to gain legal access to his Shipmates in Prison, and which was persevered in for upwards an hour, without any attention whatsoever being paid to him; should not have induced His Majesty to mitigate the heavy Mulch of three Months Wages which now stands impressed against these Men, as I feel assured nothing of the kind would have taken place, if the quiet request had been complied with.[42]

It is not clear whether Collinson or the consul had paid the fines, or whether Collinson had been obliged to sail without these men.

Also while at Honolulu,. Collinson had to concern himself with the rather mysterious case of one of the Mates, R.T. Legg. As Collinson explained the situation rather cryptically in a letter dated 26 June 1850 to Rear-Admiral Hornby, Commander-in-Chief of the Pacific Squadron,

> I have the honor to acquaint you that I have received an application from Mr. Legg, Mate, requesting permission to leave H. M. Ship under my command.

Mr. Legg had been brought before me twice by his Messmates, for making use of language unbecoming to his character as an Officer and a Gentleman, and highly provoking. On the occurrence of the second offence I directed that he should for the future mess in his cabin; and I have now acceded to his request, and directed Commander Oldham to give him a passage to Valparaiso.[43]

Among other dignitaries, Collinson met with Mr. R.C. Wyllie, Minister of Foreign Relations at Honolulu, who showed him a very important letter from Dr. John Rae, of the Hudson's Bay Company, to Mr. Anthony Barclay, the British consul in New York, which had been published in New York on 13 April; in it Rae outlined his travels with Dr. John Richardson, searching the coast from the mouth of the Mackenzie to the Coppermine River in 1848 and 1849.[44] This information was very useful to Collinson, as it made him aware of the extent of the mainland coast that he would not need to search.

Pleading that the season was "so far advanced," and contrary to his explicit orders (Clause 18), Collinson decided not to wait for *Investigator* after all, but did leave orders for M'Clure. Predicated on the assumption that *Enterprise* would reach the Arctic first, these read, in part, as follows:

So soon as Her Majesty's ship under your command is fully complete with provisions, fuel and water you will make the best of your way to Cape Lisburne,[45] keeping a good lookout for the "Herald" or casks and firing guns in foggy weather after passing the Island of St. Lawrence. The whalers also may afford you information of our progress.

Should you obtain no intelligence, you will understand that I intend to make the pack, close to the American shore, and pursue the first favourable opening west of the coast stream, pressing forwards towards Melville Island.

In the event of meeting land, it is most probable that I would pursue the southern shore; but conspicuous marks will be erected if practicable, and information buried at a 10-foot radius.

As it is necessary to be prepared for the contingency of your not being able to follow by the ice closing in, or the severity of the weather, you will keep the "Investigator" as close to the edge of the pack as is consistent with her safety, and remain there until the season compels you to depart, when you will look into Kotzebue Sound for the "Plover", or information regarding her position; and having deposited under her charge a twelvemonth's provision, you will proceed to Valparaiso, replenish and return to the straits, bearing in mind that the months of June and July are the most favourable....

Should you not find the "Plover", or that any casualty has happened to render her inefficient as a depôt, you will take her place; and if (as Captain Kellett supposes) Kotzebue Sound has proved too exposed for a winter harbour, you will proceed to Grantley Harbour, leaving a notice to that effect at Chamisso Island.

The attention of your officers is to be called to, and you will read to your ship's company, the remarks of Sir John Richardson concerning the communication with the Esquimaux, and which are continued in the Arctic Report received at Plymouth.

Your operations in the season of 1851 cannot be guided by me, nor is there any occasion to urge you to proceed to the N.E.; yet it will be highly desirable, previous to entering the pack, that you completed provisions from the whalers, and obtained as much rein-deer's meat as possible. Captain Kellett's narrative will point out where the latter is to be had in most abundance, and where coal can be picked up on the beach; but husband the latter article during the winter, by using all the drift wood in your power.

In the event of leaving the straits this season, you will take any weak or sickly men out of the "Plover", and replace them from your crew; affording Commander Moore all the assistance in your power, and leaving with him Mr. Miertsching the interpreter, together with the instructions which you have received with regard to his accommodation.[46]

Having sent numerous letters and reports to London with HMS *Swift* and having filled his water casks, taken aboard what fresh provisions he could find, and loaded about four tonnes of coal, left for him by Captain Henry Kellett of HMS *Herald*,[47] Collinson put to sea at 10 AM on 30 June, without waiting for *Investigator*. Before leaving the archipelago, however, *Enterprise* first called at Yam Bay on the island of Oueehow to purchase the vegetables, pigs, and similar supplies that had not been procurable in Honolulu. Two boats were sent ashore, but they were able to buy only a few yams; Collinson reports that the demand for labour in the California goldfields and on board the American whalers had led to a noticeable reduction in the population of the islands, and hence a relative dearth of fresh vegetables.

Collinson now had to decide which route he would follow to reach Bering Strait. Among the mail waiting for him at Honolulu was a letter from Captain Henry Kellett, who had called at Honolulu in HMS *Herald* on his way north a month earlier. In it he made the following suggestion:

> If you should be obliged to pass through the Aleutian group, by all means prefer the Straits of Seguan (Amouchta);[48] they are wide, safe and free from races, which none of the others are. I have passed through them; you will find a very good description of them in the book I have left for you, trans-lated from the French by my purser.[49]

Collinson, however, opted to ignore this very sensible advice, and instead headed west and northwest to pass around the entire Aleutian chain, that is, west of Attu Island, although this route inevitably took much longer.

In his first major criticism of his captain in his journal, Skead remarks,

> The reasons assigned for making so circuitous a course as we have done is to avoid certain NW gales which are supposed to prevail in the NW Pacific & to prevent those gales from being directly foul, which they would be on a direct course, it is necessary to get well to windward (to the West) before the region of these supposed gales is entered.... We, for fear of gales that no one else has experienced, have followed a roundabout course to reach the place, which for all we know to the contrary, might have been reached directly.[50]

Even then Collinson selected an unnecessarily circuitous route, as Skead pointed out:

> the course from Oueehow to Attu is N38°W, yet we have steered WNW & then West making so circuitous a course as to ensure the failure of the month of July before we can reach Behrings strait. Altogether I am at a loss to reconcile this route with the avowed intention and views of the Captn. who states that June & July are the best months for navigating the Polar Sea.[51]

In fact, Skead was vindicated by the course followed by M'Clure's *Investigator*. Having met a merchant captain at Honolulu who advised him to sail due north

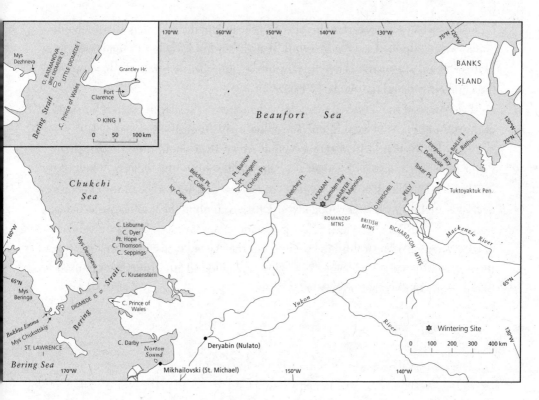

Bering Strait, Chukchi Sea, and Beaufort Sea. Area of operations of HMS *Enterprise* in 1850, 1851, and 1854. Inset: detail of the Bering Strait area.

and through the Aleutian chain, following the same route that Kellett had recommended to Collinson, M'Clure ran through Seguam Pass between Seguam and Amukta islands and encountered HMS *Plover* in Kotzebue Sound on 29 July,[52] well ahead of *Enterprise*, which had a head start of five days on leaving Honolulu.

Following the course selected by Collinson, *Enterprise* encountered only light winds and calms. As Skead noted in his journal, her passage was "remarkable for the total absence of a breeze sufficiently strong to require even a reef in the topsails."[53] She reached her westernmost longitude (166°E) at 50°N on 27 July in thick fog and rounded the west end of Attu Island on the 29th. Fog persisted for the run north across the Bering Sea and cleared only when the ship was just south of Mys Navarin on 8 August. Thereafter she had some pleasant, clear, dry weather. On the 11th the ship passed the western tip of Saint Lawrence Island, and by 5:30 AM on the 12th was within sight of Mys Dezhnev, at the west side of Bering Strait.

Numerous whales were seen in this area and three American whalers were sighted, one of which appeared to be making off, that is, flensing a whale and rendering the blubber. Soon afterwards *Enterprise* was approaching Bering Strait, the gateway to the Chukchi Sea and the Arctic Ocean.

Enterprise had thus reached the point where she would start her search for signs of the missing Franklin expedition. It was now early August.

Thus far there is little in the surviving record that would indicate that there might be serious tensions between Captain Collinson and his officers. The only indications that Skead, at least, was not entirely satisfied with some of the captain's decisions are his much later comment on *Enterprise* fouling the tug *Gorgon* at Bahia Fortescue in the Strait of Magellan (see p.36), and his criticisms of Collinson's choice of the circuitous route around the west end of the Aleutian chain (see pp. 48). But there is no evidence at this point that Collinson had found any grounds for faulting Skead or any of the other officers. ●

3

"I MUST HAVE 15 MILES"

Despite THE WEATHER BEING

quite hazy as *Enterprise* passed through Bering Strait, Mys Dezhnev, the Diomede

Islands, and Cape Prince of Wales in Alaska were all visible at once. At this point

three boats were sighted, and Collinson considered altering course to communicate

with them, but since they showed no sign of trying to head for the ship, he deduced

that they were not from Franklin's expedition, and hence he held his course.

Pushing north with a fresh easterly wind, *Enterprise* raised land on the starboard
bow in the early hours of the 13th, and by 10 AM had reached Cape Lisburne. In
the letter Captain Kellett had left at Honolulu, he had promised either to wait for
Enterprise at Cape Lisburne or to leave bottles with messages under cairns at Point
Hope, Cape Lisburne, and Wainwright Inlet. There was no sign of HMS *Herald* or
of any cairns, but what appeared to be a large white marker was spotted on shore.
Collinson, accompanied by Dr. Anderson and Mr. Edward Whitehead, the ship's
clerk, went ashore, only to find that the white marker was just a patch of ice in
a gully; vast numbers of looms (murres) were nesting on the cliffs. After having

the ship's name painted on the rocks, while Anderson and Whitehead shot large numbers of looms, Collinson and his party returned to the ship. Rather than wasting time by beating back 30 miles against a foul wind to Point Hope, Collinson opted instead to push on to Cape Collie in Wainwright Inlet.

By 15 August *Enterprise* had reached Cape Collie, a low headland at the narrow entrance to Wainwright Inlet. At this point Skead noted that the officers, on the basis of the reports of experienced arctic captains such as Parry and Ross, anticipated that they still had five or six weeks before freeze-up would end navigation in the Arctic for the season, in striking contrast to Collinson, who insisted that only June and July were suitable for arctic navigation. This view of Collinson's seems to have been derived from his interpretation of a comment by Sir Edward Parry in a memorandum solicited by the Admiralty to the effect that "Every exertion should be made to reach the ice to the northward of Behring's Straits by the 1st of August."[1] Parry was suggesting that ice conditions for getting past Point Barrow would be optimal from that date onwards, quite the opposite of Collinson's interpretation! It was presumably on the basis of this belief that, according to Skead, Collinson was talking of wintering at Hong Kong and of sending *Investigator* to winter at Valparaiso, even before they reached the Bering Sea![2]

When the fog cleared off Cape Collie on the morning of the 15th, the point was found to be close under the lee. Lt. Phayre went ashore to examine a conspicuous post, but it was found to have been erected by the Inuit, although footprints of both moccasins and boots were found—but nowhere was there any sign of a cairn or a message.

It is not clear why Collinson or his men were unable to find the cairns for which they were searching, but it was certainly unfortunate. From Kellett's messages they would have learned that *Investigator*, which had run north by the more direct route through the Aleutians, was now ahead of *Enterprise*, and since the latter did not come up with her consort before reaching Point Barrow, it could be assumed that she had pushed east from there, as indeed she had.

Enterprise encountered the first scattered ice floes in the early hours of 16 August, and later that day the crow's nest was sent aloft.[3] For the next four days the ship was working her way north and east, generally in sailing ice, ice loose enough to present little in the way of obstacles. At 4 AM on the 20th she was 25 miles due north of Point Barrow, and although the edge of the main pack was in sight to the north, stretching from horizon to horizon, there was no ice to the eastwards, water temperature 40°, and no bottom with 60 fathoms. Collinson was quite optimistic as to his prospects:

"we thought ourselves fairly on the way to Banks' Land or Melville Island, for which a course was shaped."[4] But this was not to be.

As the ship worked her way eastwards from Point Barrow, Collinson ordered Skead to map the distribution of ice in detail, an exercise which the latter (correctly) found to be totally pointless since it

> gave me much trouble in calculating courses and distances to enable the Points & bays of ice to be fixed. The compasses being almost useless & the frequency of the alterations made in the ship's courses reduced the DR [dead reckoning] to be a very questionable authority for the ship's position. It was however sufficiently accurate for a body whose position was not more stable than that of the clouds. However the bays & points were plotted with as much gravity as if they had been upon the shores of some newly discovered land.[5]

Skead and others of the officers believed that the only sensible option was to hug the coast as closely as possible, since the deep-drafted hummocks and pressure ridges in the pack tended to become grounded some considerable distance offshore, leaving a strip of open water inshore of them, with adequate depth for a ship such as *Enterprise*. It was by taking advantage of this belt of open water that M'Clure in *Investigator* had succeeded in working along this coast just two weeks previously.[6] But Collinson's views were diametrically opposed to this, much to Skead's disgust:

> we are now scared by another conclusion, viz. the coast of America close inshore is shallow, therefore the whole coast is dangerous. In consequence of this conclusion the Capt. has determined that he will go no nearer to the shore than 15 miles. On the Chart supplied to us by Captain Kellett there is a line of shoals laid down 10 or 12 miles to the NE of Point Barrow which I think has much to do with this decision. However the officers who have been on these voyages declare that our only chance of success in pushing to the eastd. consists in keeping close inshore between the land and the ice & this agrees with the judgement pronounced by Captain Parry. Upon one or two occasions when conversing with the Capt. upon the subject, I have ventured to express an opinion of the possibility of the water's proving deeper than it is supposed, but he has abruptly stopped me by saying: "I must have 15 miles." "You must give me 15 miles."[7]

In the early hours of 21 August, as *Enterprise* ran east along the south edge of the main pack, ice was also sighted to the south. When the weather cleared slightly, the zone of open water between the two ice masses was seen running off to the east, but Collinson insisted that it was "only a bight, as the water is too smooth for it to be anything else."[8] The ice mate on watch advised heaving-to until the weather cleared completely, but Collinson refused and ordered that they head back west in the hope of finding a route eastwards beyond his "safe" limit of 15 miles from shore. By noon the fog had cleared and Skead noted that from aloft Lieutenant Barnard

> saw an opening which he said would lead into water to the SEd. This was reported to the Captn. Why had he not reported it before? Barnard said he had only just made it out." Ah well," the Capt. replied, "I will not alter the course now for the men have only just got their spoons in the soup."[9]

Given the importance of trying to get east as fast as possible, this reaction would appear to be taking concern for the men's welfare much too far.

Collinson's assessment of the situation, as recorded in his published narrative, was distinctly different:

> At 8 o'clock we were within 30 miles of the land and no water to be seen in that direction from aloft. I was therefore under the necessity of determining whether I would attempt the inshore passage. A careful perusal of the Arctic voyages along the north coast of America, as well as a personal communication with Sir George Back, who was kind enough to give me the benefit of his experience previous to leaving England, had fully convinced me that I could look for no place of safety for a vessel of Enterprise's draught of water nearer than Cape Bathurst, which I could scarcely hope to reach previous to the winter setting in, and the ice closing on the shore. I therefore reluctantly gave up the examination in this direction, and made my mind up to turn the edge of the pack further to the west, where Captain Kellett had penetrated last year, and seen a promising opening, and where Captain Moore had reported the loom of land.[10]

Having run back southwestwards some 50 miles, to cover himself against any possible accusations that he had not persevered long enough, Collinson then made a show of canvassing the opinion of his officers and the ice mates (in writing), by asking them to sign an extremely ambiguous document. In hindsight, however, the wording of the declaration that his officers were asked to sign certainly makes it very clear what answers Collinson was expecting:

> Gentlemen: It is my direction that you give me your opinions as to our future progress to the Eastward under the following form:
>
> Remarks. Having traced the edge of the Pack in a SEly direction for 145 miles, from Latitude 72° 45'N, Long. 159° 5'W and being compelled to retrace our course to the SWd 50 Miles in consequence of its taking a trend in that direction leaving no signs of an opening towards the East or SE, the only open water being from SW to NNW, we consider any further progress to the Eastwd. to be wholly impracticable "Off Shore."
>
> With respect to our getting to the Eastwd. by pushing in that direction "in shore" the following facts are to be considered: 1st the wind is directly foul; 2nd the weather has just become foggy; 3rd the Ice is closely packed as far as the eye can reach (an extent of 10 miles), reducing our distance from the shore to 15 miles, together with the great improbability of our being able in a heavy ship on a shallow coast with a very doubtful passage and a foul wind to make any Easterly progress, and 4th no place for anchorage being nearer than 500 miles.
>
> All these things being considered, we are of opinion that any further attempt to get to the Eastwd. by running to the SWwd looking for open water would be a useless waste of time.[11]

All those to whom this letter was addressed (Lts. Phayre and Barnard, Second Master Skead, and ice mates Arbuthnott and Atkinson) signed to indicate that neither the inshore nor the offshore route was practicable. But they were all thinking of the prevailing ice and weather conditions at that moment and certainly were not advocating that the attempt to get to the eastward should be totally abandoned for the season.

As Skead confided to his journal, Collinson's request

> was altogether unexpected & occasioned much surprise, as we had only just commenced our labours. No one considered it in a serious light, however, but fancied it had reference to the circumstances immediately present. While surprise was being expressed as to what were the Capt.'s

motives for asking our opinions in writing I said to Lt. Barnard "Let us
go aloft & see what can be done." Lt. Barnard, Mr. Arbuthnot & myself
accordingly went aloft, from whence we had a full view of the state of the
ice, the weather at the time being remarkably clear in the South & SW.
Our vision we estimated reached to 10 miles (Mr. Arbuthnot said 15 but
we considered so great a distance to be beyond the range of vision) & this
space was covered by a close, heavy field of ice without any signs of an
opening to lead through it. We pushed the ship far into the loose ice to
the Southwd. which fringed the pack edge, so far indeed as to compel us
to return as we came or get beset. The 10 miles seen to the South & SW
which we saw to be impenetrable reached to the 15 miles from the shore
within which the Captn. had expressed his determination not to carry the
ship, & no one thought of questioning that determination, much less of
disputing it with him. The wind blew freshly from the ESE in gusts &
a dense fog rapidly approached from the Eastd. which shortly enveloped
surrounding objects in thick gloom. We therefore concluded that under
existing circumstances no Easterly progress could be made even if deep
water existed between our extent of vision & the shoals off Pt. Barrow,
of which from all accounts we had considerable doubts, and that to run
SW any longer looking for a passage which, if found, could not be made
available in the present state of the weather, would be losing valuable time
to no purpose. At 8 PM after having retreated 50 miles from our morning's
position, the Senr. Lieutt., 2nd. Lt., Mr. Arbuthnot & myself were assembled on the Quarter deck. Mr. Phayre asked "Well, gentlemen, what do
you think of it? We answered: "In the present state of affairs no progress
to the eastd. can be made either Off shore or in shore & to run away any
longer is wasting time to no purpose." Lt. Barnard said: "Had we not better
recommend the Capt. to heave-to until the weather changes?" I asked: "Do
you think we are called upon to offer advice? It seems to me that we have
simply to state whether we can get to the Eastd. or not; the Captn. will
then decide himself upon the measures to be adopted." The order for our
opinions was then read over again when Lt. Barnard said: "I think you are
right, I did not see it in that light till now." In this the others acquiesced, &
it was then decided that the Captn. should be told what had been done &
that we considered no Easterly progress could be made, & that to run SW
any longer looking for open water was uselessly wasting time. This was

delivered verbally by the Senr. Lieutt. who promised to deliver it in writing on the morrow. This was done by 8 AM but we ran to the Westd. till 9 h. when orders were given, not to heave-to but to steer WNW over the very track we had followed for the three preceding days.[12]

On the relevant pages in his own copy of Collinson's narrative, Skead later expressed his feelings as follows:

Downright humbug. The Captain had positively stated that he would not go nearer to the shore than 15 miles, as the opinion of all those in England who knew Arctic navigation was against it & we accepted his dictum loyally & without dispute. Alas! … All the time he was running to the S.W. with a strong wind.… We ran away in absurd haste & had lost many miles of Easting before he had the report or even asked for it.… The Ice Mates advised the Capt. to make fast to a big floe & wait for a change, but in vain.[13]

Later, as Skead noted in his journal, he and his fellow officers regretted that they had not clarified what they intended in their response to Collinson's "poll":

From what has since transpired it is very unfortunate that we did not put on record more fully the grounds upon which we formed our opinion as to Easterly progress "in shore," but as no importance was assigned to the signing of the paper at the time, it was drawn up without any allusion to what might take place or be practicable in a few hours, should the wind shift or the ice disperse, which it very often does in the most unaccountable manner. The "in shore" too had reference only to the limit prescribed by the Captn. & which he must have understood fully. Altho' every one thought that a chance did exist close inshore between the ice & the land no one thought of disputing the Captain's decision not to go closer than 15 miles & this is the "in shore" alluded to in the Report.…That we were about to abandon the attempt to get eastd. along the American coast no one had the slightest idea of; in short it was believed that we should either heave-to or secure the ship to an ice floe & wait for a favorable change in the weather & state of the ice, instead of which we ran away & it was afterwards made to appear that the Officers acquiesced in the necessity of such a proceeding.[14]

For a week thereafter Collinson tried to push northwards, in the hope that he would find a route eastwards well offshore. He reached his farthest north at 73° 23'N; 164°W on the morning of 28 August. Not surprisingly he found the ice becoming heavier and closer the farther he penetrated. He therefore

> hauled out to the west at noon, being compelled to come to the conclusion that this season had passed away without our being able to do anything towards the succour of the missing expedition.[15]

In other words, Collinson was abandoning the search for the season.

A few days later, on 26 August, an improvement in the weather and ice conditions encouraged Skead to risk suggesting to his captain that they might make another effort to go eastward:

> The fine clear weather & the fresh fair wind that was blowing increased the temptation so at 8 AM while putting the ship's track upon the Chart I ventured to point out to the Capt. the uselessness of our beating about the ice to the NWd while the wind was fair for Pt. Barrow & the sea open. He said: "What good do you expect by returning to Point Barrow?" I said: "Tis very probable that the water will be found deeper than it is supposed to be. If so, & the sea be open we may get to the eastd. alongshore; at all events we can examine the Point & the land in its vicinity & ascertain whether it is shallow or not, which knowledge will be all in our favour next spring, should we not succeed in getting to the East'd now." He answered: "Tis not a bad idea & I'll try it." We accordingly tacked & stood towards the Point which the wind nearly permitted us to do direct. This change in our course infused new hopes into all, particularly as the tabooed 15 miles were thrown to the winds & the "Old Polars" spoke of success as almost certain.
>
> About 10 AM while standing for the Point I walked the deck with the Captain & engaged in the following conversation with him regarding our future chances of success. For the first time he spoke something about the lateness of the season. I said: "As to that, Sir, had we been detained a few days longer to the Southd. & had only arrived as it were just now, you would not have thought it too late, I imagine, Sir." "Oh, no." the Captain answered."Well, Sir," I said, "We have only to forget having failed once if

a chance does offer to Easterly advance." He replied: "I will certainly try it again if a good opportunity offers...."

Towards noon the wind drew gradually forward & became foul for the Point, yet the sea was quite open & the speed undiminished, so by making a few tacks we still hoped to reach the Point during the next day, but upon taking the Noon position to the Captain I soon found his resolution to go close inshore had changed with the wind, for he thus addressed me: "Here! We have a foul wind & you want me to beat to windward." I said: "The wind was fair, Sir, when I suggested we return to the Eastd., but even with a foul wind I think we have a better chance of success by returning to the Point than by keeping to the NW where we have already seen that no passage exists." To this he replied: "It looks d—d foolish to run away from the Pt., then directly the wind becomes foul to beat back again. The opinion in England among those who understand most about the matter, is that open water will be found to the Nd. of 72°, so unless the wind shifts before 1 PM, I shall go about & the long board we have made will be all in our favour for weathering the SW ice we tacked off this morning."

I could say no more, seeing it would be useless & that he was determined to give the Pt. a wide berth, so I left the Cabin fully assured that all hope of success for this season was gone. This cursed <u>Polar basin</u>, which I suppose is what he meant by "open water North of 72°" is one of the phantoms which has led to our failure. We began by trying to get into it which detained us while we might have been trying to find what in all probability did exist, viz. an open channel along the American coast & we now end the season by continuing to seek for what no one save the Captain believes has any existence.[16]

It seems very likely that this show of independence by Skead, and his attempt to guide the expedition's course in a direction at odds with Collinson's stated beliefs, meant that from now on he was a marked man. Collinson's version of events, including his interpretation of his poll of his officers' views, a version that reveals that he was not trying to reach the "Open polar sea," was very different:

We got, you will see, 70 miles to the East of Point Barrow when we were headed back by a barrier resting so close to the shore as to demand my serious thoughts whether on the 21st of August we had season enough left to push for Cape Bathurst, and this being pronounced not practicable I had before me two alternatives, one to communicate with the Point and the other to try for open water further to the North. The latter I selected although I am not of the Polar Basin theory, and gained no end except a conviction that if we want to get to the Eastd. we must go in shore.[17]

Regaining open water, *Enterprise* headed south along the ice edge. Some walrus had been seen earlier, but when a herd was now seen, since there was no longer any urgency, two whaleboats were launched and managed to kill and recover three of them. Some 1200 lbs of meat was obtained, as well as three casks of blubber. Surprisingly, perhaps, given their usual conservatism concerning food, the men ate it, "pronouncing it to be very tolerable, tasting not unlike coarse beef."[18]

By 9 PM on the 30th, *Enterprise* was off Cape Lisburne, and she reached Point Hope at 6 AM next morning. Collinson and Dr. Anderson went ashore, to be met by a party of eight or ten Inupiat. While the doctor distracted them with beads, tobacco, and other gifts, Collinson walked to the end of the point, where he found a post with the message *Herald VIII. / 50 a bottle, 10 feet magn. North.*[19] On digging at this spot Collinson found a message from Captain Kellett to say that *Herald* had called here five days before and was now heading for Grantley Harbour, where it was proposed that *Plover* should winter. Furthermore, Kellett revealed that *Investigator* had reached Cape Lisburne on 31 July and had last been seen by *Plover* on 4 August off the Seahorse Islands, "standing to the NEd under a heavy press of canvas."[20]

This was the first inkling Collinson received that M'Clure in *Investigator* had reached Bering Strait before him, and that he might have passed Point Barrow and be preparing to winter in the Arctic. In fact, *Investigator* had rounded Point Barrow on 5 August 1850 and, even as Collinson was reading Kellett's message, she was passing Cape Bathurst, heading east.[21]

In a letter M'Clure wrote to the Secretary of the Admiralty as he was approaching the Aleutians on 20 July 1850, which he later left with Captain Moore in HMS *Plover* in the Chukchi Sea for forwarding to England, he makes a pretence of anticipating that he would reach Cape Lisburne after Collinson, and that, failing to connect with him, he would thereafter be operating independently. The letter in question reads as follows:

Sir,

As I have received instructions from Captain Collinson, C.B., clear and unembarrassing, (a copy of which I enclose) to proceed to Cape Lisburne, in the hope of meeting him in that vicinity, as he anticipated being detained a day or two by the "Plover" in Kotzebue Sound, it is unnecessary to add that every exertion shall be made to reach that rendezvous, but can scarce venture to hope that, even under very favourable circumstances, I shall be so fortunate as to accomplish it, ere the "Enterprise" will have rounded that Cape, as, from her superior sailing, she hitherto having beaten us by eight days to Cape Virgins, and from Magellan Straits to Waohu[22] six. It is, therefore, under the probable case that this vessel may form a detached part of the expedition, that I feel it is my duty to state, for the information of the Lords Commissioners of the Admiralty, the course which, under such a contingency I shall endeavour to pursue, and have to request that you will lay the same before their Lordships.

1st. After passing Cape Lisburne it is my intention to keep in the open water, which from the different reports that I have read, appears, about this season of the year, to make between the American coast and the main pack, as far to the eastward as the 130th meridian, unless a favourable opening should earlier appear in the ice, which would lead me to infer that I might push more directly for Bank's Land, which I think is of the utmost importance to thoroughly examine. In the event of thus far succeeding, and the season continuing favourable for further operations, it would be my anxious desire to get to the northward of Melville Island, and resume our search along its shores, and the islands adjacent, as long as the navigation can be carried on, and then secure for the winter in the most eligible position which offers.

2d. In the ensuing spring, as soon as it is practicable for travelling parties to start, I should dispatch as many as the state of the crew will admit in different directions, each being provided with 40 days' provisions, with directions to examine minutely all bays, inlets, and islands towards the N.E., ascending occasionally some of the highest points of land, so as to be enabled to obtain extended views, being particularly cautious in their advance, to observe any indication of a break up in the ice, so that their return to the ship may be effected without hazard, even before the expenditure of their provisions would otherwise render it necessary.

3rd. Supposing the parties to have returned (without obtaining any clue of the absent ships), and the vessel liberated about the 1st of August, my object would then be to push on towards Wellington Inlet (assuming that that channel communicates with the Polar sea), and search both its shores, unless, in so doing, some indication should be met with to show that parties from any of Captain Austin's vessels had previously done so, when I should return and endeavour to penetrate in the direction of Jones' Sound, carefully examining every place that was practicable. Sir, should our efforts to reach this point be successful, and in the route no traces are discernible of the long-missing expedition, I should not then be enabled longer to divest myself of the feeling, painful as it must be to arrive at such a conclusion, that all human aid would then be perfectly unavailing, and therefore, under such a conviction, I would think it my duty, if possible, to return to England, or, at all events, endeavour to reach some port that would ensure that object upon the following year.

4th. In the event of this being my last communication, would request you to assure their Lordships that no apprehension whatever need be entertained of our safety until the autumn of 1854, as we have on board three years of all species of provisions, commencing from the 1st September proximo, which, without much deprivation, may be made to extend a period of four years, as, moreover, whatever is killed by the hunting parties I intend to issue in lieu of the usual rations, which will still further protract our resources.

It gives me great pleasure to say that the good effects of the fruit and vegetables (a large quantity of which we took on at Waohu) are very perceptible, in the increased vigour of the men, who at this moment are in as excellent condition as it is possible to desire, and evince a spirit of confidence and a cheerfulness of disposition which are beyond all appreciation.

5th. Should difficulties apparently insurmountable encompass our progress, so as to render it a matter of doubt whether the vessel could be extricated, I should deem it expedient, in that case not to hazard the lives of those entrusted to my charge after the winter of 1852, but, in the ensuing spring, quit the vessel with sledges and boats, and make the best of our way either to Pond's Bay, Leopold Harbour, the Mackenzie, or for the whalers, according to circumstances.

Finally. In this letter I have endeavoured to give an outline of what I wish to accomplish (and what, under moderately favourable seasons, appears to me attainable), the carrying out of which, however, not resting upon human exertions, it is impossible even to surmise if any or what portion may be successful. But my object in addressing you is to place their Lordships in possession of my intentions up to the latest period, so, as far as possible, to relieve their minds from any unnecessary anxiety as to our fate; and, having done this, a duty which is incumbent, from the deep sympathy expressed by their Lordships, and participated in by all classes of our countrymen, in the interesting object of this expedition, I have only to add that, with the ample resources which a beneficent Government and a generous country have placed at our disposal (not anything that can add to our comfort being wanting), we enter upon this distinguished service with a firm determination to carry out, as far as in our feeble strength we are permitted, their benevolent intentions.

I have etc.

ROBERT M'CLURE, COMMANDER.[23]

These are remarkably detailed plans for M'Clure to be expounding for their Lordships, as to what his intentions would be on the off-chance that *Enterprise* had reached Cape Lisburne first and that, despite their Lordships' specific prohibition against allowing the ships to become separated, Collinson had forged ahead alone. One has a strong suspicion that M'Clure was hoping passionately that by cutting through the Aleutian chain, he would reach Bering Strait ahead of Collinson, and by pretending that he thought he was astern of the latter, he could without risk of censure, proceed into the Arctic independently.

It was when M'Clure encountered *Plover* that he discovered that *Enterprise* had not yet been seen, and he surmised that she might have passed *Plover* in the persistent fogs of the Chukchi Sea and was already somewhere farther north, since "she was the faster sailing ship, and there was no reason to suppose she had not been equally favoured in winds."[24]

Somewhat later, on 31 July, M'Clure had encountered HMS *Herald*, Captain Henry Kellett;[25] however, the latter did not share M'Clure's opinion that *Enterprise* must already have passed by, northward bound. Although senior to M'Clure, he was reluctant to order the latter to wait since, as Dr. Armstrong, *Investigator*'s surgeon, noted, he felt the responsibility he should incur, should she have passed, by detaining her consort. Captain M'Clure, too, pointed out how valuable every hour was to him, and to the important service he was upon; for he well knew the value of the arctic maxim, that a day lost often entails a whole season of fruitless labour. At last Captain Kellett consented that the "Investigator" should part company....[26]

Kellett made one last attempt to persuade M'Clure to wait, however:

> The "Investigator" had not long borne up on her solitary course under a heavy press of sail, when the signal was made, "Had you better not wait forty-eight hours?"
> The reply was characteristic: "Important duty. Cannot upon my own responsibility." In a few hours the "Investigator" was alone, the wind changing to the N.E. quarter.[27]

M'Clure had achieved his goal; he could now function as an independent command.

While Collinson was retrieving and reading Kellett's message at Point Hope, Dr. Anderson, meanwhile, had been visiting an Inupiat tent; here he obtained half a letter from Kellett (presumably the other half was in the possession of another of the Inupiat), but it was found to contain essentially the same information as the letter Collinson had dug up. As Skead noted in his journal, the surgeon's reaction was "For God's sake, Sir, go back; it is not now too late," but Collinson's response was "No, no, I must see Kellett."[28] With that remark the last chance of getting into the Arctic for the winter was lost.

Collinson's decision to turn back from Point Barrow, and especially his decision to ignore the advice of the ice mates, not to mention that of his officers with previous arctic experience, appears to have been the spark-point that developed into the smouldering conflict that arose between the captain and his officers.

Putting to sea again, by early next morning (1 September) *Enterprise* had both Cape Prince of Wales and the Diomede Islands in sight; she rounded the cape at noon, and by 7 PM had reached Port Clarence. Initially there was no sign of either *Plover* or *Herald*, but then at about 8:30 a light was spotted in Grantley Harbour (the inner, easternmost continuation of Port Clarence); at this latitude (~ 65° 30'N), it was starting to get dark by that time. Collinson burned a blue light and fired a rocket, and saw answering signals from Grantley Harbour. At 10 PM Captain Thomas Moore of

HMS *Plover* came aboard; following Captain Kellett's orders, he was making preparations to winter here at Grantley Harbour, even building a house on shore to store
supplies. *Plover* was lying in a cove on the north side of Grantley Harbour in a depth
of 2½ fathoms. However, Collinson now informed him that, since *Plover* had already
spent two winters in the area, he proposed that *Enterprise* should take her place,
and that *Plover* should head south to Hong Kong for the winter. Captain Moore
then returned to his ship, leaving his Second Master, Mr. Henry Martin, to assist in
piloting *Enterprise* into Grantley Harbour.

Next morning *Enterprise* weighed and stood in towards the bar at the entrance to
Grantley Harbour. Leaving instructions for the ship to anchor off the bar, Collinson
took a boat and went ahead to check the channel:

> Finding the latter very shoal and the channel not only narrow but crooked,
> I dropped one or two buoys and went inside Grantley Harbour to judge
> whether it was a fit place for us, and that our labour in getting in might not
> be thrown away.[29]

On reaching *Plover* he found that *Enterprise* had run aground on the bar, "the officer
in charge [Lt. Phayre] having very improperly, and against the advice of Mr. Martin,
run for the outer buoy instead of anchoring as I had ordered him."[30] Fortunately, by
laying out a stream anchor *Enterprise*'s crew was able to haul her off the bar fairly
easily and without any damage.

Next day (3 September) Captain Collinson and Mr. Arbuthnott again took a
boat inside the bar to locate a possible wintering site; it was deemed that there should
be sufficient depth of water. Collinson then made a more detailed examination of
the entrance and moored some buoys to mark the channel.

Early next morning *Enterprise* got under way, heading for the harbour entrance,
but before reaching Collinson's second buoy, she ran aground in 15 feet. According
to Collinson, although there was practically no tidal range, the water level had
dropped by about four feet from the previous day due to the wind shifting from
north (offshore) to south (onshore). This is hard to understand, since such a wind-
shift would have the opposite effect, that is, it should have caused a rise in water
level.

Work began immediately to try to heave the ship off, and in the midst of this
predicament HMS *Herald* arrived,[31] although initially she appeared so distorted by
refraction that Collinson mistook her for HMS *Investigator*, but, as Skead noted,

"those who knew Capt. M'Clure, as positively affirmed that under no circum-stances would he be induced to quit the ice before the *end* of Septr."[32] *Herald's* arrival was very fortuitous, since Collinson was able to transfer 180 tonnes of provisions and stores to her. The ship was further lightened by dropping anchors and chains overboard, after they had first been buoyed so that they could later be recovered. Then a bower anchor was led out astern, and by heaving on the cable to that anchor the ship was hauled off the shoal at 5 PM on the 5th. Berthold Seemann, naturalist on board *Herald*, was impressed by Skead's part in this operation:

> They were obliged to heave her astern, and with the bower-chain, as she had
> no stern-holes; some difficulty and delay would have been experienced in
> doing this had it not been for the ready resource of Mr. Skead (her second
> master), who placed a small anchor in the port, the arms and shank making
> a perfect lead for the cable.[33]

In the meantime, *Plover* had tried to come to *Enterprise's* help; she too ran aground, but was able to get afloat again without too much difficulty.

While *Enterprise* was aground, Skead sounded the channel independently and found depths of 3½ fathoms, whereas the buoys placed by Collinson were in depths of only 2¼ to 2½ fathoms. Skead does not mention whether he revealed the depths he had found to the Captain.

From *Herald's* officers Skead and his fellow officers were now able to confirm what they had suspected as to *Investigator's* progress. She had reached Honolulu only a few hours after *Enterprise* had sailed; she then put to sea six days later but by cutting through the Aleutians by the Amukta Pass "instead of following our blockhead of a course" (to use Skead's expression) had reached Cape Lisburne 17 days before *Enterprise*.

> What a comment is this passage of the Investigator upon our miserable
> bungle; yet it was just what we had anticipated; not indeed that the Inves-
> tigator would steer straight, but that if she did she would make a quicker
> passage than ourselves. The news of our consort's movements created
> mingled sensations of pleasure & regret amongst us: pleasure in the prospect
> of relief being afforded to the objects of our search & regret in the reflection
> that we were debarred from sharing in the glorious work.[34]

In view of *Enterprise* having grounded, "as we had so bungled about getting into Grantley Harbour,"[35] and despite Captain Moore and his Second Master insisting there was plenty of depth and even offering to pilot *Enterprise* into the harbour, Collinson decided that it was either impossible or unsafe to winter there and now reversed his earlier decision: *Plover* would remain here for the winter after all, and *Enterprise* would proceed to Hong Kong for the winter. For the next week, *Enterprise*'s men were kept busy transferring a three-year supply of provisions and stores to *Plover* and helping her men complete the house on shore.

Skead, understandably, was totally disgusted by these decisions:

> It is somewhat remarkable that the Captain's prediction uttered just after leaving Woahoo (that he should winter at Hong Kong) should be brought to pass by such an extraordinary chain of events & it now only remains for the Investigator to proceed to Valparaiso, as ordered, to present the wonderful spectacle of the Polar expedition encompassing the globe in the region of the Tropics in their endeavours to afford relief to the missing Polar Navigators! No one however entertains a doubt that the Investigator will find Winter quarters much nearer to the appointed ground for her search.[36]

Skead further noted that Captain Kellett (of HMS *Herald*) was even

> much surprised to find us in Port Clarence in the very heart of the working season & one of the lts. told me that Capt. K. had declared "he would rather have seen us upon the rocks than looking for winter quarters at so early a part of the summer season."[37]

Skead had served under Kellett previously and now had a frank conversation with him. When he expressed his dismay at the prospect of wintering at Hong Kong, Kellett tried to console him with the thought of the beneficial effect of filling up with fresh provisions, but "I told him we had everything we wanted & could get venison from the natives & be able to start in better condition than if we went to Hong Kong where the men would desert & contract disease. The Captain [Collinson] now came up & so a stop was put to this conversation."[38]

In Skead's view, at least one ship should winter at Point Barrow, where Captain Moore (who had reached it by boat from Icy Cape only weeks before) reported there was a good harbour, in which Captain Rochfort Maguire would winter in *Plover* in 1852–53 and 1853–54.[39] Skead felt that Point Barrow was

> the spot to which any party of the missing ones would make for to find assist-
> ance and relief, whereas the Plover was left at Port Clarence, a spot so far
> from the Point that any party might perish before they could reach it, even
> supposing them to know that a ship was stationed there....[40]

But before heading south Collinson decided to make one last sortie north, as far as Cape Lisburne, in case *Investigator* had run into trouble and her crew were attempting to come south in her boats. After handing mail and dispatches to *Herald*, which was now homeward bound, *Enterprise* put to sea at 8 AM on 14 September, but as she tried to round Cape Prince of Wales she encountered a strong northerly wind, a strong current, and a short sea; after several tacks it was clear that she was making no progress, and hence Collinson dropped anchor three miles offshore, between Cape York and King Island, where the ship rode quite comfortably despite some violent squalls. When the wind dropped somewhat on the afternoon of the 17th, a boat was sent ashore for firewood and some officers went along to try their luck at hunting.

At 11 PM on the 18th (17th according to Skead), *Enterprise* got under way again and rounded Cape Prince of Wales at 8 AM on the 19th. Shortly afterwards, some seven to eight miles offshore, they encountered two umiaks, whose occupants were very keen to trade for rum.

Pushing steadily northwards, *Enterprise* raised Point Hope early in the morning of the 20th, but since the wind fell light, it was afternoon before they closed with it. Here, as Collinson reported, the ship was

> visited by eight *oomiaks*, containing between sixty and seventy people, who
> made themselves quite at home, and proceeded to barter their bows, arrows
> and spears, together with their furs, for tobacco and beads. They had also
> evidently been in communication with vessels before, although we could
> not recognize a single individual of the party that were on the point when
> we visited it on the 1st inst. Lucifer matches were in great demand, and some
> good sable skins were obtained for two boxes. They gave us a pressing invita-
> tion to visit them on shore, and left the ship (after having had a most riotous
> barter) very quietly on being told. One of the party had leprosy, all were

filthily dirty, covered with vermin, some of which were transferred to our people, and caused the greater part of the purchases to be thrown overboard.[41]

Enterprise stood northwards under easy sail, with a south wind and a temperature of 38°F. She reached Cape Lisburne at 10 AM on the 21st with a fair wind and open seas. This induced Lieutenant Phayre, whom Skead offered to accompany, to volunteer to continue north to Point Barrow (presumably by boat) to check Moore's report of a good wintering harbour there:

Sir,

A doubt existing as to whether Pt. Barrow affords a proper shelter for a ship during the winter I beg to volunteer my services to solve that question, the importance of which is too well understood to require any explanation from me.

The importance of gaining any information, however slight, respecting either Sir John Franklin or our consort, added to the confidence I feel in being able to reach Point Barrow & to return to the ship before the winter sets in, induces me to offer myself for this service.[42]

Skead ruefully commented, "This proposal must have displeased the Captain as he did not condescend to make any reply to it."[43] Nor, significantly, did Collinson have his clerk copy the letter into his In-Letter Book. Had he done so, it would have provided a permanent record that he had declined this offer of Phayre's, which might have seen *Enterprise* wintering in the Arctic, rather than retreating to Hong Kong, with all that this would have meant in terms of an earlier start in the following navigation season.

But this letter appears to have influenced Collinson sufficiently that he decided to push at least somewhat further north; in the early hours of the 22nd, however, the wind shifted to the north, and it was 5 PM before the fish-drying racks on Icy Cape were sighted. By the morning of the 23rd the wind had freshened to a gale from the WNW and, as Skead noted, the temperature had dropped to 16°F,

which froze the spray as it fell on the deck.... The only inconvenience felt from the low temperature was the coating of the ropes about the bow with ice, but it was so trifling as to be scarcely worth mentioning.[44]

But to Collinson it was far from a trifling matter; in his view, by the evening of the 24th

> the ice accumulated so fast upon our bows and sponsons, increasing the top weight of the ship and causing her to labour very uneasily, that our people were employed to chip it away; this, however, proved no ordinary labour, and, it being evident we were too far north for this season of the year, I bore up at 4 AM for Cape Lisburne, off which we remained next day. And were then driven to take shelter under the lee of Point Hope by a gale from the N.N.E.[45]

During this southwards progress Skead points out that although they were standing off and on, they were always a great distance offshore, which he felt rather compromised their purpose:

> Had the boats of the Investigator been on their way to the Sd they would have kept close inshore, & of course out of sight of us, & as we fired neither Guns nor Rockets at night I could not understand the utility of our cruizing.[46]

Until 4 PM on the 30th, as Collinson noted, *Enterprise* cruised between Capes Thompson and Seppings in cold, stormy weather,

> rendering our bows, sponsons and rigging a perfect mass of ice, which we beat off from time to time, but occasionally it was so thick that the only part of the anchor to be seen was the outer pea.[47]

Having checked Point Hope one last time, Collinson started south for Port Clarence, which he reached on the afternoon of the 2nd. Earlier, *Plover* had been embedded in ice up to seven inches thick, and the crew had been able to walk ashore across the ice. This new ice had subsequently broken up but was still drifting around the harbour. Over the next few days Collinson supplied *Plover* with all the provisions and warm clothing he could spare to make her wintering as pleasant as possible; these were stowed in the storehouse on shore.

On 4 October the ship was swung, in preparation for putting to sea, but her departure was delayed by a spell of bad weather. On the afternoon of the 6th *Enterprise*'s crew was sent ashore for exercise, but when the wind shifted into the southwest, raising a heavy surf on the beach, it was impossible to re-embark them, and they were forced to take refuge on board *Plover*. They were able to get back to their own ship by noon on the 7th, and *Enterprise* weighed at 5:30 AM on 8 October, southward bound, to the disgust of Skead and most of the other officers.

As the officers saw things, Collinson had lacked sufficient drive in trying to push eastwards from Point Barrow. But probably even more irksome was the decision to winter in Hong Kong, rather than staying as far north as possible, with a view to getting an early start on their search for the missing Franklin expedition in the following navigation season. Although tensions between Collinson and his officers did not give rise to conflicts or disputes that were documented in the surviving written record until some time later, tensions must have been building on board the ship as she headed south for the winter. ●

4

SITKA, HAWAII, AND A
WINTER IN HONG KONG

After LEAVING PORT CLARENCE,

Enterprise's first port of call was Mikhailovski (now St. Michael), the Russian post near the mouth of the Yukon River. During the previous winter, while *Plover* had been wintering at Chamisso Island in Kotzebue Sound, Captain Moore had picked up persistent rumours from the Inupiat either of ships and men on the coast somewhere east of Point Barrow, or of a party of Whites somewhere well inland on the Yukon River. Moore had even sent Lieutenant Bedford Pim overland to Mikhailovski in March 1850 to try to have these rumours confirmed.

Lieutenant Barnard, who, according to Skead, "little relished the prospect of a voyage to Hong Kong,"[1] had written to Collinson, volunteering to stay at Mikhailovski for the winter to try to pin down these rumours by interviewing Indians from the interior, and to try to learn some Inuktitut, since Mr. Miertsching, due to circumstances, was still aboard *Investigator*. In the spring Barnard hoped to head inland with the Russian traders to try to locate the mysterious strangers in the interior. He invited Skead to join him, but Collinson objected, on the grounds that Skead was in poor health. Even though the surgeon pronounced Skead strong and fit, when Barnard again approached the captain requesting that Skead join him, Collinson claimed that he could not spare another executive officer. Instead, Edward Adams, the Assistant Surgeon, who was also less than keen to spend the winter in Hong Kong, volunteered to go with Barnard. Collinson also sent a seaman, Thomas Cousins, who had been a member of Sir John Richardson's party, which had searched the coast from the Mackenzie Delta to the mouth of the Coppermine in the summer of 1848 and had wintered at Fort Franklin on Great Bear Lake.[2]

By the afternoon of the 12th, *Enterprise* was running into Norton Sound past Cape Darby, and soon afterwards the tent-shaped hill of Cape Stephens, close to Mikhailovski, hove into view to the south. Collinson and his officers and men were pleasantly surprised to spot a windmill and the onion dome of a Russian Orthodox church on shore (see illustrations p. 254, 255). Collinson went ashore, accompanied by Barnard and his companions, and through an interpreter from California, Bosky by name,[3] was able to make the purpose of his visit understood by the Russian authorities. The latter offered Barnard and his party accommodation at the fort. Collinson then invited the Russian Governor on board for dinner, and as they were rowed out to the ship, the first boatload of provisions for Barnard and his party passed them heading in.

According to Collinson's account,

> Notwithstanding my anxiety to see our party thoroughly equipped, the exposed nature of the anchorage would not permit any time to be trifled with; accordingly at 8:30 we despatched our last boat, and I took my leave of them and the Russian Governor, having acquainted the latter with the proclamation and rewards offered by Her Majesty to any parties who should afford assistance or information of the missing expedition.[4]

Skead's version is somewhat different:

> The dread of difficulty & danger which has haunted us hitherto was not inactive at this place. Visions of heavy Westy. Gales & the impossibility (as alleged) of beating out of the sound, spurred us so sharply that we bundled Lt. Barnard & his party out of the ship at 11 o'clock at night during a thick snow shower, & so great was the hurry that a considerable portion of his

baggage was forgotten. At 2 AM on 13th we started with a very light air &
attempted to get out of the terrible sound before a Westy. Gale should set in.[5]

Next morning the weather was fair and, according to Collinson, he sent a boat
ashore with some of the officers "to take a last look at their shipmates, and to see if
anything in the hurry of disembarkation had been mislaid."[6] Skead's description of
the same events has a truer ring to it:

at 10 AM being just off the spot from which we had started at 2 AM the Senr.
Lt. prevailed on the Captn. to allow the forgotten articles to be sent to Lt.
Barnard.[7]

Adams himself confirms Skead's version; his description of the entire landing is as
follows:

On the 12th of Oct. at 3 PM, the ship anchored off Michalaski, and the provisions etc. were got on shore during the evening. Our party consisted of only
one seaman (Thomas Cousins) besides ourselves.

We landed at midnight at the Fort, & when the boat shoved off, we
found ourselves on the beach with our traps lying about in all directions &
surrounded by a party of Russians, none of whom could speak a word of
our language, nor did we know anything of theirs. Fortunately there was
amongst them a Californian who had been on board the "Plover", so that
with a few words of English & Spanish, & a good many signs we soon made
ourselves partly understood....

In the morning the ship again stood in & sent us a chronometer which
had been forgotten the night before. By the afternoon we had got our stores
a little together, so that we could see what we had. We soon found that
scarcely anything but the provisions had been sent. Amongst the missing
articles were Halkett's portable boat, Fur Blankets, Presents & articles for
barter etc. The ship was still but a short distance from the land, so we fired
the guns of the Fort, & sent a fast canoe after her, but all to no purpose; a
breeze sprung up & she was soon out of sight. Thus left to ourselves we
were obliged to make the best of it, indeed considering the way in which
the things were bundled on shore, I thought we were fortunate in getting
what we did.[8]

Due to light winds, *Enterprise* made little progress over the next couple of days, and she was still within sight of Cape Darby on the afternoon of the 15th, when a *baidar* or *umiak* was sighted between snow showers. Since its occupants appeared to be in distress, Collinson shortened sail and allowed the *umiak* to come alongside. Its occupants were a man, two women, and a child about two years old; the *umiak* was half-filled with snow, which indicated that they had been at sea in rather foul weather for some time. They were given water and raw walrus meat, which they devoured, the mother chewing pieces before feeding them to her daughter. By refer-ring to an Inuktitut vocabulary on board, Collinson was able to obtain a remarkable amount of information as to how they had landed in their predicament.

Five days earlier they had been tracking the *umiak* along shore near Cape Prince of Wales when the towline broke and the *umiak* began driving out to sea. The husband of one of the women, who had been towing the vessel, jumped into the sea to try to reach her but was drowned. Collinson decided to take them to Cape Nome, where there was a large Inupiat settlement, and once the *umiak* had been hoisted aboard, *Enterprise* got under way again.

This encounter provided a good opportunity to examine the *umiak* in detail, as Collinson described:

> She proved to be 36 feet long, 6 feet beam, entirely composed of walrus skins tightly drawn over a framework of wood, which was very ingeniously secured by lashings of hide and gut. The boat had no keel and was perfectly flat-floored. The mast had 10 feet hoist with a very long yard, the sail being composed of walrus gut with a patch of an old shirt here and there. The cargo consisted of deer skins sufficient for two if not three tents, together with fishing nets made of sinews, bows, arrows and spears.[9]

The visitors were accommodated in the sick bay for the night. By 2 PM next day (16 October), *Enterprise* was off the large encampment near Cape Nome. The *umiak* was launched and the Inupiat clambered down into it, having first been given a wide range of gifts. The younger of the women was given a copper medal on which the date and place where they had been picked up had been stamped.

Collinson now headed south, bound next for Sitka and planning to pass through the Aleutians by Unimak Pass, the most easterly navigable channel through the Aleutian chain. They made good time across the Bering Sea, and "on the morning of 21st the Peaks of the high mountains of Oonemak were seen towering above a dense

stratum of misty cloud which entirely concealed the lower part of the island."[10]
Making a good 8 knots, *Enterprise* headed into Unimak Pass and here, to quote
Skead, her officers experienced a pleasant surprise:

> From the given accounts of these passages thro' the Aleutian Islands by
> several Navigators we expected to find a heavy sea, strong currents, races
> & tides, & so made preparations for battening down as the Channel was
> neared, but altho' the moon was at the full we found no tide or current
> stronger than 1½ knots, no heavy sea, no races, in short we were agreeably
> surprised to find the Oonemak channel somewhat similar to channels which
> are found in most other parts of the World.[11]

After rounding the southwest tip of Unimak Island, Collinson hove-to not far from
shore at a spot where James Cook's men had caught a fine haul of halibut. *Enterprise*'s fishermen were not so lucky, however, and had to be content with some cod.

At dawn on 22 October *Enterprise* was passing just south of Sanak Island, with
the mountains of the western tip of the Alaskan Peninsula visible beyond. This land
was still faintly visible on the 23rd, but then dropped below the horizon as the ship
headed southeast. In the early hours of the 26th a strong northwesterly wind quickly
strengthened to gale force then, as Skead described,

> gradually changed its direction till it had gone right round the Compass by
> the North to NW, West, SW, South, SE and East by Noon 28th. During
> the whole of this interval the gale raged without intermission save during
> short periods while it changed its direction, which it had no sooner done
> than it blew with the same violence as before. A furious cross-sea ran during
> the time the gale lasted & it did not subside till several days after the gale
> abated. The latter part of the gale from the SE proved the termination of the
> heavy weather this passage, the wind falling light at 8 AM on 29th. At Noon
> 28th during the gale the Bar.[12] Stood at 28.66 ins.[13]

By midnight on the 31st the pressure was back up to 30.15 inches. One could
scarcely find a better description of the sequence of wild weather associated with a
deep North Pacific low pressure system.

By 4 AM on 1 November *Enterprise* was some 14 miles by dead-reckoning off Cape
Edgecumbe, the southern tip of Kruzof Island that shelters Sitka. Since the weather

was thick with a light wind and an uneasy swell, Collinson hove-to till daylight, when he closed with the land. Land was sighted about 8 AM , but since the weather was still quite foul, Collinson stood off again hoping it would clear. As *Enterprise* stood in for the land in clearer weather next morning, Mount Edgecumbe was visible for the first time, in Skead's words "a high truncated cone with vertical snow streaks down its sides shewing thro' the rain clouds occasionally. The appearance of the mountain is most remarkable & forms a splendid landmark for making the sound in clear weather."[14] Beyond it, across Sitka Sound, the mountains behind Sitka could be seen, "consisting of a chain of sharp conical peaks which were covered with snow."

On sighting the Sitka lighthouse, *Enterprise* hoisted the pilot jack. This soon produced the desired effect, as Collinson described:

> two kayaks, paddled by two men, each with a centre hole for a passenger, one of which was occupied, coming out. They were soon alongside, when it became apparent why two were required to carry one person; for, laying their paddles across, they formed a steady platform, and enabled the pilot to effect his release, and get up our side. They are so ticklish in the water, that it is almost impossible for a person to get out; but at the same time they are not only remarkably swift, but also very safe in a seaway, and often put out when boats dare not venture.[15]

The steam-tug *Nikolay I* next appeared and took *Enterprise* in tow at 3 PM; by 5 AM she was riding safely at anchor in 7 fathoms in the lower harbour. Collinson and his officers were really glad of the assistance of the pilot and the tug since, to quote Skead,

> There are some very ugly reefs in the sound with deep water close around & a long, heavy swell incessantly rolling over them. The winds, too, towards its head become very fickle, rushing down the gorges in strong gusts & imme-diately falling calm or blowing from some other quarter. While running at the rate of 5 knots under easy sail a heavy squall took us aback & before the yards could be braced round it was a calm. The Pilot told us this was a common occurrence.[16]

Captain Collinson went ashore to pay a visit to the Governor, Captain Nikolay Yakovlevich Rozenberg.[17] The latter arranged for fresh provisions to be sent aboard: rice, beans, potatoes, and butter. Collinson had also been hoping to get a supply of fresh salmon, normally abundant, but was disappointed to learn that the salmon fishery had failed that year. That evening at dinner Collinson also met Mrs. Rozenberg. Later the previous governor, Captain Mikhail Dmitriyevich Teben'kov,[18] came in; he was waiting for the annual supply vessel to arrive, aboard which he was scheduled to return to St. Petersburg. Collinson was particularly glad to meet him, since he had established the post at Mikhailovski and was very familiar with that area and the lower Kvikpak (Yukon) River. On his way back out to his ship, Collinson went aboard the Hudson's Bay Company's steamer *Beaver*, which was also lying at anchor.

At high water next morning the steam-tug again took *Enterprise* in tow and towed her over the bank separating the inner and outer harbour, which had a depth of only 12 feet at low water; there she dropped anchor immediately below the fort. It rained almost constantly, and a low, heavy overcast hid all but the lower slopes of the forest-covered mountains. The Russian officers reported that this was typical weather, although it was some consolation that in winter the temperature rarely fell below 10°F (-12.5°C).

Next day (3 November) Governor Rozenberg invited Collinson to dinner, where he met most of the officers stationed at Sitka. Indeed, the Russians were almost overwhelming in their hospitality, as Skead gratefully acknowledged:

> From the Governor (Captn. Rosenberg of the Imperial Navy), as well as from the whole of the residents we received the most unbounded hospitality. All our wants which they almost anticipated, were supplied & they feted us in the most princely style. Everything that generosity and good fellowship could prompt was done to render our visit as agreeable as possible. On Sunday 9th we all dined at the Governor's house where all the gentlemen of the place were assembled to meet us. After dinner loyal toasts were drunk with three times three cheers & Royal Salutes; then followed the Captn. & officers of the Enterprise with like accompaniments. The Governor & Officers of the establishment were entertained on board & the utmost harmony prevailed during our 14 days stay at Sitka. The recollection of our friendly reception will doubtless remain green in all our hearts for many years to come.[19]

Since *Enterprise* had now been at sea for some ten months, her running rigging was becoming frayed and worn, and hence Collinson was delighted to be able to replace much of it with cordage from the Sitka dockyard. Governor Rozenberg also invited him to select whatever spars, planking, and firewood he needed. He even had one of the only four bullocks at Sitka slaughtered for the ship's use. Collinson fully expected to have to pay for all this material and provisions, but to his amazement Rozenberg charged him only for imported items; anything produced locally was a gift.

Rozenberg also offered what might well have been a significant direct contribution to the search for Franklin. He promised to send orders to the Aleutian Islands that eighteen Aleuts with 20 kayaks be detailed to be sent north to Port Clarence where they would be available to reinforce *Plover*'s crew for her cruise the following summer, or else to man the house at Grantley Harbour in her absence.

Collinson also received a great deal of valuable information from Captain Charles Dodd, in command of *Beaver*.[20] The latter had twice received letters at the head of Lynn Canal (via Indian couriers) from Mr. Robert Campbell, also with the Hudson's Bay Company, who had established a trading post at Fort Selkirk at the confluence of the Pelly and the Yukon, or the Lewes as he knew it. Together with information from Captain Teben'kov Collinson was able to unravel many of the mysteries and misunderstandings about the geography and river systems of the Yukon and Alaska. Having been in communication with Mr. Alexander Murray, who had established the Hudson's Bay Company's post at Fort Yukon at the confluence of the Porcupine and the Yukon in 1847, Campbell had determined that the Lewes and the Yukon were the same river. And now from Captain Teben'kov Collinson was able to determine that the Yukon was the same river as the Kvikpak, as the large river ending in the vast delta near Mikhailovski was known locally. Most importantly, from all this Collinson was able to correct the earlier misapprehension that the Upper Yukon and the Colville, debouching into the Arctic Ocean, were the same river.

The local Tlingit Indians made a less than favourable impression on Collinson and his officers. Skead's comments are typical:

The Natives of this locality are a treacherous race of Indians, requiring to be strictly looked after by the Russians whose negotiations for intercourse with them are necessarily very severe. Their huts are built of logs on a site adjoining the Fort to the Westd. In their persons & habits they are very filthy, the soil about & even inside their huts reaching up to the ancles (sic) so that it is requisite to be provided with water boots when visiting them. The "lip ornament" described by Kotzebue seems to have gone out of fashion, as we saw only one very old woman so adorned. All the younger women were ornamented at the under lip by a small silver pin which projected about one third of an inch beyond the junction at the lip & chin. This is a decided improvement upon the ancient fashion which is inconceivably hideous and disgusting, the under lip swinging backwards & forwards, & when brought to perfection covering nearly the whole of the face. Great numbers of Natives of both sexes visited the ship, many of whom were, notwithstanding the inclemency of the weather, almost in a state of nudity. With an old blanket wrapped around their crouching forms they appeared the most miserable beings (save the Fuegians) in existence. They were not ill-made, nor ill-favored in features, but from being smeared & streaked over with Coal tar & red ochre, from which not even their hair was exempt, they presented the most revolting appearance conceivable.

Some of the young women were decidedly pretty & were neatly dressed in habits made of colored blankets ornamented with rows of pearl buttons which had a pleasing effect; others wore an old shirt only, or a pair of inex-pressibles, but the greater number wore nothing but a piece of Blanket thrown carelessly over their shoulders & fastened at the neck. Just before our arrival[21] an outbreak of measles was making savage ravages amongst them, when the Governor caused them all to be brought into hospital & cured; those who concealed their malady received a sound flogging. The result of this was at the time of our visit the disease was almost unknown. This was an act of true benevolence on the part of the Russians, & was no doubt grate-fully appreciated by the victims whose condition is wretched enough in all conscience without the addition of this white man's curse. The practise of beautifying themselves with Coal tar & red ochre is common to both sexes, but the ladies glory in the decoration to a greater extent than the men.[22]

From Captain Dodd Skead learned that he never let his guard down when dealing with the Tlingit:

He frequently makes voyages to the Southd. among the islands & between them & the main land, trafficking with the Natives for furs. So stout are they in all their intercourse with the Natives that their arms are always kept ready for immediate use, boarding nettings spread, & only a certain number of Natives are permitted on board at a time. Altogether a very unfavourable account of these people was given by the Capt. of the Steamer.[23]

On the morning of 14 November, the tug *Nikolay I* towed *Enterprise* out to sea until an ESE wind began to blow, when she cast off the tow. But then the wind freshened to gale force and the fore topsail sheet carried away. Soon afterwards the Bentinck boom[24] and the mizzen topmast also carried away, several sails were split, and the fore roundhouses were washed overboard. Collinson and his officers were extremely glad of the supply of cordage they had obtained at Sitka, since the running rigging kept giving way.

Strangely, once the wind had moderated considerably, the pressure continued to drop to an extreme low of 28.20" on the 19th, and everyone was expecting a further severe gale, as Skead noted:

> We were however agreeably surprised to find a moderate SW wind only, following this remarkable fall in the mercury. A mountainous sea ran during the gale, & did not subside with the wind but continued to run for some days after. I have never seen so heavy a sea in any part of the world I have visited; it was not an angry one & it seldom broke on board. It was in fact more remarkable for the height & magnitude of the waves than for its fierceness.[25]

For the next three weeks *Enterprise* was battling strong winds and heavy seas out of the west and southwest, as Collinson's heartfelt assessment makes clear:

> during the fall of the year, this north-west coast of America is worse to navigate, as far as the wear of the hull and rigging is concerned, than either Cape Horn or the Cape of Good Hope. The weather appears never settled; you have scarce got sail made on the ship when the squalls return with a violence which renders it necessary to shorten sail again immediately; and then they are accompanied by so much wet weather that it is extremely harassing to the people. This showed itself very plainly by increasing the number of our sick to nine previous to the 8th.[26]

During this period of heavy weather the main topmast had been sent down, and on 8 or 9 December all hands were called to send it up again. During this operation Lt. Charles Jago fell foul of his captain. Once the mast had been fidded,[27] but before the job of setting up all the rigging was completed, Jago, who did not have the watch, went below. On discovering this, Collinson accused him of neglect of duty. In extenuation of his leaving the deck Jago replied that upon a previous and more important occasion, viz. the turning in and setting up of the lower rigging, the officers (with the exception of the 1st Lieutt., Officer of the Watch and 2nd Master) were not only not required to attend, but that some of them were smoking which was not then objected to and therefore I did not consider it neglect of duty being absent on the occasion when the topmast rigging only was in hand.[28]

Collinson's response to this letter was to issue a general order to all officers:

I require every officer immediately to repair to his station whensoever all hands are turned up at sea. And for the future prevention of irregularity the period when the people are at Meals and the latter dog watch are assigned for those Officers who are in the habit of smoking.[29]

In a written reply Jago begged leave to remark

that you have entirely misunderstood the statement I made upon that occasion, which was an endeavour to place my view upon the subject in question in a clearer light before you, and not to charge any of the Officers with neglect of duty.... I would therefore most respectfully beg to request that you will cause that part of your order which states that I charged some of the Officers with neglect of duty to be cancelled.[30]

But Jago's appeal cut no ice with his captain:

Sir,

I regret to inform you that I cannot comply with the request contained in letter of the 22nd Inst.

You state that on a former occasion I dispensed with the attendance of some of the officers while the rigging was being set up at sea. This surely must have been a proof to you, that when you were sent for on this occasion, I considered your presence necessary. You are aware that in consequence of the attention of the Senior Lieutt. and Second Master being occupied with placing the main Topmast, that the flying bobstay[31] was eased up contrary to orders, which could not have occurred had an intelligent and active officer been at his post on the forecastle.

It would, I have to assure you, afford me infinitely more satisfaction had I to report to their Lordships, that your strict attention to your duty, and cheerful obedience to my commands had met with my approbation instead of having to acquaint them that at a period when the Ship's Company were much debilitated by sickness, and the hands were turned up to perform an important and necessary duty, you were found absent from your post, and on being sent for told your Captain that you had no right to be on deck, that it was not your business to see the rigging set up, and conducted yourself with such impropriety, that I was compelled to reprove you in the presence of the Senior Lieutt.

I have thus, Sir, placed my view of your conduct plainly before you in the hope that it will have the effect of rendering you more careful in the future and not to give me the disagreeable and painful necessity of acquainting the Commander in Chief in China, that I have an Officer on board who will not work with a Will but only on compulsion.[32]

Jago refused to be browbeaten, however, and he replied on the same day:

With reference to the contents of your letter, it is a subject for the decision of the authorities to whom you may think to submit it; at the same time I would remark that the precedent I have pointed out to you, together with the permission of the first Lieutenant to go below after the Main Topmast was fidded, renders it impossible for me to allow that I was guilty of neglect of duty upon that occasion.

In conclusion I beg respectfully, yet firmly, to protest against the misstatement at the head of your order dated the 9th Inst., which charges me with having accused some of the Officers of this ship with neglecting their duty.[33]

Not surprisingly, Collinson's order greatly restricting the times when the officers could smoke, which was a by-product of this contretemps, was extremely unpopular, and the officers concerned complained vigorously. The result was a memo from the Captain the very next day:

In consequence of its having been represented to me by some of the Officers of this Ship that the recent restrictions I have placed upon smoking has in a great measure deprived them of one of the few comforts that are at their Command in a Voyage of this description, I am induced to rescind it.[34]

Collinson had been intending to head west for the Bonin Islands, staying as far north as possible, with a view to stocking up on fresh provisions and water, and to assessing the possibility of doing so again on the way north in the spring, but in view of the persistent westerlies and southwesterlies, he was forced to abandon this idea. Instead, he decided to head southwards for Hawaii again, aiming particularly for Hanalei (Honlai) Bay on Kauai (Atooi). Here again Collinson's almost paranoid excessive caution drove Skead nearly to distraction:

At 6 PM on 16th while standing to the Southd. for this Island which was 55 miles distant, a sudden fear possessed the Captain that the chronometers were not correct.[35] For my part I had not the least suspicion that anything could be wrong when 7 or 8 chros. agreed together as nearly as possible; however we tacked off shore for 2 hours with a speed of 5 & 6 knots till 8 when we again put the Ship's head towards the Island which at daylight on 17th shewed itself 30 miles off, by which time the wind had all gone. By the clever manoeuver of the preceding night, for which we had not the excuse of bad advice, we lost our chance of making the harbour, which chance did not again offer till 22nd when we succeeded in getting into the bay where we anchored under the lee of a ledge of rocky reef which runs partly across the bay from the Eastern cape forming a small natural Breakwater. It is almost needless to say that the fears respecting the chros. was nothing but a bugbear, the hobgoblin that has frighted us & scared us at every place we have yet visited. Two miles was the extent of error in our Longitude by Chronometer.[36]

Since the navigation of the ship represented a major part of Skead's duties as Second Master, this unfounded worry of Collinson's about the chronometers was undoubtedly particularly frustrating.

The island was in sight by daylight on 17 December, but due to light winds and currents (according to Collinson), it was not until the 22nd that *Enterprise* picked up a pilot and successfully made the harbour, anchoring in the lee of a rocky reef in a depth of 6 fathoms.

The pilot had warned that during November, December, and January this anchorage often experienced very heavy seas that broke across the reef; soon after anchoring on the morning of the 24th they were provided with proof of this statement, as Skead described:

[The rollers] set in with great fury breaking in one tremendous wave right across the harbour's mouth. It was a magnificent sight, wave after wave rushing with inconceivable fury towards the beach, their heads crested with foam & leaving behind them a long train of feathery spray which had the appearance of a light cloud. I had no idea of what surf in its full fury was till then. I have seen surf at its height at Madras & have stood on the rocks at C. L'Agulhas[37] & watched the tremendous surges of the Southern Ocean as they were dashed against the shore during a heavy SE gale, but I have no hesitation in asserting that neither can give more than a faint representation of the terrific grandeur of these Cordilleras of the Pacific Ocean. Had we been nearer to the shore & more under the shelter of the reef, the rollers would not have caused us much inconvenience, but being exposed to the ends of several which broke, we parted from our anchor and drifted farther into the breakers than was either safe or pleasant. A second Anchor fortunately brought us up, & we laid partly exposed to the ends of the rollers. An enormous quantity of water was thrown into the bay which raised the sea above the common level & produced a strong outset; this doubtless proved our salvation, as it caused us to lie broadside to the waves, & we were able to steer the ship, by which the Cable was kept slack. Had she been exposed end-on to the sea without the outset no Cables could have held her for an instant. We rolled our Yard arms nearly to the water, & as the rollers struck the weather side of the ship they were thrown back by the sponsons[38] in a broad sheet, instead of rolling on board which they would have done in a common-sided ship. The people on shore gave us up for lost when they saw we had parted.[39]

When the first anchor cable was hauled in, it was found that the shank of the anchor had broken.

Before the surf had risen, work had started on watering the ship and on obtaining fresh vegetables. The latter were not as plentiful as they had hoped. Both Collinson and Skead ascribed this to the problems the landowners had in recruiting labour, since the native Hawaiians were not particularly keen on working. Skead makes reference to attempts which had been made to recruit Chinese labourers for the coffee and other plantations and predicted that coffee would become an important crop of the islands if these attempts were successful—an interestingly accurate prediction.

Also, before the surf became a problem, Collinson had taken the opportunity to repair the damage to the rigging suffered in the heavy weather on the way from Sitka: the fore-topsail yard, which had sprung, was replaced, and one of the spars obtained at Sitka was sent up as a new fore topgallant mast.

By Christmas morning the surf had largely abated; the ship was warped[40] back as close as possible to her original anchorage and in the afternoon Collinson "turned our people on shore for a run after their long cruise."[41]

On the 27th the surf began to rise again. A small junk-rigged vessel from Honolulu, which was sharing the anchorage, was carried under *Enterprise*'s bows, so close that the latter's jib boom carried away her mizzen mast. Then next day one of the ship's whaleboats, which had been used for watering and fetching provisions and was still moored alongside, was capsized by a wave; a further wave broke her cable and she was carried away alongshore.

In the midst of this excitement, between 9 PM and midnight on the 29th a frighteningly puzzling death occurred on board. William Luxford, quartermaster of the middle watch, was found dead in his hammock when he was called to stand his watch at midnight. Collinson himself had seen him in apparently perfect health at 6 PM when he came down from aloft where he had been keeping an eye on the drifting whaleboat for as long as possible. He had not mentioned being unwell to the men who slept on either side of him when he climbed into his hammock at 9 PM , and he had made no sound to waken them before dying. His body was buried at sea with the usual ceremony on the evening of the 30th.

On the 31st six live cattle were taken aboard and boats were sent ashore to complete the watering operation. Skead was in charge of one of the boats and (along with the crew of his boat, no doubt) enjoyed a memorable encounter:

While pulling up the river…a young woman came down to the bank, & standing within a few feet of the boat she gazed for a few moments at us, & then with the greatest unconcern slipped her arms thro' the open front of her gown, & stood before us in the simpler & more respectable looking garb of Eden. While remarking upon the improved appearance in her dress, she rolled the garment into a ball, which she held above her head, & plunging into the river shot rapidly over to the other side. After shaking the spray

from her limbs & fully gratifying her curiosity by a more lengthened stare
at us she slipped into the bed gown again & disappeared amongst the trees.
At first there was something rather startling in this proceeding, especially to
a boat full of youthful mariners, but we soon got used to it, especially when
it was found to be the common method of crossing the river, the bridge, in
short which nature has provided; however as these people are supposed to be
civilized, 'tis a pity they should continue to practise their ancient customs in
the presence of Europeans, & that too without a blush. True, this chocolate
colored Venus might have blushed under the skin but we could not see it.[42]

The rather prudish tone of the last few sentences scarcely rings true, and one suspects
that the boat's crew certainly would not have shared the attitude expressed there.

Enterprise was ready to put to sea by New Year's Eve, but had to wait for a land
breeze to carry her out beyond the surf; there was no sign of such a breeze on New
Year's morning either, and since Collinson deemed it impossible to tow the ship with
the boats through the surf, he decided to wait a little longer. In the meantime he sent
the crew ashore to wash their clothes and bedding and gave some of the officers
shore leave. The land breeze started to blow around 1 PM, but it was 4 PM before
everyone was back aboard, at which point *Enterprise* weighed and put to sea.

After leaving Hawaii, Skead's patience as a navigator was to be tried even more
by Collinson's incomprehensible behaviour on the run westward:

After getting into 17°–18° N, we shaped a course along the parallel for
Hong Kong. This route, which has become the common thoroughfare of
the Pacific has had the numerous "doubtful" reefs and shoals which are
marked upon the old charts expunged long since by Beechey, Wilkes &
other voyagers. Notwithstanding our Capt. was pleased to consider our
track to be beset with reefs & islands inaccurately laid down & by using
a chart published 30 years ago a complete resurrection of defunct dangers
took place. We were supplied with Arrowsmith's chart of 1848 upon which
no doubtful shoals or islands were marked & Beechey & Wilkes had both
searched for them in vain. However we raised them all up again & having
failed to find Sir J. Franklin it was resolved that our long voyage should not
be altogether unproductive, so for the "benefit of future Navigators" we slew
these thrice-slain dangers & now I fancy the route may be safely followed by
all Navigators without dread.[43]

At first *Enterprise* encountered northwesterly winds, but then at noon on 3 January at 21° 50'N; 161° 30'W she picked up the Northeast Trades and headed west for Hong Kong along the parallel of approximately 17–18°S, as Skead noted. At these latitudes the Trades were not as constant or as strong as had been hoped, and Skead ventured the opinion that they would have had more reliable Trades a little farther north at about 20–21°N.

It was during this passage through the tropics that Collinson inflicted a further source of irritation on his officers. In his night order book, in the entry for 17 January, there appears this order: "The attention of the officers is called to their Lordships' circular dated June 20th /46 in accordance with which I shall require their work books to be laid on my table before the 31st inst. R. C."[44] Less than two weeks later (on 30 January), this was followed by a peremptory reminder: "The officers in the course of the day will bring me their work books, with the reckoning for the last 24 hours."[45] The work books in question were the notebooks in which the ship's latitude was calculated from sun-shots, usually taken at noon, and the longitude by comparison of the chronometers.

Lieutenant Phayre and Mr. Skead evidently felt that this was an inappropriate demand. In the entry for the night order book for the following day we find the following notation:

> Lt. Phayre & Mr. Skead not having complied with my order relative to their work books, will do so tomorrow and at the same time give me their reasons in writing for not complying with my demand. Lt. Jago will until further orders bring me his work daily; Mr. Arbuthnott taking charge of his watch while he is calculating the ship's position; but he is not to interfere with that officer's meal hours. R.C.[46]

Both Phayre and Skead complied with Collinson's demand for an explanation in writing of their failure to submit their work books. On 1 February Phayre wrote,

> Sir,

> In answer to your order requiring me to state my reasons in writing for not having complied with your order of yesterday's date, I beg leave to state that from the nature of the Service in which we were to have engaged, viz. the searching for the Missing Expedition under Sir John Franklin in the arctic

regions, I did not imagine that the minute requirements of the Service in a regular Cruizer would have been required, consequently I did not provide myself with the books necessary for working Navigation.

Moreover, in a servitude of 22 years I have always seen the Senior Lieutenant exempt from the sending in of a daily reckoning, consequently I did not deem the order to apply to me.[47]

Skead replied,

In obedience to your directions contained in the night order book of yesterday's date, I beg leave to observe that being charged with the duty of Master of this Ship & having by the regulations of the service to produce the same documents as a Master, I do not consider that their Lordships' Circular dated June 20th 1846 to which you have directed the attention of the Officers had any reference to me.

In assigning a reason for not having obeyed your commands I beg leave to state that I had no idea that the order to which you refer (the existence of which was only known to me by hearsay) required me to produce for your inspection the Work books with which I have navigated the ship for the past year, which books together with this statement I now most respectfully lay before you.[48]

When asked to express an opinion on Collinson's orders regarding work books, Dr. Alan Pearsall suggested that Collinson's demand would indicate a personality clash and that no captain would normally make work for himself by checking his officers' work books on a daily basis.[49] When one considers that it was now over a year since the expedition left England, during which time Collinson had presumably made no mention of wanting to see the officers' work books, suddenly making an issue of it now appears to be simple harassment. The same would also apply to a reprimand Lieutenant Phayre received from his Captain a week later, for what the latter deemed neglect of duty while Phayre was Officer of the Watch. Phayre was moved to reply in writing:

With reference to the reprimand which you have given me in your written order of last night, I beg most respectfully to observe that it was I who noticed the Ship to be wide of her Course and that I did so the very instant she was swung off, also that I was not at all neglectful of my duty on that occasion. The man at the wheel says his eyes were dazzled for a moment and that he did not distinctly see the points of the Compass when her head was off to the SE; and I do not doubt his word as I have always found him attentive to his duty. In short the swinging off of the ship for an instant was an accident for which I cannot conceive myself censurable.[50]

The mainland coast of China was sighted on the evening of 13 February, 44 days out from Kauai. Off Tung Lung Island a Chinese pilot came aboard and offered to guide the ship through Lei Yue Mun narrows into Hong Kong harbour for $4 or $5; Collinson demurred, however, not wishing to risk the narrows by moonlight, and anchored for the night in the lee of Tung Lung. Next morning *Enterprise* ran through the narrows and dropped anchor off the city at 9:30 AM on 15 February.

Since leaving Plymouth on 20 January 1850, just over a year earlier, *Enterprise* had sailed 35,225 miles in 343 days at sea, her course taking her from 49°N to 52°S in the Atlantic and from 53°S to 73°N in the Pacific/Arctic oceans.[51] The health of the ship's company was generally good, only two officers (Mr. Skead and the clerk-in-charge, Mr. Whitehead) and one seaman being on the sick list.

Almost the first news they heard was that traces had been found at Cape Riley and on Beechey Island (on southwest Devon Island) of Franklin's expedition having spent the winter of 1845–46 there, but that there was no indication of where *Erebus* and *Terror* had headed thereafter, so there were still grounds for continuing the search. The news of the discoveries had been relayed from the American search vessels, *Advance* and *Rescue*, which had been involved in making some of the finds,[52] to Captain Charles Forsyth, leader of Lady Franklin's private expedition aboard *Prince Albert*. Forsyth, considering this news sufficiently important, had headed back to Britain in the fall of 1850.[53]

Collinson also learned that HMS *Herald* had also called at Hong Kong and had left for England only six weeks earlier. She too had called at the Sandwich Islands (Hawaii) where she had picked up some boxes of balloons, which had been dispatched from England via Panama and were intended for *Enterprise*. These balloons, which were supplied to many of the Royal Navy's search expeditions, were filled with hydrogen, with a long tail of slow match[54] attached, to which messages were tied and released in the Arctic. As the slow match burned, the messages were released and, it was hoped, might be found by members of the missing Franklin expedition. An example of these balloons may still be seen in the Museum of the Scott Polar Research Institute in Cambridge, England.

Having paid his respects to Admiral Sir George Bonham, Admiral on the China station, Collinson made arrangements for work to begin on refitting his ship. Her sails, which were on the whole the same as those used aboard the ship during Sir James Ross's earlier expedition to Prince Regent Inlet in 1848–49,[55] were by now in rather poor shape. Since there were no suitable sails in store, a new suit of sails was now specially made for her (mainsail, topsail, jib, driver, and topgallant sails). The sail-making operation was carried out aboard HMS *Minden*, and part of *Enterprise's* crew was also accommodated on board that ship while *Enterprise's* hull was being caulked.

An examination of the ship's stores revealed that some of the casks of beef had started; that is, they were leaking. Although Skead has a different story to tell, Collinson maintained that the meat was still found to be in excellent condition, and that all that was required was for the brine to be topped up. Even Collinson admits, however, that since the casks had been stowed with coal, this was "a troublesome and dirty operation."[56]

Over the next few weeks Collinson applied to the Naval Storekeeper for a whole range of items and services, from the help of the coopers at the Victualling Yard in repacking provisions and the provision of saucers for the galley, carpenter's axes, bastard files, Newcastle coal, and ammunition boots.[57] Finding that the coal available from the dockyard was not particularly good and that Newcastle coal was not available, Collinson purchased 14 tonnes of coal from a junk from Chi-Lung in Formosa (Taiwan), paying about what he would have paid for top-quality coal in London.

Collinson also provisioned his ship for three years. On 20 March *Enterprise* took delivery of 2400 lbs of tobacco from HMS *Cleopatra*, which had arrived from Manila; this was to replace what had been used by *Enterprise's* crew or given to HMS *Plover*. Finally, just before sailing, *Enterprise* took delivery of eight live steers with fodder for a month.

Although, clearly, a great deal of work had to be taken care of, during the six weeks in Hong Kong officers and men were allowed on shore quite liberally. Collinson himself enjoyed a particular treat on 22 February. On that date Admiral Sir George Bonham was installed as a Knight Commander of the Bath, and Collinson, with all the other Navy captains, was invited to the ceremony and subsequent festivities. He was quite inebriated when he came back aboard, something which, then and subsequently, was a matter of comment among the officers, as Skead would later regret bitterly.

In mid-March the officers and crews of HMS *Enterprise, Reynard,* and *Royalist* were able to make a significant contribution as firefighters when a fire broke out in Victoria.[58] They managed to extinguish the fire, which must have been a relief to the people of Hong Kong, given the crowded nature of the town and the flimsy construction of most of the buildings.

Enterprise's prolonged sojourn in tropical waters produced all the deleterious results that Skead had predicted:

> Our stay at Hong Kong was, as had been foreseen, productive of disease & desertion amongst the crew; and our prolonged stay in the tropics proved very injurious to the provisions, public as well as private. We lost 10 men by desertion, the places of whom were filled by men from HM Ships and from the jail. We completed provisions & water & repacked & repaired the casks of salt meat which had been burst from the heat of the holds. On one occasion I found the Tempr. of the after hold to be 92° Faht. In the Fore Peak the heat was so great & the air so foul that a man could not remain down in it for any length of time, & after a few minutes the body was covered with profuse perspiration. A candle would not burn until an air-pumping apparatus had been used which cleared out the foul air from the bottom of the compartment....
>
> Our visit to Hong Kong was most ruinous to all of us. We lost a large stock of mess stores by exposing them to heat of the Tropics, & to replace them we had to purchase dollars at 5 shillings a piece, but this was the least of the evil occasioned by leaving a working ground to the North; it has engendered a spirit of strife & discontent amongst all that argues very badly for our future success, if indeed any success can attend upon a voyage which is assuredly too late by the year we have lost.[59]

As we have seen, tensions between Collinson and his offices appear to have been mounting ever since *Enterprise* left the Arctic, but especially since leaving Sitka. All the officers were frustrated at Collinson's decision to run all the way south to the Tropics and to winter in Hong Kong, instead of wintering at some convenient location north of Bering Strait, from where they could get an early start on their objective, a search for the missing Franklin expedition, in the 1851 navigation season. In this atmosphere, what might otherwise have been seen as minor irritations, in terms of the captain's demands, quickly ballooned into serious infringements of the officers' rights and privileges. Even at this early stage in the voyage, the battle lines had been drawn. ●

RETURN TO THE ARCTIC

On 2 April HMS *Cleopatra*'s boats towed *Enterprise* out of Hong Kong harbour, since it was a flat calm. Despite the oarsmen's efforts, however, *Enterprise* ran foul of an American brig, doing some damage to her sails as well as carrying away her own flying boom,[1] an accident that Skead characterized as "our usual clumsiness."[2] Then, casting off the tows, Collinson beat to windward to and through Lei Yue Mun narrows. The weather was foggy, and the lookouts had to keep a sharp eye out not only for land and rocks, but also for the numerous Chinese fishing vessels.

On the afternoon of the 4th the wind steadily freshened from the northeast; soon *Enterprise* had to shorten sail to double-reefed topsails and reefed courses. The rough seas were "very distressing to our cattle," and also ruined much of the fodder that had been shipped for them. So much fodder was lost that, after only about another week, soon after passing through the Bashi Channel south of Taiwan, Collinson was thinking that he might have to put in to Okinawa or some other island close to the ship's course, for fear that the fodder would not last for the long reach across the

open sea to the Bonin Islands (now Ogasawara-Shoto), the next scheduled port-of-
call. But by repacking the ship's supply of wine bottles and other bottles in oakum,
the original straw packing could be used as emergency cattle fodder. The hot weather
was also very deleterious to the ship's supply of potatoes, much of which was found
to be rotten and had to be pitched overboard.

During the run east to the Bonin Islands, an incident occurred that brought the
simmering feud between Skead and Collinson to a head. On 18 April, by an entry
in his night order book Collinson ordered Skead daily to stand a watch on the forecastle head under the Officer of the watch. Skead responded with a very strongly
worded objection:

Sir,

With reference to an order contained in the Night order book of yesterday's
date directing me to keep a watch on the Forecastle under the Officer in
charge of the Watch, I beg leave respectfully to observe that I deem the order
at variance with the Regulations & customs of the service & to point out its
contrariety thereto. That I hold the position of the Master of this ship, responsible under yourself for the safe Navigation & Pilotage of her, I believe you
will not dispute, for you have frequently reminded me of that responsibility.

If the ship is in Pilot water, amongst reefs & Islands which are incorrectly
laid down, it becomes my duty to be on deck whenever these dangerous spots
are approached, which duty I cannot perform if I am bound to a particular
watch, for it may happen (& did so on a previous occasion of my keeping
this watch by your order) that a dangerous spot is approached or passed
over during my watch below, added to which I conceive it to be contrary
to the custom of the service to place the Master of the ship in a watch upon
the Forecastle under another Officer, more particularly too at a time when
circumstances demand his unremitting attention to the ship's Pilotage.

Circumstances have transpired with which you are acquainted, that
have thrown me into great perplexity as to what duty I am to perform so that
I may at least avoid your censure. Under the impression that you had, by
the order to which I have referred, suspended me from the duty of Piloting
the ship, I refrained from interfering, more particularly as you had taken that
duty solely upon yourself, keeping myself however in readiness in case you
required my services. This occasioned you to find fault with me & threaten

to report my neglect of duty to the Admiralty. Now that I am anxious to perform the duty which your disapprobation convinced me you expected me to do, I have a duty imposed upon me which renders it impossible for me to fulfil the duty of the Master, & lays me open to another charge of neglect.

I take this opportunity of stating with great respect (& which I have previously done verbally) that the inconsistencies in your line of conduct towards me renders it impossible that I can perform the duties of my station with that exactness which your repeated references to the Printed Instructions seems to require, & to request that if you persist in my keeping a Watch under another Officer, you will give me a written order to that effect, that in case of anything's happening to the ship during the time I am resting from my watch I may be exonerated from the charge of neglecting the duty of the station which their Lordships have appointed me to fill.

I beg also, in conclusion, to state with great earnestness, as well as with deference that it is not extra duty of which I complain, & to declare that the whole of my energies, both of body & mind, & even life itself, have been & are still faithfully devoted to the noble cause in which I voluntarily embarked, but the order you have given me, imposing a duty upon me which seriously hinders me in the performance of my own, is the cause of my addressing you, & to request that you will be pleased to reconsider the order, & permit me to fulfil my proper station, & instead of mixing them up with those of an irresponsible Officer.[3]

But rather than a rescindment of the order, all this request of Skead's elicited from his captain was the threat of a discharge back to England and an insulting listing of the duties he expected of Skead, including a daily schedule:

Sir,

As you do not appear satisfied with the reasons which I have given you on a former occasion for placing you to keep watch on the forecastle during the night while we are in the vicinity of dangers incorrectly laid down, but have written me a letter on the subject where, instead of a ready & cheerful obedience to my commands, you cavil at the orders you have received, I have to inform you that as soon as the ship arrives at Port Clarence, I shall discharge you into the Plover to wait a passage to England, where you will have an opportunity of explaining to their Lordships, that your ideas relative to the duty of a Second Master do not agree with mine.

In the mean time to relieve you of the perplexity you state you are under relative to the duties you have to perform, I lay down the following rules for your guidance.

Daily

Before 8 am Inspect the holds & storerooms, report their condition to the
   Senior Lieutenant & superintend the issue of fuel & water, 0.30.
At 8. Assist in comparing the chronometers & compute the ship's position
   by D.R.[4] 0 h.40.
At 9. Observations for the ship's position, variation of the compass &
   working the same. 0 h.40 m.
During the forenoon. Examination of rigging, security of casks, boats,
   anchors, etc. 0 h.15 m.
Noon. Observation for latitude, writing the ship's log. 0 h.30 m.
pm Writing the Admiralty six monthly log, computing & taking afternoon
   observations. 0 h.45 m.
8 pm Reckoning at 8 pm 0 h.10 m.
Night watch at present 4 h.0 m.

Occasional duty

To be present at the opening of all casks & to see that the number & contents of them, as well as the candles & issue of oil out of the tanks are correctly entered in the log, for which purpose you will place your initials against the articles in the purser's/steward's number content book. The spirit room is only to be opened in your presence & should other urgent duty call your attention from it you are to acquaint the Senior Lieutenant thereof, before you permit the keys to be taken from your cabin. The sail room will be examined by you weekly or oftener should it be necessary & you are to report your having done so to the Senior Lieutenant and acquaint me should there be occasion for airing the sails or slops.[5]

You will be a check upon the Warrant officers in the expenditure of the stores of which the utmost economy is necessary & if you witness any waste whatsoever you are immediately to report the same & carefully overhaul their expense books before they are brought to me. Whatever stores or provisions are received on board it is your duty to make yourself acquainted therewith; see that they are carefully stowed away & enter a full & particular account of the same in the ship's log.

The 16th article of their Lordships' instructions to Masters points out that under the direction of the Captain they are to have charge of navigating the ship; and whenever the ship is approaching the land or any shoals he is to be on deck & is to keep a good look out. That an Officer who professes that the whole of his energies both of body & mind, even life itself! have been & are faithfully still devoted to the noble cause in which he voluntarily embarked can assert that the keeping of a first or middle watch hinders him in the performance of his duty in this respect, I cannot understand, as in the course of my service I have for a period of six months kept my regular watch both at sea & in harbour, besides performing the duty of Master, keeping the Warrant Officers' accounts, the Meteorological Register, the error & rates of 17 Chronometers. I have thus laid before you plainly your duty & I trust that by a steady endeavour to perform what has been allocated to you I shall not have the pain of adding to the complaints which I have to transmit to the Admiralty against you.[6]

Probably with little hope of persuading the Captain to change his mind, but clearly convinced that he was in the right, Skead penned an eloquent riposte:

Sir,

In reply to your letter of yesterday I beg most respectfully to state that from its general tenor, you have in some measure misapprehended my objective in addressing you. Instead of cavilling at your orders I only followed the injunctions laid down in the Printed Instructions which enjoin any Officer who receives an order which he considers to be at variance with the rules of the service to point out in writing wherever that variance lies. This I did most respectfully.

You state it to be your intention to send me to England, that I may have an opportunity of explaining my ideas regarding the duties of a 2nd Master to the Lords of the Admiralty. Even if my Lords required them I have no new idea to offer upon the subject; but an opportunity of rebutting publicly whatever charges you may choose to exhibit against me will undoubtedly be a great boon since I am certain I can prove my duties to have been well performed from the day I joined the ship. Yet I would beg to say that I am eager as ever to have an opportunity of doing all in my power towards the furtherance of the great object in which the ship is engaged.

As you repeat the order that I am to keep a night watch upon the Forecastle, I cheerfully obey; but at the same time I beg to request that you will be pleased not to insist upon my doing so under the junior Watch keeper (Mr. Parks, Mate) while two Ice Masters, my junior Officers, do duty above me—Mr. Atkinson almost Officer of the Watch, Mr. Arbuthnott as Mate of the 2nd Lieutenant's watch. I had at least hoped that my position in the ship & my length of service would have entitled me to occupy the highest station in this respect—not to be degraded to the lowest.

I have learned the duty of Second Master & of Master by service in both capacities in many ships, & I have hitherto discharged these duties in such a manner as not only to escape from censure, but to obtain the Commendation of the Officers under whose command I have had the honor to serve, & I am totally at a loss to comprehend the line of conduct you have chosen to adopt towards me since we left the ice—those constant censures which have rendered that period of my service in this ship the most intolerable portion of my life.

Up to that time all went well as far as regarded my duties. I did no better then; I have done no worse since & I can only repeat "that my best energies of body & mind & even of life itself, are still faithfully devoted to the cause I volunteered to serve."

When I stated the perplexity in which I was placed, it was not to obtain a code of Instructions for my hourly guidance, but in the hope that you might relieve me from many minor duties which interfere with the duty of Master which you rigidly require to be performed by me in addition to those of the Second Master.[7]

When asked for his assessment of Collinson's insistence on Skead standing a watch on the forecastle, Dr. Alan Pearsall expressed the view that this would be extremely unusual, and that, if anywhere, the Second Master's place was on the quarter deck, rather than on the forecastle: "To put him in a subsidiary position on the forecastle when he was responsible for navigation was curious: again it looks like Collinson was attempting to put Skead in his place."[8]

During a period of fair winds and fine weather from about 20 April onwards, *Enterprise* made excellent progress, and Collinson took advantage of the favourable conditions to have the carpenters build lockers on the lower deck for the men's clothes. This meant that their sea chests, which cluttered the lower deck and prevented it from drying properly, could be stowed elsewhere.

At 2 AM on the 28th, Bailey Island, one of the Bonin group, was in sight, and Collinson altered course for Port Lloyd on Peel Island, his planned destination. The island had been named after Sir Robert Peel and the harbour after Bishop Lloyd, the Bishop of Oxford, by Captain Frederick Beechey during his visit in HMS *Blossom* in June 1827.[9] As *Enterprise* approached the harbour, a canoe put out under sail; its occupant came aboard introducing himself as Harry and offering to pilot the ship into the harbour, which was very sheltered and appeared to be the crater of an extinct volcano. He also offered pigs, yams, onions, and turtles for sale. *Enterprise* anchored in Ten Fathom Hole, in a sheltered corner of Port Lloyd. Spreading the purchases among various of the settlers in the community, the ship was now stocked up with fresh provisions, as Skead reported:

> We procured Fruits, yams, sweet & Irish potatoes, onions & palm cabbage in abundance & at moderate prices. Firewood was also plentiful but we found some little difficulty in getting water. A hundred fathoms of hose was required to convey it to the casks in the boat & the watering place was at an inconvenient distance from the ship, being in the sandy bay near the south side of the harbour's mouth. A few goats & wild hogs are to be obtained from the islands outside by shooting them; we were only able to secure three goats after several attempts. Abundance of fish swim [in] the head of the "Ten fms. Hole." We took 600 fine mullet in one haul of the seine. ....[10]

Port Lloyd had long been a favourite port-of-call for American whalers for stocking up on water and fresh provisions, particularly green turtles, which could be kept alive for long periods on board, turned upside-down on deck. During his visit in 1827 Beechey had noted that the turtles "were so numerous that they quite hide the colour of the shore" on some of the sandy beaches.[11] The going price for turtles was

$2 each. *Enterprise* also laid in a stock of cabbage-palm shoots, both as an antiscorbutic vegetable for the crew and as fodder for the cattle. According to Lieutenant George Peard, who was at Port Lloyd with Captain Beechey in HMS *Blossom*, "when well boiled it eats like sea kale or asparagus."[12]

During his visit in 1827 Beechey had "declared [the islands] to be the property of the British government by nailing a sheet of copper to a tree, with the necessary particulars engraved upon it."[13] At the time of *Enterprise*'s visit the sheet of copper was "still preserved, & was shewn to us as a curiosity."[14]

Over the period from September 1849 until January 1850, the islanders had suffered the depredations of the crews of the Hong Kong junk *Saint Andrew* (Captain Barker) and the cutter *Maid of Australia* (Captain Young). On their first arrival the settlers had given them every assistance in repairing storm damage to their vessels and in reprovisioning, but then the two captains and their men had gone on a rampage, stealing cash, provisions, clothing, and equipment from both the white settlers and the natives and kidnapping two women, although in one case the term "kidnapping" is not entirely appropriate. She was quite young and her American husband, Mr. Savory, quite elderly and apparently, in Skead's words, "this youthful Helen was not averse to the abduction, &...informed her captors of the whereabouts of her 'lord & master's' money bags."[15]

Captains Barker and Young had sailed for San Francisco and, with a view to trying to bring them to justice, Captain Collinson took depositions from many of the victims of their plundering and forwarded them to General Miller, the British consul at Honolulu. Also, before leaving, Collinson supplied the settlers with a Union Jack and some ball cartridges, "strongly advising them to show some confidence, and stick by one another, in the event of Commodore Barker, or any other marauder, visiting them in future."[16]

Having loaded a good stock of cabbage palms and grass for the five remaining steers, increased the number of pigs to 35, stowed 20 live turtles on deck, and stowed a good supply of yams, potatoes, and onions, some of which, it was hoped, would still be in sufficiently good condition to transfer to *Plover* at Port Clarence, *Enterprise* put to sea on 6 May. One unexpected problem was that the "Bonin Island pigs proved a quarrelsome set, fighting and biting one another, while the Chinese were much quieter and better behaved."[17]

But Collinson and his officers soon had more serious problems to deal with. Alerted by a falling barometer and a rising wind, Collinson reduced sail, and by 3 PM on 11 May the ship was carrying only a close-reefed main topsail, main trysail, and a fore staysail. But even with these precautions, that evening the ship plunged her bows deeply into a wave, burying the jib boom; as she rose on the next wave the jib boom snapped and took with it the fore topmast and main topgallant mast, the latter in three pieces. Since the wind had moderated a little, it was possible to clear the wreckage from the bows by midnight, but as there was still a very heavy sea running, it was not until the 15th that a new topmast could be sent up.

The livestock suffered from the ship's violent motion; one pig and a turtle were lost, and one steer had to be killed. Over the next few days the foul weather and heavy seas continued, staving-in one of the whaleboats and twice carrying away the tiller ropes. With all the wet weather and the temperature dropping steadily, the Sylvester stove was set up and lit, and this greatly improved conditions below.

During this leg of the voyage Collinson no longer insisted that Skead stand watch on the forecastle, which simply strengthened the latter's earlier conviction that this earlier insistence had been purely for the purpose of harassing him:

> Altho' we have zealously declared our object to be the "benefit of future Navigators" in confirming or otherwise the existence & positions of doubtful reefs & islands, yet we have so cleverly managed the business as to pass (with one exception) every reef & island which is still retained upon the Charts, during the night, when the extent of vision was so limited as to render our report almost if not quite useless. From the Sandwich Islands to Hong Kong there is one reef or island for every 800 miles of distance on a zone 120 miles in width. From the Madjucasimch Ids. to the Bonin group upon a similar zone there is one for every 120 miles. During these passages, instead of doing my proper duty as Master of the ship, I was put to keep a look out man's watch on the Forecastle as our way was beset with dangers as well as "for the benefit of future Navigators." I remonstrated with the Captn. which gave such mortal offence, that I was threatened to be sent to England. After leaving the Bonin group, there was one Island or reef upon the 120 mile zone, for every 45 miles, but here our solicitude for the "benefit of future Navigators" ceased, at least I fancy so since the look out on the Forecastle was declared to be no longer necessary. During the last period the weather was thick & squally, but on the two former passages the nights were almost as light as day. I fear the "benefit of future Navigators" is less cared for than the persecution & annoyance of present ones.[18]

On 23 May (25th, according to Skead) *Enterprise* entered the Bering Sea via the wide passage between Attu Island and Ostrov Medniy (Copper Island), the easternmost of the Kommandorskiye Ostrova (Commander Islands). To Skead's bafflement and irritation, he discovered that Collinson was now excluding him from his real professional functions on board, with worrying results:

> he has long since ceased to treat me as the Officer in charge of the navigation, not even acquainting me with the alterations made in the ship's course at sea. As we were entering the Sea of Behring, by mere accident I discovered that the ship was steering a course for Attu Id. when it was intended that we should sight Copper island [Ostrov Medniy] (a difference of 3 pts.). Upon further enquiry, after we had run 7 hours & gone over 40 miles, I found the Capt. had altered the Course without my knowledge, & had <u>allowed the variation the wrong way</u>. Such being the position I hold I can only conjecture what are the objects & motives of our somewhat strange proceedings.[19]

On the 31st, on crossing the 180° meridian, Collinson changed the date; he had previously changed it at Sitka on 9 November to be in accordance with the Russians who, even there, stayed on the same date as Russia. *Enterprise* thus experienced 31 May twice.

In the Bering Sea the expedition encountered numerous whaleships, especially American and French. Several captains came on board and reported that there were in excess of 100 whaling vessels waiting at the ice edge for ice conditions to improve so that they could push on northwards. On 4 June, as *Enterprise* worked her way east along the edge of the ice, she spotted a dead whale (presumably killed, but not recovered, by one of the numerous whaling vessels) and informed the captain of the New Bedford whaleship *Champion*, which they encountered soon afterwards; the latter immediately went off to try to locate this windfall. Another American captain who came on board, Captain Caleb Strong Holt of *Armata*, offered Collinson a spare spar to replace the missing flying-jib-boom, and declined payment.

By noon on 5 June *Enterprise* was beset in heavy ice and being carried towards Mys Bering. Collinson took the opportunity to water the ship from pools on the ice, taking aboard eight tonnes.[20] Large numbers of seals of an unfamiliar species were spotted on the ice; since it was unfamiliar, several attempts were made to shoot one, but it was not until the morning of the 7th that one was brought aboard. These were ribbon seals (*Phoca fasciata*).

Thereafter the ship was subjected to a slow easterly drift; by the 16th she was seven miles off Mys Acchen, and by the 21st seven miles due south of Mys Chukotskiy. One unfortunate result of the delay caused by this besetment was that Collinson was obliged to have the last two steers killed since the fodder was exhausted; he had hoped to put them ashore at Port Clarence for the use of *Plover's* crew, with the expectation that they would have found enough fodder there at least until winter. The last of the turtles from the Bonin Islands were suffering severely from the cold, and they too were killed at this point.[21]

It was also during this besetment off Anadyrskiy Zaliv, on 18 June, that the clerk-in-charge, Edward Whitehead, died. Collinson's version of his death in his published narrative reads as follows:

> We had however the misfortune to lose Mr. Whitehead, clerk-in-charge, during the middle watch. ... He had been suffering for a considerable time from rheumatism, which had also rendered him a cripple, and was scarcely able to do any duty all the time we were at Hong Kong; previous, however, to our departure from there he rallied considerably, and a medical consultation on his case being held, they arrived at the conclusion that he was in a fit state to go, with which I was very well pleased, as having served in the ship under Sir James Ross, his experience would have been of value and I had also every reason to be well pleased with the manner in which he had discharged his duty. It was, therefore, with very melancholy feelings that we bore his body across the floe and committed it to the deep.[22]

Collinson included some greater detail in his report to the Secretary of the Admiralty:

> Sir,
>
> I regret to inform you that Mr. Whitehead (clerk in charge) put an end to his existence on the 19th of June. He had been suffering from acute rheumatism for a considerable period which it appears at length to have reached the brain & caused temporary insanity during which, notwithstanding the constant care & attention of the surgeon he managed to secrete a razor & commit suicide. His previous conduct had given me every satisfaction & by his care & attention to the stores & provisions under his care & anxiety to

attend to my wishes had entirely gained my confidence & caused me greatly to regret his loss.[23]

As we have seen, however, according to Lt. Sharpe of HMS *Rattlesnake*, it was common knowledge on board *Enterprise* that Whitehead's suicide had resulted directly from Collinson's intolerable treatment of him.[24] To replace Whitehead, Skead was ordered to take charge of the victualling accounts until further notice, on top of all his other duties.[25]

On several occasions during this period, parties of Chukchi came off to the ship; they paddled along leads where they could and hauled their *baidars* (umiaks) over the ice where necessary. They were quite familiar with the fact that *Plover* (Captain Thomas Moore) had wintered in Bukhta Emma on the Chukotka coast in 1848–49[26] and were able to recite the names of some of the officers.[27] Some had walrus tusks and furs to trade, preferring especially tobacco or alcohol in exchange. When one of them was given about one-eighth of a pint of rum, he swilled it several times around his mouth, then squirted it into his neighbour's mouth, who then passed it on to the next in line, including women, so that they could all get at least a taste.

Several attempts at freeing the ship by blowing up the ice with gunpowder were made, but to no great effect. The technique was, however, useful in trying to free the rudder to unship it, although in one case when the charge was placed a little too close to the ship, it blew off some of the copper sheathing and broke the lower pintle.[28]

On reaching open water on the 21st Collinson headed northeast towards Bering Strait. With the ship making about five knots, Skead and his fellow officers were surprised to see several Chukchi *baidars* overtaking her, the paddlers sweating freely, although the temperature was only about +1 °C.

Around 11 AM on the 22nd some streams of loose ice were encountered, and by midnight the ship was again among heavy ice. Next day she made some 6–8 km by sailing and warping, but by midnight on the 24th she was again solidly beset. Both King Island and Cape Prince of Wales were in sight, tantalizingly close but unreachable. *Enterprise* was carried steadily north-northeast at a rate of 14–15 miles per day and was not released until the 30th. As she drifted towards the Diomede Islands on the 29th, there were serious fears that she might be driven onto one or other of the islands. The crew were set to warping the ship to try to get her into a safer position, but to no avail. At one point *Enterprise* was heading steadily towards Little Diomede Island, only about 2.5 to 3 km away, but fortunately the drift direction then changed and she passed within about 1.5 km of the island; the sight of floes being driven violently ashore must have given all on board reason to feel very fortunate.

The ship finally reached open water at 6 AM on the 30th June and headed south toward Cape Prince of Wales. Soon after she passed that cape and was running east for Port Clarence, an *umiak* came alongside. Among its occupants was the Inupiat woman who had been in the *umiak* that had been rescued in Norton Sound the previous October. She did her best to express her gratitude, which Skead found to be very commendable, but remarked, "Our interest in the woman was probably heightened by her being very good looking as well as good humoured."[29]

Enterprise reached Port Clarence at 4 AM on 3 July, to find *Plover* lying, ready for sea, at the mouth of Grantley Harbour. Captain Moore soon came aboard *Enterprise*, with some disturbing news. Edward Adams had returned to his ship only two days before, Captain Moore having sent the ship's launch to Mikhailovski to pick him up. He reported that Lieutenant Barnard had been killed by Indians. Late in December 1850, accompanied by the interpreter, Barnard had taken advantage of the fact that the Russian governor of the post at Deryabin (now Nulato; see illustrations p. 257, 258) on the lower Yukon was returning to his post from Mikhailovski to accompany him, to see if he could gather any information about the rumours of white men having been seen farther up the Yukon. On 25 February 1851 Adams, who had remained at Mikhailovski, received a note from Barnard say that he had been seriously wounded when the post had been attacked by a band of Indians who had come from some distance away. They had attacked in the middle of the night on 15 February and, having first killed the Russian factor, had next attacked Adams and the interpreter. Adams had put up a vigorous defence, breaking the stock of his gun in the process, but had been stabbed nine times; the interpreter had also been badly injured. After leaving the post, the attackers had rampaged through the nearby Indian village, killing every person they encountered (a total of 57) and setting fire to the village.

On receiving Barnard's note, Adams travelled to Deryabin as quickly as he could, but found that Barnard had died in the interim. He buried him nearby and took the wounded interpreter back to Mikhailovski, but despite Adams's best efforts, he also died, of a fever.[30]

Barnard's death was a serious loss to the expedition, in that he was one of the few officers with previous arctic experience, having been (like Edward Adams) on HMS *Investigator* under Captain Edward Bird on Sir James Ross's expedition of 1848–49. Understandably, Collinson was fully cognizant of the seriousness of the loss of this officer; writing to Sir Francis Beaufort, the Admiralty Hydrographer, he noted, "I have to lament the loss of an able and intelligent officer, to whose ability and good-ness of disposition I had looked forward as one of the main stays of the expedition."[31] To replace Barnard, Collinson promoted the Mate, Mr. Murray Parkes, to Acting Lieutenant.[32] Adams and Thomas Cousins, the seaman who had accompanied him, returned to their own ship on the 4th.

It was probably in part because of the loss of Lieutenant Barnard that Collinson did not carry through with his threat of transferring Skead to *Plover* for transport back to England. The captain claimed that he had considered transferring the Second Master and the Clerk-in-charge from *Plover* in place of Skead and the late Edward Whitehead, but changed his mind since these potential replacements had already spent three winters in the Arctic, and "I saw the idea of spending two or more winters among the ice too disheartening."[33] Later Skead claimed that he would have left *Enterprise* quite happily, "foreseeing nothing but failure."[34]

Also on 4 July, a French whaler, *Nancy*, and the American whalers *Lagoda and Sheffield* dropped anchor in Port Clarence. The latter was commanded by Thomas Roys who, in 1848 in *Superior*, had been the first to go whaling north of Bering Strait; in that season he had taken 11 bowheads in the Chukchi Sea,[35] and had quickly been followed by many other whaling ships. He provided Collinson with a great deal of information about whaling in these waters, reporting that there had been 100 whaling ships in the Bering and Chukchi seas in 1850; he anticipated that this number would rise to 150 in the 1851 season. Roys also presented Collinson with a box of potatoes, part of a cargo that an enterprising schooner captain had hauled north from Hobart.

Despite Skead's misgivings, most on board were probably looking forward to finally getting into the Arctic and getting to grips with their task. They could at least hope for messages from, or traces of, the missing Franklin expedition. But that anticipation must have been offset, at least among the officers, by the tensions between them and the captain. While Skead appears (from the surviving documents) to have borne the brunt of Collinson's displeasure and his unreasonable demands during the circuitous voyage around the North Pacific over the winter, one strongly suspects, from their earlier confrontations with the captain, that others of the officers, such as Lieutenant Jago, had also been the objects of his displeasure. The atmosphere in the gunroom was far from happy as its occupants finally prepared to push north into the Arctic. ●

6

PAST POINT BARROW AND AROUND BANKS ISLAND

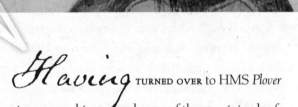

Having TURNED OVER to HMS *Plover*
all the remaining live pigs, plus onions, pumpkins, and some of the remaining beef,
Collinson made preparations for heading north. One of the marines, James Adams,
who was clearly suffering from a pulmonary disease (probably tuberculosis) was
transferred to *Plover*.[1] The plan at this point was that *Plover* would now head for
home; in fact, while Captain Moore and his men (along with James Adams) were
sent home in another vessel, *Plover* was to spend a further two winters in the Arctic
(at Point Barrow) with a new captain, Captain Rochfort Maguire, and a new crew.[2]
On 10 July *Enterprise* weighed anchor and headed west for Bering Strait.

By now Collinson was treating Skead with open contempt:

> Altho' I have not been sent to England as the Capt. threatened I am still
> treated in the nondescript manner I have before mentioned. As we left Port
> Clarence the charge of the ship was given to Mr. Atkinson, Ice Mate, & the

Capt. went to bed. I was within a few feet of them both when the orders were given, & was treated with as much indifference as if I had been the Purser (only) instead of the ship's Master.[3]

For the first leg of the voyage, as far as King Island, *Enterprise* was carrying some passengers: an Inupiaq named Chimuak, whose *umiak* was hung from the after davits under the ship's gig, his wife, another man named Kaimoki, his wife and child, and two other men. On reaching King Island the ship was surrounded by *umiaks*; from one of them the woman they had rescued the previous fall again came on board, along with the man who had also been rescued on that occasion. He presented Collinson with a large walrus tusk as a token of his gratitude.

Enterprise rounded Cape Prince of Wales on 12 July, and Collinson set a course for Point Hope. Soon, however, the ship encountered progressively heavier ice and was forced to swing east into the mouth of Kotzebue Sound to avoid it. Approaching the coast near Cape Krusenstern, she was able to take advantage of a shore polynya[4] 8–10 miles wide, and thereby to work her way northwest towards Point Hope. [5] In the early hours of the 15th an *umiak* came off from shore, and its occupants offered about 150 looms (murres) for sale. As the ship approached Point Hope a few hours later, there was a strong white glare over the water between the ice and the land that Collinson interpreted as an ice blink,[6] but that proved not to be, disappearing as they got closer. Collinson sent Lt. Phayre ashore at the Point to leave a message.

By noon on the 16th they were off Cape Dyer, and in the evening Collinson sent Lieutenant Phayre in one of the cutters to work his way north along the coast to shoot looms from the cliffs. He reported the results as follows:

In the middle watch the next morning we could hear quite distinctly peal after peal of firearms reverberating from the cliffs, which were distant more than three miles, showing that our shooting party had commenced the work of destruction. At 7, being off Cape Lisburne, two more boats were sent, and we remained standing off and on until 4 PM , when all parties returned, bringing with them 524 birds.[7]

By noon on the 18th they were abeam of Icy Cape, which, as described by Skead, certainly lived up to its name:

Several heavy grounded floes were passed & the shoals off Icy Cape were crowded with enormous masses of Ice 40 to 50 feet high. Some of them consisted of Floes forced up by pressure, others were small berg masses perfectly clean, with sharp angles, & some of their faces perpendicular as if totally broken from some parent berg, but where to find parents for such masses as these I know not; we never saw any that could bear such offspring. Some of the grounded masses lay in 15 fm, but they were small in extent in comparison to their neighbours which crowned the shoals off Icy Cape. The Cape must have been similarly crowned with ice when seen by Cook[8] since, if I remember rightly it was named Icy Cape in consequence. When we visited it last year in Septr. not a particle of Ice was to be seen, & yet to judge from its present state one would say that it could scarcely ever be clear of it. So little are conclusions which are drawn from partial observations to be relied on, particularly where Ice is concerned.[9]

By 8 AM on the 19th the ship was passing abeam of Wainwright Inlet, where ten or a dozen *umiaks* came alongside. Their occupants were very keen to trade, and many of the crew purchased skin parkas and *kamiks*[10] in exchange for tobacco. Later that day, as the ship approached Point Belcher, the strip of open water between the pack ice and the shore narrowed menacingly. Captain Collinson sent Lieutenant Phayre in the whaler to see if there was enough depth for the ship to squeeze past the cape; he returned with a negative report. According to Skead, the ice mates recommended that they moor with ice anchors to a grounded floe and wait for the ice to open, since otherwise there would be a real risk of becoming beset.[11] The captain refused this advice, however, and instead began beating about near the ice edge until the current carried the ship into it. By 4 AM next morning *Enterprise* was solidly beset and drifting steadily to the east-northeast, embedded in the ice.

For the next few days the steady drift towards Point Barrow continued. Occasionally, when there seemed some prospect of getting into a nearby lead, sail was made, but never to any effect. On the evening of the 23rd, as noted by Skead, the ship experienced some pressure, "giving her a slight list (15° or 16°) to starboard. The floes, which were 5 to 6 feet thick, were forced up against us until they reached a vertical position when the ice sponsons gave them an outward inclination & they fell back again clear of the ship."[12] Later that evening a group of Inuit, including some women, walked out to the ship. Skead describes them: "Upon being refused admittance they revenged themselves by exposing their persons & performing ludicrous & indecent gestures. The morals of these people have not improved by intercourse with the Whalers."[13]

To landward of the drifting ship lay a ridge of grounded floes, rising to a maximum height of 60–80 feet, with a lane of water between it and the shore. As the ship passed Point Barrow in the early hours of the 25th, she was carried along alarmingly close to this grounded barrier, to Skead's evident dismay: "At 1 AM on 25th the rate of drift had increased to 3 knots when we drove past a stupendous mass of grounded ice, the flying-boom scarcely clearing the face of it."[14]

There was a large Inupiat settlement on Point Barrow, and, as Collinson describes, its residents gathered to watch this unusual sight from the barrier,

> on which nearly a hundred natives had assembled, shouting, waving and trying to keep up with the ship, which the rapid rate we were driving at, and the rugged nature of the ice they were on, would not permit. Some in vain sought a place where they could cross on to the packed ice we were in, but the lane of water, although narrow between it and them, ran like a mill-stream; others, embarking in their oomiaks paddled down in the clear water between the barrier and Point Barrow, which was about one and a half miles wide, and thus getting ahead of the ship, perched themselves on the pinnacles so as to get a good view; and most likely with the same feeling that used to animate the Cornish wreckers in olden times.[15] We were, however, not destined to be a prize to them this time, but drifted on to the E.N.E. , parallel to the shoal and never more than a quarter of a mile from it, but not having less than 12 fathoms of water; so that it must be very steep-to.[16]

Enterprise drifted steadily eastwards, beset in the pack, but fortunately suffered no damage, and as Skead reported:

> At 3 AM on the 31st after a few severe shocks against the ice we emerged from the pack & entered a broad sheet of open water which extends to the land as far to the Eastd. as can be seen. C. Christie bore ESE 5 or 6 miles....[17]

Thus, although she had run a serious risk of colliding with the grounded ice masses, *Enterprise* had achieved, with no particular effort on the part of her crew, what they had struggled for days to achieve during the previous summer: they had safely rounded Point Barrow. Skead was fully aware, if no one else was, of how lucky they had been:

As it is we are fortunate, but it is the result of an experiment that few men would try at all, & none I fancy attempt a second time. Besides the risk of being crushed against the grounded ice, there is the great probability of being detained in the Pack for an indefinite period of time & carried no one knows whither.[18]

Beating eastwards along the strip of open water about 3–5 miles wide between the land and the edge of the pack, by noon *Enterprise* was abeam of Pt. Tangent (see illustration p. 259). Lt. Phayre was sent to check a post on shore, but he discovered it was an Inuit marker.

On the afternoon of 1 August two *umiaks* came off from shore; their occupants traded some geese and caribou meat for tobacco. Skead reported another proposed transaction that was not concluded: one of the women accepted an offer to buy her daughter, aged about 13 or 14 and very pretty, for a few sticks of tobacco; both seemed very disappointed when it was explained to them that the offer had been made only in jest.

Next, two more *umiaks* put off from shore, their occupants again offering geese, ducks, and caribou meat for sale. One of the women had a box containing one of the dolls presented to the expedition by a Mrs. Washington to give to the Inuit, the intent being that if any members of the Franklin expedition subsequently ran across them, they would realize that help was somewhere relatively close at hand. Collinson had distributed some of these dolls at Point Hope and Port Clarence the previous fall; however, he did not discount the possibility that Captain M'Clure in *Investigator* might also have been handing out some of Mrs. Washington's dolls. Skead reported that the owner of the doll was allowed to visit the gunroom "& from the break-fast table she very dexterously filched two silver forks";[19] when confronted with this misdemeanour she relinquished the forks and seemed to think it a great joke.

Slowly but steadily, *Enterprise* worked her way eastwards, tacking between the edge of the pack and the coast, occasionally stirring up the mud as she tacked near the shore, or more accurately near the shingle bars, strewn with driftwood, that parallel this coast. At noon on the 3rd they were off Pt. Beechey, and that afternoon they sighted the Franklin Mountains. Fog was an ongoing problem, and on the 4th, while working in fog past Return Reef, the ship collided with a grounded mass of ice, breaking the stock of the port anchor and the bollard head.[20]

On 5 August an offshore breeze raised the temperature several degrees and brought the welcome smell of tundra vegetation. Next morning, however, the wind dropped so that Collinson had to have recourse to ordering two boats to tow the ship. Skead, however, was disgusted that all hands and all boats were not set to towing or warping:

> 6th [August]. At 4 AM our fair wind deserted us leaving us becalmed. Now was the opportunity of testing the strength & stamina of the crew by setting them to warp or to tow. With all hands I doubt not that a considerable distance might have been made, but we sent two boats only ahead, one of which was nearly useless, & these were of course insufficient to produce any effect upon the ship....[21]
>
> It was some consolation that the weather was marvellously clear & afforded us a fine view of the Romanzoff mountains which in appearance joined the Franklin & were lost in the distance to the West. The outline of the Romanzoff chain was clearly defined, & shewed extensive glaciers of a light blue tinge, the beauty of which was heightened by the sun's rays falling upon them from an almost cloudless sky.[22]

Around 6 that evening, just as the ship was about to tack, she ran aground. Several kedge anchors were laid out, but the ship refused to budge, until a fortuitous squall struck her from the landward side, and with the help of the kedges, drove her back into deeper water. That night she passed Flaxman Island and, next morning (7 August), Barter Island. By then the British Mountains were in sight, although quite severely miraged. Next day *Enterprise* passed Point Manning, but since the wind had died, only by dint of warping. Once again Skead was amazed and annoyed that the crew was not pushed harder:

> The wind was too light & fickle to allow much progress to be made under sail alone, but with the boats towing, or the crew warping a considerable distance might have been gained. After some trouble the Senr. Lt. prevailed upon the Capt. to try the warps at 6 PM. Instead of putting the whole strength of the ship to work, the watch only were employed, & they too unfortunately were sulky, having had bad tea issued to them. I tried to infuse a little life into them by hauling myself & proposed a song but I might as well have tried to infuse life into a corpse."We can't sing upon salt water tea," was the response to my proposal. It was mortifying to see such favorable chances allowed to pass without taking advantage of them. In a short season & such

precarious Navigation as prevails here, every opportunity for making a mile ought to be seized with eagerness but we are quite indifferent, & our only progress is & will be such as Providence provides fair winds for.... [23]

During this period, as Skead reported,

> Loud reports were frequently heard during calm, quiet weather. At first I was at a loss to account for them, but I had an opportunity of seeing the cause this day. A large, lofty mass of ice was passed with its base at the water's edge wasted away by the warmth of the waves which beat against it. It had the appearance of a monster Mushroom. All at once the stem broke & the large overhanging mass fell into the sea with a loud crash & these were the reports we so often heard. [24]

Finally, around 8 PM on 10 August, *Enterprise* emerged into open water, but unfortunately the winds were now quite light and variable. Yet again Skead felt that the captain was too easy on the crew:

> 11th. Open water in all directions.... Light airs which were insufficient to give us steerage way attended us, with fog & gloomy W[eathe]r until 9 PM on 13th.... As no efforts were made to get to the eastd. our progress could be no other than very scanty. I have always understood Navigation to be attended with constant hard labour. I have no hesitation in saying that I have never seen men have easier times on board any ship in which I have served than the crew of the Enterprise enjoy at present. As we make so little progress when there are so few obstacles to our advance I am afraid to think of what we shall do if we meet with difficulties from Ice. Poor Sir John! God help you, for you'll get none from us. [25]

Thus by the morning of the 14th Herschel Island was still about 15 miles to the southeast of the ship; beyond the island, the British, Buckland, and Richardson mountains were in sight. Skead estimated that they had covered only 15 miles in the preceding 48 hours!

With light, variable winds, fog, and perplexing currents, the next few days were quite frustrating, as the ship slowly but steadily pushed eastwards. On the 16th, it was found that the water was almost fresh, a result of the massive discharge of the

Mackenzie River into the shallow waters of the Beaufort Sea. On the 17th an entire tree was spotted floating in the water, complete with its roots. When trimmed of its roots and branches, it made a useful spare spar, 45 feet in length.[26] On the evening of the 19th, Pelly Island was in sight to the south-southeast, and next day the north end of Richards Island, badly distorted by a mirage.

By noon on the 22nd *Enterprise* had Toker Point in sight to the south; both Collinson and Skead commented on a "remarkable knob on the land," this being Toker pingo, one of the hundreds of pingos that dot the Tuktoyaktuk Peninsula, steep-sided, ice-cored hills that rise abruptly from the tundra. That afternoon, on two successive tacks, the ship passed over a shoal with only 3½ to 4 fathoms of water; this was about 30 miles north of Toker Point.[27] Passing Cape Dalhousie, Collinson steered a course across the mouth of Liverpool Bay, rounded Cape Bathurst some 50 miles off and thus without seeing it, and continued east across the mouth of Franklin Bay until he raised the Booth Islands and the hills of Cape Parry at 1 PM on 26 August.

From here Collinson swung northeast, across the mouth of Amundsen Gulf. The weather became foggy and rainy, but in the evening it cleared temporarily, and around 8:30 PM the lookouts reported land to the northward, a bold coast with sheer cliffs. Snow and mist then obscured it again, and many thought it a mirage or a fog bank or, as Collinson called it, "Cape Flyaway." But Lt. Jago, who had the watch, insisted it was land. Around midnight he was proven right when the weather cleared again, revealing land about 25–30 miles to the northwest. In Skead's words,

> Its Wn extreme was high and cliffy, a feature which continued to the Ed for many miles. The cliffs were stratified & the highest part stood over the bold cliff head which formed the Southn. Point of the land. It appeared to me to be about 1000 feet. A light mantle of snow covered the whole & the ravines & hollows were filled with it. Here & there at the water's edge dirty masses of ice adhered to the cliffs. It was a beautiful & interesting sight & the weather cleared up as if to indulge us with a view of a territory never perhaps visited by civilized man.[28]

As he would soon discover, his last assumption was incorrect. Nonetheless, this is an excellent description of the imposing headland of Nelson Head, the southern tip of Banks Island (or Baring Land, as Collinson named it); Collinson, however, called it Cape Erebus.

Even at this point land could be seen to the eastward (the western coast of Victoria Island) and, as *Enterprise* beat northeast along the coast of Banks Island all next day, to Skead, the land to the east "appeared continuous trending SEd towards Wollaston Land to which I cannot help thinking it is joined."[29]

The waters between the two converging coastlines narrowed, yet everyone on board began hoping that this was perhaps a through-channel that would lead to Barrow Strait. On the evening of the 28th, near the eastern shore, they reached a small island where, to Skead's delight, "A large Polar Bear sat near the beach watching our movements with much complacency & cleaning his face with his paw just as a Cat does."[30] the island, now called Ramsay Island, was named Bear Island.

Enterprise now started beating northeastwards down what still promised to be a strait, rather than a bay. During the morning of the 29th Collinson went ashore on the eastern shore (Victoria Island):

> On arriving at the crest I had the satisfaction to see a clear open strait, as far as the eye could reach, in a northeasterly direction: and while taking the necessary bearings heard our Newfoundland dog, Neptune, give tongue, and soon saw him in chase of three deer [caribou], which fortunately he turned between Mr. Adams and my coxwain and ourselves, and passing within shot of the former, one was immediately knocked over. Having skinned our prize, and each one taking a load, we set out for the beach.[31]

Skead adds a further piece of information as to the captain's state soon after his return:

> Being in a condition which totally prevented him from attending to the ship* [Footnote: *Drunk] the Capt. placed me in charge & directed me to run to the Nd. into the bight for an opening he has seen from the hills & which had the appearance of a channel.[32]

The wind was now fair, and the ship ran on all night to the northeast, assisted by a favourable current. At 2 AM on the 30th, Skead, who had the watch, but who had serious concerns that *Investigator* might already have explored this strait,

> Made out what I took for the tops of two hills standing nearly in Mid-channel. This was another damper but our speed was kept up, & we shortly

found that our misgivings about our new discovery were not without cause when upon the summit of the largest hill which proved to be Islands nearly in Mid-channel a Flag staff & Beacon had been erected—by whom—save our consort? [see illustration p. 260] All our high hopes were thus thrown into the mud. My own disappointment was not very great for I had prepared myself for some such discovery. We hove to off the island & the Capt. landed to examine the beacon, which was a black ball upon a lofty spar supported by guys.

On the Nn face of the island a boat & 39 casks of provisions lay stored up and a Notice left which informed us that the Investigator had spent the previous winter in the Pack 4' [miles] NE from the largest island, being frozen in on 18th September. She had discovered the NW passage on 26th October by sending a party over the ice to the Nn entrance to the strait in Lat. 73° 31'; Long. by lunar 114° 11'W. The crew were all well in June & had had "abundance of game." No traces of the missing ships had been found. To the Southd. 90 miles an inoffensive tribe of Natives had been met by a travelling party from the ship. These Isds Capt. McClure had named Princess Royal Isds....[33]

The message gave no indication of where M'Clure had headed after leaving this wintering site.

The strait to the northeast was almost totally free of ice, and so Collinson continued to explore it. Towards evening the strait opened out into a major east-west channel (M'Clure Strait), and at 8 PM a cairn was spotted on Peel Point, the eastern entrance cape of Prince of Wales Strait. Lt. Phayre took a boat and went ashore to examine it. In it he found a message, left there by a sledge party from *Investigator* in April, but it provided no new information. From the cape Phayre could see a shore lead about 1 mile in width running to the east-southeast along the north coast of Victoria Island, but apart from that, M'Clure Strait appeared to be solidly choked with ice.

On the boat's return to the ship, Collinson got under way again and headed north to examine this ice more closely. After only a few tacks *Enterprise* was brought to a halt by close, heavy pack at 73° 35'N; 114° 18'W at 3 AM on 31 August. This was, in fact, the stream of multi-year pack ice that constantly drives out of the Central Arctic Basin and down M'Clure Strait, Viscount Melville Sound, and McClintock Channel as far southeast as King William Island.

Collinson next examined a small bay on the Banks Island coast as a possible wintering site, but found that it had filled with ice since the afternoon; next he tried a bay on the Victoria Island coast, but it was too shallow. Since it could be assumed that M'Clure would have searched all the shores of Prince of Wales Strait, Collinson next determined to run back south to Nelson Head (Cape Erebus), around that cape and north up the west coast of Banks Island.

By 2 AM on 1 September the ship was back at Princess Royal Islands; a boat was sent ashore to leave a message and to get some more water, since the water derived earlier from floes was somewhat brackish. Getting under way again, *Enterprise* continued running to the southwest down the strait. Off the southeast coast of Banks Island that evening a bear was spotted on a floe; the ship was hove-to and Lt. Phayre was sent with the whaler to try to kill the bear to provide some fresh meat. The bear raced across the floe and plunged into the sea but Phayre managed to shoot it as it was clambering out onto another floe. It measured 7' 8" and weighed about 900 lbs.[34]

At this point Skead had charge of the ship, but was finding the captain's behaviour very unsettling:

At 8 PM [on 1 September] I was once more put in charge of the ship, the Captain being unfit to do the duty himself* [Footnote: *Drunk]. I was told to look for some place on the Wn. shore that would afford quarters for the winter. …. The Captn. had come on deck again & he ordered the stud[ding] sails[35] to be set & course steered that would soon take us out of sight of land. As soon as he went below I prevailed upon the Officer of the watch to alter course & take in the stud[ding] sails, for it was evident the Capt. was not conscious of what he was doing. We hauled to the wind again & at 1 AM on 2nd reached near enough to the land to enable us to see whether there were any harbours or not, but in the meantime we had missed a considerable distance of the Western shore by running out to sea. The point of land was the Nn. entrance to a deep indentation about 15 to 20 miles across at its entrance. I called the Capt. at 1 AM & enquired whether I should work into it or stand across making long tacks."Do what you think best," he said & went to sleep again.[36]

When *Enterprise* stood into the wide bay (De Salis Bay) next morning, it was discovered that what Collinson had hoped was a secure harbour was only a low gap between quite high hills with a shallow lagoon bordering it. At 6 AM on the 3rd Collinson went ashore to check the lagoon. He found numerous muskox skulls, some with the tips of the horns cut off, indicating that Inuit had been here, and an old weather-worn paddle well above high water mark. There were also numerous stone meat-caches and, to Collinson's pleasant surprise, large numbers of flowers. Having established that there was no suitable anchorage for the ship, Collinson got under way again, and by noon *Enterprise* was lying becalmed under the impressive cliffs of Nelson Head.

Rounding the headland, the ship followed the coastline, beating to the north and north-northwest, in which directions the cliffs continued for about 50 km. On the morning of the 4th, large flocks of waterfowl and shore birds were seen heading south. By the morning of the 5th, a light southeasterly wind allowed the ship to run northwestwards, parallel to the shoreline of Thesiger Bay. Somewhere near the mouth of the Masik River, Collinson sent Lieutenants Phayre and Jago ashore to check for possible wintering sites and cairns. Lt. Jago, accompanied by the Newfoundland dog Neptune, started walking alongshore, while the boat, under Lt. Phayre, kept pace with them. Two bears (mother and cub) were spotted; they "tried hard to get into the sea & the dog stuck so close to the mother that the shooters were afraid to fire. After a while they succeeded in getting clear of the dog & into the sea when we sent a boat & shot them both."[37]

A second cub was then spotted on shore, but since the hunt had already lasted an hour, Collinson, afraid of losing the advantage of the fair southeasterly wind, decided not to pursue it. That afternoon a lagoon (Sachs Harbour) was sighted, and Mr. Skead was sent ashore to examine it. He found

> the approach to a moderately sized inlet with a low alluvial island on its Nn side to be very shallow. Horns of the Musk Ox were found on the Island which was about 3 miles in circumference, & separated from the main by a shoal, narrow channel.[38]

After Skead returned to the ship at about 4:30 and reported the unsuitability of this inlet as a wintering site, the ship continued along the shore, which now tended west-ward to where it ended in a long, low recurved spit, Cape Kellett. Next morning, on 6 September, Collinson sent two boats ashore to examine the bay inside (i.e. on the north side of) the recurved spit as a possible wintering site, one of these boats again being commanded by Mr. Skead. On shore a surprise awaited him:

Upon landing upon the spit end, which is in Lat. 72° 03'N, Long. 125° 35'W, we nearly ran the boat's nose against a cask which, upon it being opened, was found to contain a notice of our consort's visit only 18 days previously. It was dated Augt. 18th & stated that she had left P. of Wales strait on 16th & had coasted it thus far in two days with a fair wind....

The space inside the spit promised well to afford shelter for the winter. Several large masses of ice were lying aground from which I inferred that the water was deep enough for us. I had been told to sound it, but as I found we were in the midst of our consort's finished searching ground I hastened on board with a copy of the notice. As I pulled off to the ship I found 3 & 4 fms, but off the entrance to the space inside the spit the water was deeper. The harbor certainly appeared to afford shelter, but it was poor, being 6 or 7 miles from the mainland [i. e. the higher land at the east end of the spit].[39]

While recognizing that this was potentially a suitable wintering site, Collinson decided, first to push northwards along the coast in order to lay a cache of supplies at some appropriate point where they might be used by sledging parties either in the fall or the spring.

Getting under way again, northward bound, the ship had not gone far when she ran aground at noon at 72° 07'N; 125° 45'W, some three or four miles west of a cliffed headland, at the point where the coast changes from a north-northwest-erly to a northerly and even north-northeasterly alignment. Fortunately the sea was calm and the bottom soft sand, and at 7 PM the ship was warped off without having suffered any damage.

With a wind out of the east-southeast, *Enterprise* now ran to the north-northeast parallel to the coast, but around midnight she began to encounter loosely scattered ice floes. Soon she was running north in a coastal polynya with heavy, multi-year pack to the west; Skead correctly surmised that this was the same multi-year pack that had brought Parry to a halt in M'Clure Strait during his voyage of 1819–20. By 9 AM on 7 September they had reached a small island (Terror Island) off Meek Point; at this point the edge of the heavy pack to the west was converging towards the land. According to Skead,

We hove to off the Island & sent the Senr. Lt. (Lt. Phayre) on shore with a small quantity of provisions, some fuel & to build a beacon. The island lies about ¾ of a mile from the land in Lat. 72° 50'N; Long. 125° 10'W. The

Senr. Lt. & the Medical Officers, both of whom accompanied him, report a snug looking harbour at the SEn end of the island sufficiently large to hold the ship. They also report open water in shore as far to the North as the eye could reach. The Provisions (20 days for 10 men) were deposited on the island & the beacon erected by Noon when the boat returned. The open water was reported to the Captn. But we put the helm up & ran away to the SWd for the spit harbour where the Investigator's cask was found.[40]

Collinson's interpretation of the situation was markedly different, reporting that he

found the main body of the ice close to it [the island], and the open water so strewed with floes, as to render it very doubtful whether we could turn to windward among them. I therefore determined on returning to the south, believing that a westerly wind would cut off our retreat to the only harbour we had seen, and leave us exposed on a shoal shore.[41]

Furthermore, since he had not found any message from M'Clure here, he somehow concluded that he, too, had turned back at this point and had followed the edge of the pack southwards and westwards towards Point Barrow. In fact, M'Clure had continued north along the west coast of Banks Island, and at that point *Investigator* was temporarily beset in the ice off Ballast Beach on the north coast of the island.[42]

By 8 PM on 8 September *Enterprise* was back at Cape Kellett, and Collinson again sent Mr. Skead to reconnoitre the bay inside the recurved spit:

We Anchd. off its outer point in 5 fms, the spit being about ½ a mile distant. I left at 8:30 PM in a boat to sound the inlet. From the ship into the land in a Wy direction I found 5 & 4½ fms. From this to the bottom of the bight formed by the shingle crescent, the same depths were carried, there being 4½ & 3½ fms close to the shingle spit itself. We picked up some drift wood on the spit & brought it on board. From its centre the bay was open to the North but close to the spit it was sheltered & land-locked. At 11 PM I returned on board carrying 4½ & 5 fms close round the spit end.

9th. At 3 AM we weighed & stood into the bight to have a better view of the place for a winter station. I sounded close to the main & found it shallow. The Capt. did not like the look of the place which, from being 6 or

7 miles from the high part of the land was in all conscience dreary enough, altho' I doubt not of it being sufficiently safe.[43]

Collinson now decided to investigate Bear Island as a possible wintering site. Skead was not unhappy at this decision, since while they knew the west coast of Banks Island had been searched by M'Clure, there was at least a chance that the coasts around Bear Island (the southwest coasts of Victoria Island) were as yet unexplored. Progress back around Nelson Head was slow, due to foul southerly winds, and it was 10 PM before they rounded the cape; in the forenoon, when they were quite close inshore, Collinson had sent Lt. Phayre ashore with a boat to get a barrel of water and to leave a message somewhere on the shores of Thesiger Bay. *Enterprise* got back to Bear Island at noon on the 13th. Skead was sent to look for a harbour and to sound on the landward side of the island, if it looked at all promising. He found, however, that a long line of breakers extended all the way from the east end of Bear Island to the mainland of Victoria Island; there was no possible sheltered anchorage anywhere around the island.

Collinson now stood to the southeast with light winds, and at 4 AM on the 14th Skead was again sent ashore to examine what appeared to be several inlets on the coast of Victoria Island:

I left the ship in a calm, & after a long pull, landed upon a point under a high Dome-shaped hill which stood between the entrances to what appeared to be two deep inlets [Jago Inlet and Winter Cove]. From the summit of the Dome there were many places in sight like harbours from which to choose. In the Nn inlet I saw two or three snug-looking places, & I conjectured that the hill I stood upon was an island, in which, however, I was mistaken, as it afterwards proved to be a peninsula, the isthmus that connected it with the main being 3 miles across. Numerous recent foot prints of the Reindeer were seen & white bears sported about in abundance. We also saw the remains of Esquimaux encampments; they were old & moss-covered. We pulled into the NEy inlet, or rather towards it, with a view of examining an apparent harbour it contained, but after pulling a few miles I landed & walked up a hill to have a better view. On the Nn shore of the inlet a promising harbour was seen towards which we pulled & found it all that could be wished for. Admirably adapted for winter quarters by being sheltered from all winds, it had the additional advantage of deep water close to the beach.[44]

Skead got back to the ship at 4:30 and reported that he had found an ideal wintering site. The tone of his annotation concerning this trip in his personal copy of Collinson's narrative is one of intense frustration, however: "I was thus 12 hours away from the ship in an open sea in a whale boat in search of winter quarters in the height of the work season."[45]

Enterprise dropped anchor in the inlet he had selected at 7:45 PM; initially Collinson expressed his total satisfaction with this location but soon changed his mind, to Skead's annoyance:

> On the following morning, however, the Capt. discovered by some marks upon the beach that the place was exposed to ice pressure. For my own part I could see nothing amiss with the place. 'Tis true that the shingle on the beach was furrowed, & lay in ridges like sand on a wave-washed beach, but I saw the same thing at different elevations all along the coast, some of which were 50 & 60 feet above the sea level. To my mind these furrows told the tale that the land has risen gradually, retaining the marks left upon its surface by the beating of the waves & the grinding of ice against its successive water lines.[46]

This is an accurate and very perceptive observation; due to postglacial glacio-isostatic rebound, the uplift of the land following the removal of the weight of Pleistocene glaciers, raised beaches are a very common feature of very large areas of the Canadian Arctic.

Collinson therefore weighed anchor again, and on 15 September, having dispatched Lt. Parkes back westwards to survey the coast as far as Bear Island (Ramsay Island) and to erect a cairn on the mainland opposite that island with a message as to where *Enterprise* would be wintering, ran eastwards about eight km to the head of Winter Cove to a harbour Collinson deemed more suitable, leaving a shooting party on shore at the first anchorage. In the interim it had started snowing and, with the reduced visibility, the shore party did not notice that the ship had shifted her anchorage and returned to the first anchorage. Skead was sent back to rescue them at 8 PM. By firing a few volleys he managed to make contact with them, all badly chilled since they were quite lightly dressed. However, they had shot two hares and cooked them over a driftwood fire. Some warm clothing and a glass of grog each soon made a vast difference. Skead got back on board with the missing men around 3 AM on the 16th. The ship now settled down to begin her first arctic wintering.

It cannot have been a very attractive prospect for the officers. Not only were they frustrated by the fact that M'Clure in HMS *Investigator* had forestalled them, in that he had already searched every section of coastline that they had thus far visited, but, as Skead's remarks make clear, he at least was convinced that Captain Collinson was not pushing the crew hard enough, in terms of trying to make the best possible speed to reach areas where the missing Franklin expedition might conceivably be found. Another source of frustration for Skead was his feeling that they had gone into winter quarters when the open-water season was far from over, and that they were thereby missing further opportunities to continue the search.

Perhaps the most troubling revelation from this period of the expedition of the fall of 1851 was Skead's accusations (on 29 August and 1 September) that the captain was drunk and, as a result, giving orders that were likely to compromise the effectiveness of the expedition and even the safety of the crew. And one should recall also that one of the accusations that the officers from HMS *Rattlesnake* had heard from the officers of HMS *Enterprise* when they went aboard her in Port Clarence in 1854 (see p. vi) was that Collinson had on occasion been drunk during the expedition In other words, Skead was not the only officer who had made this accusation, and the captain's drunkenness had probably not been confined to a single occasion. The officers, at least, cannot have approached the prospect of a long arctic winter under these conditions with much enthusiasm. ●

WINTERING
AT WINTER COVE

Preparations FOR THE
wintering were begun immediately. On 16 / September the ship was careened to
allow the carpenters to repair the copper sheathing, the uppermost five strakes of
which were gouged and ragged from impacts with the ice. At the same time, a party
on shore was cutting turf for use in building an observatory.[1]

Next day Collinson went ashore on the south side of the inlet and hiked to
the top of Mt. Phayre, the conspicuous dome-shaped hill lying between Winter
Cove and Minto Inlet to the southeast. The captain got his first view of the latter
inlet on this occasion. On returning to the ship, he found that a shooting party had
encountered some Inuit who appeared to be very scared; nonetheless, one of them
had been persuaded to come aboard the ship and was put ashore again later with a
number of presents.

These were members of the Kangiryuarjatmiut, the most northwesterly sub-
group of the Copper Inuit from around Minto Inlet (see illustrations p. 261, 262).[2]
The Copper Inuit, so-called for their widespread use of native copper from the lower
Coppermine River and elsewhere in making tools and weapons, occupied an area

embracing southeastern Banks Island, the whole of southern Victoria Island, and the mainland from Dolphin and Union Strait east to Perry River. The Kangiryuarjat-miut's core area was Minto Inlet, but they also hunted on southeastern Banks Island in summer and interacted with their neighbours, the Kangiryuarmiut, to the south.

Typically all sub-groups of the Copper Inuit spent the winter in quite large villages of snow houses on the sea ice; these might house anywhere from 50 to 150 people. During the winter they lived almost exclusively on seals, mainly ringed seals (*Phoca hispida*), and polar bears (*Ursus maritimus*). The seals were killed with harpoons, by the technique of waiting, if necessary for hours, at the seals' breathing holes, or by stalking them as they lay on the ice in the spring. In summer the Copper Inuit wandered inland, either on Victoria Island or the mainland, in small extended family groups. It was just such a group that the shooting party from *Enterprise* had stumbled across. In the summer they lived in caribou-skin tents and subsisted on caribou, ducks, geese, and fish. The latter, mostly arctic char, were caught with lines through holes in the lake-ice, until the latter completely melted, or by means of fish spears (leisters) at stone weirs built across rivers and designed to corral arctic char as they headed back upriver in late summer or early fall. Caribou were killed with bows and arrows.

By nightfall on 17 September Lieutenant Parkes still had not returned from his trip to Bear (Ramsay) Island, and hence muskets were fired every two hours all night, since it was now getting quite dark at night, to guide him and his party back to the ship.

The weather was quite mild, and the surface water temperature was 36 to 38° F, with absolutely no ice in sight. Skead felt that the decision to start the wintering was very premature and that the ship should have continued south to Wollaston Land (now Wollaston Peninsula of Victoria Island) to link up with the area searched by Dr. John Rae by dog sledge in the spring of 1850.[3] He felt that they would be able to find winter quarters somewhere in that area, or, failing that, would have time to return to the site Collinson had already selected.

Since the captain's mind was clearly made up, on the 17th Skead volunteered to take a whaleboat and search the coast south to Wollaston Land, and then Minto Inlet on his way back north. Collinson said that he would leave this to his discretion and that "when he gave an officer orders to perform any service 'he never interfered with the manner he thought fit to carry it out.'"[4]

Collinson stipulated that Skead should wait till Lt. Parkes returned, in part so that he could use the same boat, and in part for the sake of the surveying instru-ments Parkes had with him. When Parkes did get back at 8 AM on the 19th, his

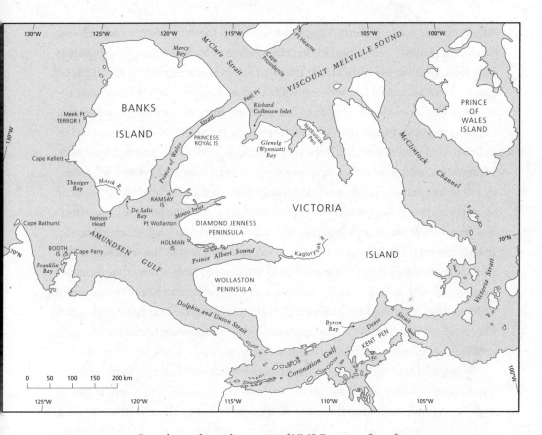

General map of area of operations of HMS *Enterprise*, 1851–1854.

whaleboat was leaking quite badly, but the carpenters soon had it repaired, and by 9 AM Skead was on his way, with permission to be gone for a week. But when he checked his orders he discovered that, rather than directing him to search to the south, to Wollaston Land, he was instructed simply "to examine the bay to the Southd. & Eastd," that is, Minto Inlet. But since there was no way of telling how far the inlet ran to the eastward, Skead decided he would make the best of it.

Collinson spent the next few days surveying around Winter Cove. On the 18th he established from the hills on the south side of the cove that Minto Inlet ran at least as far inland as Walker Bay, and that only a narrow neck of land appeared to separate Winter Cove and Boot Inlet. Also on that date, a flagstaff was erected on the hill above the ship as a guide to shooting parties or the Inuit.

Next day, along with Mr. Adams, Collinson headed up the valley at the head of Winter Cove then circled round to the south. A herd of ten caribou came to within musket range but escaped unharmed. From the hills he was unable to see the head of Minto Inlet. Then on the 20th Collinson walked across the isthmus to Boot Inlet, opening off Minto Inlet. Initially there was some debate as to whether it was a lake or an arm of the sea, probably because, given its convoluted shape, the entrance may not have been visible. But once the party reached the shoreline, the doubters were convinced that it was salt water by tasting it, as well as by the clear indications of tides and of driftwood. On the 22nd Collinson returned to Boot Inlet, taking a tent with him so that he could spend several days surveying. Meanwhile, he left orders that the crew should lighten the ship by ferrying provisions ashore to allow the carpenters access to the iron plates that reinforced the bows, some of which had been badly damaged by battering through the ice. As the captain was returning to the ship on the 23rd, a group of Inuit was just leaving. His impression was that they were poorly supplied with food and clothing and only a few of their arrows were tipped with iron. Next day Lt. Jago took a boat round to Minto Inlet to fetch driftwood, which was more abundant there than in Winter Cove. Some of the crew meanwhile started housing in the upper deck with a canvas roof, while others were cutting more turves and building the observatory.

Having left the ship on the morning of the 19th, Skead and his party rounded Mt. Phayre and started east along the north shore of Minto Inlet, camping for the night about four miles into the inlet. After they had started again next morning, one of the crew reported that he had found the recent embers of a fire, producing some charred pieces of wood to back up his story. Skead conjectured that this must have been the campsite of one of the travelling parties from *Investigator* in the spring. Before leaving their campsite on the morning of the 20th, Skead had the ship's name painted in red paint on a high rock and left a cylinder with details of his visit.

Since the moderately strong east wind made a foul wind for heading up Minto Inlet, Skead decided to run south across the mouth of the Inlet to the most westerly point on its south side (Point Wollaston), getting under way at 6 AM. As the easterly wind soon freshened, raising a fairly rough sea, the boat threatened to broach-to and forced Skead to haul more to the wind; as a result, his landfall on the south shore was about five miles east of the point. He landed at about 10 AM and, since everything was wet, took advantage of the abundant driftwood to start a large fire to dry the clothes and gear.

With this taken care of, since the wind had moderated and was now fair, Skead ran west to Point Wollaston, the headland now named Cape Ptarmigan, the westernmost tip of Diamond Jenness Peninsula:

We landed in a small nook amongst the rocks at the Point, when I ascended a small hill which stands over the Pt. to take a look round & see what was to be seen. When half way up the hill one of the men called out "We are too late here, Sir." I looked up & saw something very like a beacon on the summit. "That is a European mark & no mistake," added the seaman & in a few minutes we had gained the top. A small pile of earth & stones was crowned by a very roughly made Copper cylinder which caused me to exclaim as I took it up, "This has been left by Rae or Pullen." I did not give our consort a thought especially as I believed the Cylinders she was supplied with were made of tin like our own. Upon reading the Notice I found it to have been left by the Investigator's travelling party in May last. Our consort had thus done more in the way of search than we had given them credit for.... I consoled myself with the hope that our consort while <u>reaping</u> a rich harvest in the fields they had explored, had left the deep inlet that lay before us as <u>gleanings</u> for the "Enterprise."[5]

The message had indeed been left by a sledge party from *Investigator*, namely that led by Lt. William Haswell.[6] Skead spotted a large snowy owl on Point Wollaston and tried to get a shot at it, but it was too wary to allow him to get within range.

Constrained by Collinson's orders, he now set off back to the northeast into Minto Inlet:

With such favourable, tempting opportunity for further search to the SEd it was galling in the extreme to be tied by written orders to the bay to the Eastd; however there was no help for it so late in the afternoon we started....[7]

They camped for the night after covering about ten miles.

For the next two days Skead and his men coasted along the south shore of Minto Inlet in mild, fair weather; Skead characterized it as "a very pleasant trip, quite like a sea Pic-nic."[8] During excursions on shore he and his men shot gulls, hares, ptarmigan, and ducks, "all of which were thrown into the pot, & produced a mess not to be despised at any time or place."[9] Moderate amounts of driftwood along the shore provided plenty of firewood. Several herds of caribou were also seen grazing.

At noon on the 22nd Skead went ashore on the east entrance cape of a deep bay on the south shore of Minto Inlet; getting a noon sun shot, he established its latitude

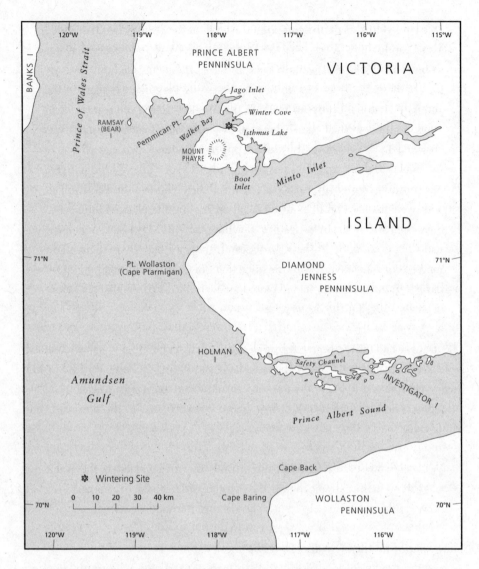

Southwestern Victoria Island; area of operations of HMS *Enterprise*, winter of 1851–52.

to be 71° 24' 30"N and estimated its longitude to be 114°W (actually closer to 116°
10'W). They camped that night about 60 miles from Point Wollaston:

> From a high hill in the vicinity I clearly saw round the bottom of the inlet.
> It was shallow & on the South side opened into a large lagoon that was
> in the midst of an extensive swamp. A chain of mountains ran round the

head of the inlet some distance inland which, with what I saw convinced me there was no outlet to it. The head of the inlet is about 70 miles from the Pt. Named Wollaston....

Towards the head of the inlet & about the place of our 4th encamp-ment the mountains present a wild & rugged appearance; composed of dark rock & stratified regularly that had all the appearance of artificial walls of masonry. Some of the cliffs literally overhung the sea.[10]

Anxious not to exceed the week the captain had allotted to him for this trip, and especially concerned that the captain might send a boat to look for him if he were away any longer, Skead started back west on the morning of the 23rd, coasting along the north shore of Minto Inlet. A strong head wind with fog and rain made progress slow, although occasional excursions ashore to shoot hares made for welcome breaks. Since they were making such poor progress, Skead ran the boat ashore at noon and even pitched the tent for a couple of hours while they ate some lunch. Getting under way again at 2 PM, he found that they were actually losing ground, no matter how hard the men rowed, so he ran back east for half a mile and put ashore again for the night. All this time Skead was trying to console himself with the thought that he was exploring new ground, that none of *Investigator*'s parties had examined Minto Inlet, but he had a nagging feeling that he was being over-optimistic.

Next morning they got under way at 5 AM in greatly improved weather, but around 9 AM a fresh NNWerly wind got up, and soon raised a short, choppy sea that forced Skead to down sail and pull for the land, landing at noon "as wet as it was possible for us to be."[11] Here Skead's worst fears were realized:

while searching for driftwood we found the remains of a European encamp-ment close to the beach. The half of a Pemmican tin precisely similar to those we were supplied with pointed out that even here we were too late, as our consort's travelling party had evidently been here some 5 months before us. The tent had been circular, as we saw the holes for the centre pole & those for the tent pegs outside a circle of stones, used I suppose to keep the flaps of the tent down. Some chips of wood & pieces of twine that lay scattered about shewed, even without the pemmican tin, that a party of Europeans had encamped there. I sought very diligently for some record of their visit but none could be found. The spot was about 40 miles from the Nn entrance to the inlet. We have thus found traces of our consort at the beginning, the midst & at the end of our boat journey. Verily we are too late for the fair.[12]

That afternoon and throughout the next day, the boat party had to contend with snow showers. They rounded the Dome (Mt Phayre) in the early evening of the 25th and camped 8–10 miles from the ship. A fairly heavy fall of snow was in part offset by a blazing fire. They got back aboard at 10 AM on the 26th, just in time to forestall a boat being sent with provisions for them. Once again, however, in his later annotations to his personal copy of Collinson's narrative, Skead expressed his frustration that they should already have selected a wintering site: "Not a particle of ice was visible from the tops of the hills, yet we had taken up winter quarters 8 days before."[13]

On the following day Collinson found fault with some of his officers on a relatively minor matter, but nonetheless the matter probably rankled with some of them:

> Some of the officers having of late absented themselves from the public worship of Almighty God I have to acquaint them that such conduct is highly improper & to direct that should occasion (except duty or ill health) prevent their attendance in future that I am informed thereof.[14]

On the 29th Collinson continued with his survey while Lts. Phayre and Parkes went over to Minto Inlet on a shooting trip, expected to last three days. Meanwhile, on board ship part of the main hold was cleared out, the casks being moved ashore to leave sufficient room for the Sylvester stove, which was lit for a short period every day from now on.[15] By the end of the month Collinson had all but completed his survey of Winter Cove, apart from taking soundings. The bay was still not frozen, but the freshwater lakes were, the ice being thick enough to walk on; the ice, still without a snow cover, was transparent, allowing the lake bed and swimming fish to be seen.

On 2 October one of the marines, George Deverill, came back from Lt. Phayre's hunting camp with six hares, then set off again with a day's provisions for the party. Next morning Parkes came aboard to report that Deverill had not turned up at the hunting camp. Lt. Jago was sent back to the camp to relieve Phayre, while Skead was sent off to where the Inuit were known to be encamped on Minto Inlet to search for Deverill and to see whether he might have landed up there. On the 4th Collinson, at the head of another search party, made a wide circuit in search of the missing man, ending up at the hunting camp. While taking a rest on the way back, he and his men heard three guns being fired from the ship, indicating that the missing man had returned. Deverill could not explain how he had lost his way, and Collinson concluded that he had gotten drunk on some of the liquor included in the provisions he was taking to the hunting camp.

On 7 October the first experiment with balloons was made, a large and a small one being released. The balloons were an attempt to communicate with the missing Franklin expedition and were released by several of the search expeditions. The technique, as described by Lieutenant Sherard Osborn from his experience on board HMS *Pioneer*, was as follows:

> a balloon of oiled silk, capable of raising about a pound weight when inflated, was filled with hydrogen evolved from a strong cask fitted with a valve, into which, when required for the purpose, a certain quantity of zinc filings and sulphuric acid was introduced. To the base of the balloon, when inflated, a piece of slow match five feet long was attached, its lower end being lighted. All along this match at certain intervals, pieces of coloured paper and silk were secured with thread, and on them the information as to our position and intended lines of search was printed. The balloon when liberated sailed rapidly along, rising withal, and as the match burnt the papers were gradually detached, and falling, spread themselves on the snow, where their glaring colours would soon attract notice, should they happily fall near the poor fellows of the Erebus and Terror.[16]

On 10 October a strong east wind made conditions on deck rather unpleasant, and hence the next day the main deck was covered over with a canvas housing. Two more balloons were released on the 23rd. Next day, a channel was cut in the newly formed ice, and the ship was eased close to shore, her final wintering position being only 300 yards from shore in 5 fathoms of water.

Skead, however, was still fuming because they had sought winter quarters so early, long before freeze-up:

> We went into Winter quarters on Sept. 13th & waited 5 weeks for ice to make! A marvellous proceeding considering Franklin was perishing for want of food & shelter.… The ocean outside was clear of ice for fully 6 weeks after we went into Winter Quarters, and this he calls eagerness to aid Sr. J. Franklin!!! Mirabile dictu![17]

On 25 October an arctic fox was trapped. A collar was then fitted to its neck, to which was attached a message as to the ship's position and the date, this being another rather optimistic attempt at communicating with the Franklin expedition. It was hoped that the fox might travel a considerable distance and be trapped or shot by a member of the missing expedition.

By 27 October the sea ice was strong enough to bear loaded sledges, and hence on that date Collinson set off for Minto Inlet, intending to investigate the bay opening from its southeast corner, which Skead had not investigated to its head; the captain took provisions for ten days. He was accompanied by Lt. Parkes, with three days' provisions on an empty sledge; he was to bring back a load of firewood from the stack accumulated by Lt. Jago. Collinson does not mention how many men he had with him, but he had three dogs to assist them. Crossing the isthmus to the head of Boot Inlet posed few problems, but they

> had more trouble in crossing the lakes than in any other portion of our route, the ice on them being so slippery that it was almost an impossibility to walk except in moccasins. Our dogs, however, made up for it, three of them drag-ging the sleigh themselves when we arrived at a smooth tract.[18]

They reached the head of Boot Inlet in two-and-a-quarter hours, and soon afterwards encountered a party of nine Inuit, including children, with two sledges, and bought a small amount of caribou meat from them. On reaching Minto Inlet, it became clear that the sea ice was all on the move, and that there were several leads and polynyas close inshore. After lunching at the east entrance to Boot Inlet,

> we set forward again, but almost immediately fell into a crack; the dogs refusing to jump baulked the sleigh, and thus we got our clothes and some of our provisions wet, so were compelled to camp where we were and dry our skin dresses and blanket bags as best we could. Driftwood being scarce, and our fire an economical one, we succeeded but indifferently.[19]

Next morning they had gone only two miles when the sledge broke through the ice again; they managed to unload it and rescue the sledge, but Collinson decided that this trip was premature and started back towards the ship. He and his men spent the night at Parkes's camp, using some of the driftwood he had collected to build a big fire to thaw and partially dry their blanket bags. On the way back to the ship next morning, they found the Inuit in a cluster of snow houses on the shores of one of the lakes, where they were fishing through holes in the ice; they attracted the fish with a shiny lure then speared them. Collinson bought two fish of 10 and 12 lbs weight, which turned out to be arctic char, for an awl and two needles.

On 30 October Phayre, with sledges and dogs, headed south across the isthmus, meeting Parkes halfway with a load of firewood. Also on that day, some of the Inuit from the lake on the isthmus came aboard the ship. An elderly man, named Ip-pee-ra, who could only move around using two sticks, was offered the choice of a boarding pike or a knife and chose the latter. He appeared to be the leader of the group, which totalled 25 individuals. With him were his sons-in-law and his wife.

Around this time, a tide gauge was set up and was read every two hours thereafter; a meteorological station was also set up at this time, and its instruments, too, were read every two hours for the entire winter.

On 1 November Lt. Phayre crossed the isthmus for another load of firewood, and returned with Lt. Parkes, who had dismantled his wooding camp on Boot Inlet. Next day (Sunday) some Inuit again came aboard and, as Collinson observed, "remained at first very quietly during Divine Service, but went away before it was concluded."[20] It would be fascinating to know what the Inuit made of the formalities of a Royal Navy shipboard church service!

On the 5th, on his way to do some surveying on the north side of Winter Cove, Collinson found the Inuit's cluster of snow houses that "have certainly a very clean and comfortable appearance when first built, but they soon get abominably filthy." Next day a new group of Inuit arrived at the snow house village; among their possessions were a small axe and part of a pemmican tin, presumably acquired from *Investigator*'s sledge party the previous spring.

On the 7th the entire group, now numbering 45 or 50, crossed the bay and built another snow house village about three miles from the ship. Some of them came aboard on the 8th, and although they were offered saws and knives in exchange for caribou meat, they could produce only a small amount, presumably because they had little surplus to spare. Collinson makes an interesting observation on their appearance: "Some among the tribe were of very different features to the others, the face being oval and the nose aquiline."[21]

This group appears to have been Kangiryuarmiut, from Prince Albert Sound to the south. Among the group was a young eight-year-old lad, named Pamiungittok, who came aboard *Enterprise* with his father. Sixty years later, in May 1911, in a snow-house in Prince Albert Sound, he recalled that visit during a lengthy conversation with Vilhjalmur Stefansson. He reported that "The white men were excellent people and paid well for water boots etc. They threw away much valuable stuff which the people picked up."[22] By 1911 he was the only Inuk still alive who had encountered Collinson and his men.

Also on the 7th Lt. Parkes and Mr. Skead walked to a hilltop about five miles west of the ship. It was a clear day, and the sea was frozen as far as they could see, but there was a dark water sky to the west. This first ice soon broke up, however; when Lt. Jago and Dr. Anderson climbed Dome Hill (Mt. Phayre) on the 10th, they found that the ice edge was only about a mile to seaward, with open water beyond that.[23]

Various preparations for wintering were now made. To insulate the ship, snow walls were built against the ship's sides as high as the sponsons (see illustration p. 263). As the captain reported, regular schedules for laundry and for airing bedding were established,

> by devoting one day to each quarter watch, and one day for the officers. We managed to dry by far the greater portion round about the hot air pipes in the main hold. The men always brought what they had washed to divisions in the morning, which ensured their having a clean suit weekly, and also that they were thoroughly wrung. Having a spare cabin on the port side of the lower deck, it was devoted to the airing of the bedding, each man's bed clothes being spread daily in rotation.[24]

On 18 November the sun disappeared and, since there would be little daylight thereafter, the quarter deck was also housed in on the 22nd. A system for providing fresh water was already established; blocks of ice were cut from one of the nearby lakes and hauled to the ship by dog team, making one or two trips per day. Two holes were cut in the ice and kept open constantly: one was for the tide-gauge, while the other, near the ship, was the fire-hole, which provided quick and easy access to water in case of fire. A further winter activity was the establishment of a "school" for the crew members. It was started in the last week of November, one watch attending in the morning and the other in the afternoon. In addition to academic subjects, two of the petty officers also gave training in tailoring and shoe-making.

Keeping the crew occupied was one of the greatest challenges on all the Navy's wintering expeditions, and Collinson tackled the problem with a great deal of imagination. In December he initiated the practice of sending the crew out for a walk on Thursday mornings; Thursday afternoons were set aside for making and mending clothes. Collinson's unique initiative in this area was a skittle alley that

> was built of snow alongside, which soon became a favourite resort, affording not only healthy exercise, but giving them something to do of their own accord. Sometimes coming off from the observatory, with the temperature below −30°, I have heard the balls rolling at midnight.[25]

The Inuit left the area, heading south, on 9 December, and Skead took the opportunity to make the following remarks about them in his journal:

> Their united numbers amounted to 36. We made them a few presents: iron hoops & other (to us) rubbish, which they valued highly. They were all well clad in seal & deer skins & appeared to have no lack of food. They carried an odour about with them any thing but fragrant to our untutored nostrils yet they were neither so filthy in their persons nor so strong in their smell as at Pt. Barrow & the natives in that vicinity. Their arms were made of Copper which they appeared to be well supplied with. We got one or two lumps of the metal in its native state. It is nearly pure.[26]

In October caribou had been seen almost on a daily basis, but always well out of range. Then in early December they appeared to leave the area. As a result, much to everyone's disappointment, they had no venison for Christmas dinner. Nonetheless, Christmas was celebrated with all the traditional features, double rations being issued to the entire crew. The "game list," recorded since leaving Port Clarence, totalled three bears, one caribou, 45 arctic hares, 21 arctic foxes, four seals, 524 murres, 21 gulls, four ducks, and 29 ptarmigan. Arctic foxes and two ravens that hung about the ship were the only living things seen during the winter.

On New Year's Eve Collinson announced that theatrical performances, the Wollaston Theatre, would begin the following Thursday, and these were thereafter a weekly event. Unfortunately, Collinson gives no details of what plays were produced or who the performers were.

Soon afterwards, however (on 11 January 1852, barely halfway through the long, sunless arctic winter), Collinson launched an attack on all his officers that predictably produced a very strong reaction:

The Gunroom lights are to be put out at 10 PM, and as I consider playing with dice for dollars to be gambling, that mode of shortening long & weary hours is forbidden.[27]

The predictable reaction came in a strongly worded letter, signed by all officers except Lt. Phayre, on 12 January:

Sir,

A reproach from you, directed to us, has been delivered by the Senior Lieutt., to the effect that no "gambling" should henceforth be carried on in the gunroom.

Without misunderstanding, we hope you would have forborne to direct a censure, not only offensive, but so unmerited.

The heaviest "gambling" that has ever occurred in this ship, to any of the officers, you have partaken of. After some seven months of playing, off and on, Messrs. Jago and Anderson arrive with a difference of 16 shillings sterling.

On Friday night when the playing, which gave rise to your censure, occurred, the entire sum exchanging hands amongst three players amounted to 30 useless Dollars.

If it should again occur that you find occasion to reprove us, for what may appear to be misconduct, we must respectfully beg you to enquire, whether or not any misconduct has really taken place.

No one in this mess has any inclination to "gamble" and we are much pained to have so harsh a term applied, to what we had thought an innocent enough mode of shortening long and weary hours.

We have the honor to be, Sir,
Your most obedient humble servants,

CHARLES T. JAGO, LIEUTT.

F. SKEAD, 2ND MASTER

MURRAY T. PARKES, ACTG. LIEUT.

ROBERT ANDERSON, SURGEON

EDWARD ADAMS, ASST. SURGEON.[28]

Since a number of hares had been seen on shore, Collinson relaxed the usual regulations, which specified that all game brought in should be added to the general "pot";
now two men from each mess might go out hunting in rotation and would be allowed
to keep whatever they brought back. This served the double purpose of providing
both fresh meat and exercise. In case these hunting parties were caught out in a blizzard, one of the Inuit snow houses was turned into a refuge, a buffalo robe, some
fuel, and some provisions being left there in case of any such emergency.

The returning sun was spotted from the flagstaff on the hill near the ship on 24
January. Thereafter the length of daylight increased rapidly, allowing the shooting
parties to roam further afield, this being necessary since all the hares in the immediate area had been killed.

On the evening of 6 March, the conversation in the gunroom somehow drifted
onto the topic of the events of the celebration in Hong Kong on 22 February 1851 to
mark the installation of the Admiral Sir G. Bonham as Knight Commander of the
Bath, a celebration to which all captains of naval vessels in the harbour, including
Captain Collinson, had been invited. It was to be a fateful conversation as far as
Skead was concerned, since his running fight with his captain was about to come
to a head.

On 10 March Collinson included the following memorandum in his Night
Order Book:

It having been represented to me by Lieutenant Phayre that on Saturday the
6th instant the Second Master of this ship made some observations upon
his Captain's conduct at the gunroom table & that on his [Phayre's] sending
for this officer [Skead] on the following morning he, the Second Master,
behaved himself not only with contempt, but had recourse to reproachful
speeches.

Having investigated the matter and the Second Master having alleged in
defence of his conduct that no disrespect was intended by the observations
he made use of at his Mess Table, but at the same time he refused to admit the
impropriety of his conduct to the Senior Lieutenant; moreover in my presence made use of most provoking & (from the evidence of Lieutenants Jago
& Parkes) unjustified language—stigmatizing the Senior Lieutenant's charge
as false & malicious, I consider his conduct highly reprehensible & this being
the fifth complaint of a similar nature which he has committed during the
period he has been under my command, I have deemed it advisable to place

him under arrest until such time as I can ascertain their Lordships' pleasure, but as a considerable period must elapse before an opportunity for doing so occurs, he is to be considered a prisoner at large & allowed such indulgencies as his behaviour will admit. At present he will abide by the following regulations. Permission is granted to him to resort to his Mess place, the gunroom, between the hours of 8 AM & 8.30 PM, after which period he is to retire to his cabin, where he may admit one person at a time, provided the door of the cabin is shut and the conversation maintained at a low tone. No conversation across the steerage is to be permitted; nor are any persons to gather about the door of his cabin. His lights are to be extinguished at 10 PM.

The Port side of the Quarter deck is allotted as the place for him to take exercise between the hours of 7 AM & 8.20 PM. While there he is in no consideration to enter into conversation with the officer of the watch or any person engaged in the duty of the ship.

The papers related to the gunner's stores (except such as are necessary for the passing of his accounts) with a schedule containing an account of these are to be delivered to the Senior Lieutenant during the forenoon of the 12th inst.; those relating to the Master's department on the 13th. And in like manner those belonging to the Victualling & Purser's accounts on the 15th inst.

Mr. Arbuthnott will take charge of the Victualling & Purser's stores, as well as the ship's Log & assist me in navigating the ship; the after cabin on the port side will be allotted to him as an officer as soon as the travelling parties have left. Joseph Page (Gunner's Mate) will take charge of the gunner's stores.

RD. COLLINSON, CAPTAIN.[29]

Clearly Skead had somehow made an enemy of Lieutenant Phayre as well as his captain, but no evidence for the cause of that enmity has survived.

Skead's journal ends abruptly at this point, but it is possible to follow the details of this remarkable development from the correspondence in the captain's Letter Book and In-Letter Book. Almost immediately (on the 11th), Parkes (and possibly Jago, but if so the text of his letter has not survived) had the courage to write to the Captain to say that he (Collinson) had misconstrued his remarks:

Sir,

I beg to repeat in writing the evidence I gave on the deck on the 8th inst. which was to this effect: that I was not paying particular attention to what was being said, but as well as I remember and understood, the Conversation turned on the installation dinner at Hong Kong. Dr. Anderson I think commenced it, and Mr. Skead said that the Captain, Cm. Bate, and Captain's Steward came on board in the same boat very jolly (or used words of the same meaning). I was then asked by Mr. Skead if I considered any disrespect was intended. I said certainly not.

The following passage from your order of the 10th Inst.: "moreover in my presence made use of most provoking & (from the evidence of Lieutenants Jago & Parks) unjustifiable language, stigmatizing the Senior Lieutenant's charges as false and malicious," has induced me to write this as I fear what I said may not have been sufficiently clear.[30]

Skead was somewhat dilatory in complying with his captain's orders about handing over various documents, and on 19 March the captain issued a reminder in writing:

Documents relative to the Gunner's stores, Master's Duty, Pursery & Victualling accounts not having been given in agreeably to my orders of the 10th inst. by the Second Master, I have to call his attention thereto, & to desire he will immediately deliver up the same, affording such excuse in writing as is in his power.[31]

Skead attempted to satisfy his Captain that he had done his best to conform with these orders concerning Gunner's, Master's, and Victualling accounts:

Sir,

In compliance with your order of this day's date, directing me to "afford such excuse in writing as is in my power" for not having delivered up certain papers connected with the Gunner's, Master's & Victualling Accounts agreeably to your orders of 10th Inst., I beg respectfully to state-that the order to which you refer directs me to deliver up the papers connected with those accounts "except such as are necessary for the passing of my accounts."

This order I have obeyed, having delivered to the Senr. Lieutt. the Gunner's papers on the 12th, the Master's on the 13th & placed upon your table those relating to the Purser's on the 15th Inst.

I have only retained the papers that are requisite for the passing of my accounts, but as you have called for several documents that I do not possess I beg to remind you that upon your requesting me to furnish you with Quarterly Accounts for the Quarters ending June, Septr. & December 1851 I mentioned that I feared it would render the Purser's accounts very complicated if I attempted to make out papers that I did not understand & told you that I had consulted the clerk in Charge of the Plover upon the subject, whose advice was that I should only keep a clear & simple account of the receipt & Expenditure of the Pursery stores & not intangle myself amongst the numerous Printed forms. You did not object to my following this advice at the time but merely desired me to try to make out the Quarterly accounts, which I did.

I have kept all the documents that are necessary for accounting for the receipt and expenditure of the Pursery stores since they have been in my charge, & I trust that I shall be able to give satisfactory explanation to the Comptroller of Victualling for omitting the forms that are required from a Paymaster & Purser.

The papers which you require & which I do not possess are the following: Victualling Book, Public Letter Book, Quarterly Account Book & Store Account Book. Those which I have retained are as follows: Daily Transaction Book, Mess Book, Weekly Account Book & Gunner's Abstract Statement. The duplicate account of the Saving of Provisions I will reduce as early as it can be made out.

The Chronometer journal is already in your possession & I have but one track chart which is unfinished. A Remark Book, such at least as I conceive you require me to deliver up, I do not possess. Upon leaving England you addressed a copy of their Lordships' orders to the Officers, directing them on the paying off of the ship to deliver their Journals, Charts, etc., etc. sealed up, to you for transmission to the Admiralty—in consequence of this I kept a Journal in which my private observations were incorporated with the remarks made upon Winds, Currents, etc., etc during the voyage, with a view of delivering it to you sealed up, in compliance with their Lordships' instructions. This Journal I must respectfully decline to deliver up to you until the ship arrives in England, when I shall be ready to obey their Lordship's commands. I can extract for your information from the Journal of which I have spoken such portions as you may require.

With regard to the journal of my proceedings between 19th & 26th Septr. I beg respectfully to remind you that shortly after my return from the examination of the coast to the Southd. & Eastwd., I applied to you for the stations which you stated you would give me, to enable me to put upon paper the outline of the land I had passed in the boat, requesting you to let me have them at once, as I was afraid of forgetting the particulars connected with each day's proceedings. To this you replied, "You shall have another opportunity of seeing the same place," & did not provide me with the stations. From this I concluded that you did not attach any importance to the works I had done, & have in consequence drawn up only a brief outline of my proceedings. This I will deliver to the Senior Lieutenant in obedience to your directions as soon as I can write it out from my private journal.[32]

On 1 March snow had been seen to be melting against the black surface of the ship's side, and by 16 March there were more than 12 hours of daylight. Wolves were now seen quite frequently, often coming close to the ship at night, judging by their tracks. Collinson's Newfoundland dog began running with the wolves, and since he was "on too good terms with them," Collinson was obliged to tie him up. The last theatrical performance was given on 18 March, since all hands were now needed for removing the snow banking around the ship and for building sledges. On 23 March the housing over the quarter deck was removed to "let a gleam of sunshine down the main hatchway on to the lower deck."[33] Then, on the 25th, the crew was sent out on the ice to practise with small arms, firing at targets, although, as Collinson confesses, it was "cold work."

Another project pursued during March was the replacement of some of the battered iron plates at the ship's bow. For this the carpenter dug and chopped an ice "coffer-dam" around the bow to a depth of 4 feet 2 inches; this gave him access to the damaged plates.

Another of the winter activities, the school classes, was also wound up in late March. For men who had performed particularly well, and for good conduct generally, Collinson awarded as prizes six pairs of knitted stockings, six pairs of mitts, and eight clasp knives.

Having allowed what he probably hoped was sufficient time to elapse for Collinson to "cool off," on 1 April Skead responded with a letter in his own defence:

Sir,

The severe & multiplied punishments you have inflicted upon me, the long, indefinite period to which they must of necessity extend before the Lords of the Admiralty can be appealed to, and a deep sense of their injustice all impel me to address you in the hope that you may be pleased to reconsider the matter, & more thoroughly to enquire into the truth or falsehood of the charge exhibited against me by the Senior Lieutenant. You declined to have all the evidence I desired to advance in defence of myself, & I respectfully maintain that your decision is not in accordance with what you did listen to, for the Officers who gave evidence endeavoured to explain to you that you must have misunderstood them, as their testimony did not support the conclusion you had drawn from it & which was set forth in the order book as the cause of my being made a prisoner. The following statement of the conversation that took place in the Gunroom, & upon which Mr. Phayre founded his accusation against me, is the same as that which I repeated to you on the quarter deck in Mr. Phayre's presence.

The conversation having turned upon the great dinner given at Hong Kong on the investiture of the Governor with the Order of the Bath, Mr. Anderson remarked that he had been reading in the library that day, & upon leaving had walked around the tables that were laid out for dinner, that the preparations were grand & that he understood the affair had become rather boisterous towards its close, some one having told him that Captn. Massie went down stairs during the small hours singing "He won't go home till morning" & that most of those who had staid were equally well on. I remarked: "I should like to have heard the speeches that were made." Then, recollecting that I was sick at the time, said that I remembered your coming on board at 3 AM with Capt. Bate, your servant & Bate's boy, & being thirsty I asked your servant for a glass of water but he brought me two oranges saying "They will do you good, my dear. We've had a glorious party & we all had as much to drink as our masters." Both he and Bate's boy were jolly drunk & I heard you laughing & speaking very loud & supposed you were glorious as well as the rest. I am not certain that I used this form of expression. I might have said "was jolly drunk" or "had a skin full," but I mention them all because I have no desire to conceal any part of the language I may have employed. Mr. Anderson then said: "It is right for every one to be jolly on these occasions, for 'tis a poor beast that never rejoices," & enquired if Bate was jolly too. I answered "No, no. Bate never does those sort of things."

If I have not stated the whole of the conversation that took place it is because I ceased to think of what had passed a few moments after it ended & should not again in all probability have thought of it, but for the purpose that Mr. Phayre has thought to turn it to.

I most respectfully request that you will be pleased to examine those who were present, & ascertain whether I have stated the conversation correctly & whether my observations can by any means be twisted into a charge of drunkenness against you, i.e. the offence Mr. Phayre has accused me of. To charge as if to accuse of some criminal act. I spoke of the installation dinner & its conclusion as an amusing piece of conviviality—nothing more—& no one knew that better than Mr. Phayre, who had heard the same story told before, without complaint, if not with pleasure, but it suits his purpose this time to make it appear otherwise. He knew what he was about to accomplish, for he stated just after the events of Jan. 14th that "he would recommend me to be upon my guard as he was certain you would be on the look out to lay hold of me, if you could only get a chance." Until very lately I had been upon friendly terms with Mr. Phayre but circumstances, quite unconnected with the matter, led to a suspension of all friendly intercourse between us, & in preferring this accusation he gratified his ill will towards me, & by his own showing took a step that he judged would be acceptable to you.

In requesting a hearing I only ask for what is accorded to the vilest criminal, not as a boon but as a right. This right I trust you will not deny me.

I am in arrest because I stated that Mr. Phayre's charge against me was false & malicious, because I spoke the truth in my own defence. I was required to retract what I had said & to apologize to Mr. Phayre, to do what I knew would be false & pusillanimous, an act from which my very soul revolts; for refusing to do this I am deprived of the emoluments arising from the charge of the Purser's and Gunner's stores. I do not ask favor or clemency at your hands, but respectfully claim what is my due, an impartial hearing, & in conclusion I beg to declare that I do not desire to address you in a disrespectful tone but conscious of my innocence of the charge for

which I am punished, & galled by its injustice I am constrained to speak
clearly & earnestly, & I trust that you will be pleased to receive this appeal
in that light & grant me the hearing I desire, when, if I be found guilty I
will not complain of the punishment, severe as it is, that you have inflicted
upon me.[34]

It seems almost incredible that such a trivial "offence" should have called forth such a
severe punishment, but undoubtedly tensions had been building between Collinson
and Skead for some time, and Collinson had probably been waiting for an excuse
to put Skead in his place. In light of this it comes as no surprise that Skead's argu-
ments now failed to move Collinson, the latter responding as follows on the 2nd :

Sir,

Having come to the conclusion that you are guilty of impropriety in
commenting upon your Captain's conduct at the Gunroom Mess table, & that
had the Senior Lieutenant permitted such observations as it appears you made
use of, to pass without reproof, that he would have been reprehensible. Also
that on his sending for you & pointing out the folly of your making ill-natured
remarks, your conduct was contrary to the discipline of the service, not only
treating your superior Officer with contempt but adding reproachful speeches.

On my enquiring into the affair, instead of quietly making your Captain
acquainted with the circumstances of the case, you burst out into language
which in my general order book suspending you from duty I have already
expatiated on. But in consequence of your letter of yesterday's date I have
again taken the affair into my serious consideration and am pained to inform
you that I can *find no cause therein to alter the regulations I have established*.[35]

In the light of this uncompromising attitude, Skead wrote again, with a degree of
desperation, on 6 April:

Sir,

The conclusions at which you have arrived cut me off from the means of
clearing myself from the charge Mr. Phayre has made against me, yet in
justice to myself I humbly beg once more to appeal to you & for the truth-

fulness of the following statements I pledge my honor & would if it were possible make solemn declaration to the same effect.

1. I did not comment upon your conduct at the mess table. The only comment made (if it can be called such) was by Mr. Anderson, who used the language I have stated in my letter, or words of similar import. As I had committed no offence, reproof from the Senior Lieutt. was not necessary.

2. Mr. Phayre did not "point out to me the folly of making ill natured remarks." How could he when no ill natured remarks were made? He at once accused me of "making a most serious charge against you." Had he been honestly engaged in maintaining the discipline of the service, he would have reproved me for any breach of it upon the Quarter deck, instead of seeking the concealment of the Skittle alley upon the plea of "wishing to have a few words with me."

3. I did not even repel the accusation with the indignation it was so calculated to excite. I replied that if he thought fit to prefer it against me, I would answer him in your presence. I appeal to your sense of justice to decide the amount of respect Mr. Phayre was entitled to when engaged upon such work & in such a place as the Skittle alley? The "reproachful language" too has suffered as much distortion under Mr. Phayre's hands as the other parts of my conduct & it is not for me to enquire upon what grounds you would yield implicit belief to Mr. Phayre's unauthenticated assertions, where you have set my words at nought, even those that are supported by Lieuts. Parks & Jago, who publicly affirmed that I did not use disrespectful or improper language when speaking of you.

4. I distinctly declare that I did not "burst out into unjustifiable language in your presence." In answer to your question "What had I to say to Mr. Phayre's charge?" I calmly but firmly stated that it was false & malicious, & related to you as fully as I was able, all that occurred, nor can I see that I did wrong, for when a malicious falsehood had been fabricated for my injury, I submit to you whether I had not a right to stamp it with its proper name.

I beg respectfully to observe that my object in addressing you on 1st Inst. was not to request you to alter the "regulations you have established" for my confinement. I merely appealed to you for an impartial hearing. If you deny me this I have only to endure what you have imposed upon me until appeal to higher authority can be made, when I have no reason to think I shall be denied the right of disproving Mr. Phayre's accusation, by the testimony of

my messmates, who heard the whole conversation, & who I feel certain are
well convinced that Mr. Phayre has no foundation for the charge he has
exhibited against me.[36]

Collinson remained unmoved, and Skead found himself faced with the demoral-
izing prospect of being under arrest for probably several years.

Collinson had hoped to have laid out some depots in support of the main spring
sledging trips in March, but the extremely cold weather had prevented this. The
weather warmed up considerably in April, however, and the depot-laying parties
were able to set off. Lt. Jago and a sledge crew set off on 2 April to establish a depot
on Point Wollaston to the south; Lt. Phayre accompanied him for two days to assist,
and Collinson and some men helped them across the isthmus to Minto Inlet. Lt.
Phayre returned to the ship on the 4th, and on the 5th Mr. Parkes and a sledge party
set off for the point opposite Bear Island to leave a depot for the parties that would
later be heading north.

In the interim, Collinson had been making a reconnaissance inland "with a
view of gaining the eastern watershed, and if possible to get sight of the sea in
that direction."[37] He appears to have thought that they were on a relatively small
island; in fact, the east coast of Victoria Island lay some 300 km to the east. Having
started out on the morning of the 3rd, he was back at the ship by mid-afternoon
on the 6th, having penetrated only some 40 km into the lake-strewn interior of
Prince Albert Peninsula and having been unable to "detect any signs of an easterly watershed."

Lt. Jago returned next afternoon, after establishing his cache on Point Wollaston,
and Lt Parkes late that evening. Many members of both depot-laying parties were
suffering from snow-blindness, and as many as 18 men were on the sick list.

It was about at this time that the Senior Lieutenant discovered that even he
could not meet his Captain's standards. On 11 April Collinson wrote to him:

In directing Mr. Arbuthnott, ice mate, in charge of Paymaster & Purser's
stores to issue savings of provisions in kind due to the Gunroom Mess, you
have acted contrary to the Queen's regulations for which it becomes my
duty severely to reprimand you. I have also, I regret to state, received a report
from that Officer, that you caused some of the provisions in question to be
changed for others of a superior description, thus benefitting the Gunroom
Mess to the prejudice of the remainder of the crew.[38]

This certainly appears like poetic justice, and Skead must have derived great pleasure from this reprimand to Phayre, if indeed it came to his notice.

Lieutenant Jago, leading a party of seven men, set off with the sledge, *Victoria*, to search the coast to the south, early on the morning of 12 April. On the sledge he had equipment and provisions sufficient for 40 days. As Collinson recorded, this load (typical of that on the other sledges also) consisted of the following:

Tent, buffalo robe, raccoon skin and foot-cloth, 5 boarding pikes [for tent poles], 8 blanket bags, 3 kettles, 1 musquet, 2 fowling pieces (private), 3 axes, 1 saw.

Provisions: Pork, boiled, 160 lbs.; preserved meats, 160 lbs.; pemmican, 72 lbs.; biscuit, 320 lbs.; potatoes, 240 lbs.; rum, 12 gall.; sugar, 60 lbs.; tea, 12 lbs.[39]

Total weight was about 200 lbs. Lt. Phayre, with two other sledges, *Investigator* and *Assistance*, was to accompany Jago's party for two days, hauling the supplies that Jago and his men would consume during that time. And, as before, Collinson and a party of men assisted them across the isthmus to Minto Inlet.

On the way back Collinson spotted the first snow-bunting of the season, while two days later a seal was seen basking on the ice, also the first of the season. Then, on the 15th, as a further sign that the winter was over, the housing over the main deck was taken down, letting daylight reach the lower deck via the forward hatchway. That afternoon Mr. Phayre returned.

Next day (16 April), the northern sledge party, consisting of the sledge *Enterprise*, led by Captain Collinson, and the sledge *Resolution*, led by Lieutenant Parkes, set off at 6:40 AM. They were to travel together as far as Point Peel at the northern entrance to Prince of Wales Strait; from there Parkes was to head north to Melville Island, while Collinson explored the north coast of Victoria Island eastwards. Each sledge was pulled by seven men, although Collinson also had three sledge dogs with him, Daddy, Sandy, and Joe. A fatigue party of nine men helped them for the first morning. The rations per man were as follows:

Morning, before starting, 1 pint of cocoa, ½ lb. of biscuit, ¼ lb. of pork. Noon, ¼ lb. of biscuit, ¼ lb. of pork, ½ gill of rum. Night, after camping, ½ lb. of preserved meat, $^3/_8$ lb. of preserved potatoes, 1 pint of tea, ½ gill of rum, ¼ lb. of biscuit.[40]

Any game shot during the day was added to the preserved meat at the evening meal, or failing that, some pemmican to improve the flavour.

They reached the depot opposite Bear Island at noon next day and picked up most of the provisions cached there, then pushed on again. Despite some minor cases of frostbite and attacks of snow blindness, they made steady progress, travelling between 11 and 20 miles per day. They reached the Princess Royal Islands on the evening of the 28th and found the depot intact, although there were tracks of a bear and cub around the main island. Having replenished their supplies from the depot next morning, they got under way again at 8:20 AM. Peel Point, at the north end of Prince of Wales Strait, was reached on 5 May, and here the two sledge parties separated, *Resolution* continuing north across M'Clure Strait and *Enterprise* swinging east along the north coast of Victoria Island. Thus far each of the sledges had had the assistance of the dogs on alternate days, but now Sandy and Daddy accompanied *Enterprise*, and Joe *Resolution*.

Heading east and southeast, Collinson crossed the mouth of the major embayment of Richard Collinson Inlet. By 11 May he found himself heading southwest by south as he followed the coast, and next day, spotting land to the east, realized that he was in another large inlet, which he named Glenelg Bay (now Wynniatt Bay). The next day was devoted to exploring the bay. Collinson, accompanied by Charters and Marshall, struck northeastwards across the bay towards Natkusiak Peninsula but, after travelling for six hours, estimated that it was still a further eight miles to the land ahead of them, and started back. Meanwhile, Hester and Murray were sent south up the bay. After covering about 14 miles, they got the impression that the bay swung more to the east.

The reunited party started back next morning (14 May). By noon on the 20th they were back at Peel Point, where Collinson had arranged to rendezvous with Parkes on the 22nd. Since there was no sign of the other sledge, Collinson and his men now had a two-day rest. The game-bag that day included three arctic hares, seven ptarmigan, and one snow bunting, which must have been a pleasant addition to the menu for their brief holiday. Next day the blanket bags were hung out in the sun to dry and air.

When there was still no sign of Parkes's party on the morning of the 23rd, Collinson set off northwards in search of them. A couple of hours after starting, they spotted a black object on the ice; leaving the sledge for the moment, they hurried towards it, thinking it was the missing sledge party, only to find that it was a seal sunning itself on the ice. Next morning they had quite an exciting awakening:

The dogs barking at 4 AM roused us up in the hopes that it would prove to be our companions; on looking out, however, it turned out to be a bear. The musquets were outside the tent near the sleigh, but were soon got in and loaded with ball; Daddy in the meantime keeping the animal at bay, and annoying him so much that he frequently turned round with a spring. The dog had a narrow escape, as we found his back scratched by the claws. Sandy kept at a distance, which surprised us all, as he was generally looked upon as the first in the fray, and Neptune's principal antagonist. After 9 or 10 shots from Hester and Marshall all of which took effect in the forequarter or muzzle, the great brute rolled over; but we should not have got him if it had not been for the manner in which Daddy stuck to him, as after the first two discharges he made off, and we were only able to get ahead of him again by the dog worrying him. When he fell he was three-quarters of a mile from the tent, and when we first saw him his footmarks were 19 paces from the door. Having cut off his head, and brought the sleigh for his carcase, we got it to the tent.[41]

Leaving the rest of the men in camp to skin the bear, Collinson, Bosquet, and Gowan headed northeast and came across Parkes's second camp on his outward journey; from there they travelled east till noon, at which point they could see both Banks Island and Victoria Island, but no sign of the overdue sledge party. Collinson and his men then headed back to their tent. In the evening he sent two men out to the east about eight miles, but they too found no trace of Parkes's party.

Next day Collinson and his men headed back to their depot at Peel Point, where there was still no sign of the overdue party; then on the morning of the 26th Collinson started back south. They were supplementing their rations with bear meat, which Collinson found "palatable, but uncommonly tough. The smallest portion of its own fat gave it anything but a pleasant taste to me."[42]

By the late afternoon of the 28th they were back at the depot on the Princess Royal Islands and stayed there for the following day. Their bread and potatoes were practically exhausted by this time. As a replacement, using flour from the depot they cooked a batch of "pemmican cakes" with flour, potatoes, and pemmican. One of the casks left by M'Clure augmented their supply of salt beef. Some of the men found a cask of rum among the supplies left by M'Clure and acted predictably: "I found two of my men drunk, which was extremely vexatious, as otherwise they had conducted themselves to my satisfaction."[43]

There was still no sign of Parkes with the sledge *Resolution* next morning (30 May), and hence, since he had told Lt. Phayre he would be back at the ship by the first week of June, at 7:30 AM Collinson and his men got under way. First, however, he had left a message for Parkes at the flagstaff.

They reached the Bear Island depot at 11:00 AM on 4 June and were in the process of pitching the tent for the night near Pemmican Point when they saw some movement on the shore opposite. This was Lt. Jago with a team of dogs, which he had acquired from the Inuit, on his way to meet Collinson with a load of provisions, since Lt. Phayre had realized that Collinson's provisions must be running very low. Jago was in the habit of travelling at night when, with the lower temperatures, snow conditions were better, and was just in the process of striking camp when Collinson spotted his camp. Collinson now instructed him to continue north for one day's travel beyond Bear Island, to wait there until the end of the week, and to assist Parkes and his men if they should turn up. He also gave Jago some of the bear meat for his dogs.

By 4:30 on 6 June Collinson and his men were back aboard *Enterprise*, having been met by Lt. Phayre and most of the crew, as well as some Inuit, about a mile from the ship.

In Collinson's absence Lt. Phayre had taken care of a range of what might be described as housekeeping tasks. The carpenters overhauled the bends,[44] which had been badly splintered by the ice during the previous navigation season. Then, when part of the deck beneath the galley was found to be in poor condition, it was replaced. On 3 May the housing over the fo'c's'le was dismantled, although this may have seemed premature when there was a heavy fall of snow that afternoon. Thereafter the carpenters were kept busy caulking the upper deck and the bends, and the running rigging, which had all been stowed in a house on shore, was brought back aboard.

In the latter part of May the head of the mainmast was hauled aft by ten inches and that of the mizzen mast by 1 ft. 2 in, which Phayre hoped would improve the ship's performance in rough seas. Then, finding that the starboard fore yardarm was sprung, he had it sent down and fished. [45]

Fairly regularly throughout this period balloons were released. Towards the end of the month, a shooting party was sent off to camp about four miles from the ship, presumably since the game had all been eliminated closer to the ship. On the 14th they shot a small caribou, which weighed 43 lbs. dressed; the meat was shared among all hands. On 25 May the same group of Inuit who had been in the vicinity in the fall returned and set up camp on the ice about two miles from the ship.

A less happy event occurred on 14 May, when the ship's cook, William Driver, died. In reporting his death, Collinson's tone is almost apologetic:

> He had been suffering from general debility, and was too old a man for such an expedition; but being an old shipmate of mine, and considering that the duty he would have to perform would not call for much exposure, he was entered. I had left him very ill, and scarcely could hope to see him again.[46]

On 30 May Lt. Jago and his party returned to the ship from the south. Having left the ship on 12 April, accompanied initially by Lt. Phayre, Jago and his men had crossed Minto Inlet, then headed west along the coast towards Point Wollaston. Lt. Phayre and his support party started back on the morning of the 14th, and that evening Jago and his men reached the depot they had left earlier, a mile short of Point Wollaston. Next morning, while rounding Point Wollaston, Jago checked the cairn that the party from *Investigator* had built and in which Skead had left a message, only to find that the message cylinder had disappeared.

From here the coastline swung towards the south-southeast. Blizzard conditions on the 16th and 17th kept the party weather-bound, but on the 18th they got under way again. That night, from the low headland on which they camped, they could see an island to the south-southeast "separated from the main by a narrow channel abreast of a high bold cape."[47] This was Holman Island, and this description could scarcely be bettered.

They reached the island on the evening of the 20th; Jago climbed to its summit and realized that he was at the northern entrance of another major embayment (Prince Albert Sound). Although he could not see its head from his vantage point, he could see the land on the opposite shore (Wollaston Peninsula) about 30 km away. Next morning, going ashore on the mainland opposite the island, Jago found a pemmican tin and traces of a camp—Lt. Haswell from HMS *Investigator* had been here too!

Jago now followed the coast round into Prince Albert Sound, first east-south-east, then east, then even east-northeast. On the morning of the 23rd he and his men woke to find another blizzard blowing, which kept them tent-bound until the afternoon of the 28th. The ice they encountered that day was very broken, making man-hauling very strenuous and slow. That evening one of the men, sent ashore to find driftwood for fuel, reported on his return that the land immediately to the north of their course was an island, and that there was a channel inside it, with much better ice. Hence, on the 29th, Jago took advantage of this "inside passage," now known as Safety Channel, which runs east-west for some 50 km. On the following afternoon Jago made another disturbing discovery: on an island ahead (now named Investigator Island) he spotted a cairn. In it Haswell had left yet another cylinder with a message, identical to the one on Point Wollaston.

Nonetheless Jago decided to push on eastwards along the north shore of Prince Albert Sound. On the afternoon of 9 May he spotted an Inuit camp on the ice: these were Kangiryuarmiut, this being the core part of their traditional territory. They are the direct ancestors of most of the present residents of the community of Holman, who are now known as the Ulukhaktokmiut. [48]

> I went out to them, but found none of our old friends were there, and they having nothing to barter I left them; but they followed me to where I encamped. They behaved very well, and were very much taken with the vocabulary, offering anything they had in their possession for it. I purchased two dogs of them, also some reindeer's meat, and fish, and when I made signs to them that we were going to sleep, they perfectly understood me, and we parted very good friends. [49]

Next morning (10 May) Jago found that three of his men were completely snow-blind and two of them partially blind, and hence he decided to make this his turning point, leaving them in camp for the day while he and the other two men walked some distance farther eastward. On encountering a large group of Inuit (45 men and two women), Jago became somewhat apprehensive about the disabled men he had left back at camp and decided to turn back, but not before he had built a cairn and left a cylinder with a message. Of the Inuit he remarked,

> The natives had no traces of having communicated with any Europeans, with the exception of a few beads, which appeared to be the same kind as we got in Hongkong. They wanted us very much to come up to their encampment, which was about five miles to the eastward, but as they mustered upwards of one hundred in number, I thought we had better keep away. [50]

By Jago's calculations the cairn at his farthest point was located at 70° 34'N; 110° 15'W. This longitude, however, would have placed him well up the Kagloryuak River valley past the head of Prince Albert Sound. Judging by his error in the position of Investigator Island, his longitudes appear to have been almost 2° too far east, so his true longitude at his farthest point was around 112°W. He and his men experienced fine weather on the way back to the ship, which they reached without incident on the morning of 30 May.

With Skead still a "prisoner-at-large," the atmosphere in the gunroom must have been extremely strained, especially since this situation was directly the result of Lt. Phayre's machinations. It is hard to imagine that his fellow officers were not giving the latter the cold shoulder, yet this does not appear to have had any effect on him. On 10 June Collinson addressed a memo to Edward Adams, the Assistant Surgeon, in his Night Order Book:

> It having been represented to me by the Senior Lieutenant that on the morning of 26th May you made us of the terms "funk" and "cowardice" at the gunroom mess table, during a discussion of measures which were taken the previous evening for the prevention of the Natives coming on board the ship;
>
> I call upon you to give me in writing a distinct avowal that the observations you made use of had no allusion whatsoever to the precautions which were thought proper to be taken on that occasion.[51]

Evidently Adams was able to allay Collinson's suspicions, since the phrase "Cancelled in consequence of Mr. Adams's explanation" was later written across the memo.

As we have seen, after meeting the captain's party near Pemmican Point on 5 June, Collinson had sent Jago on westwards to Bear Island, to watch out for Lt. Parkes and his party. Jago returned to the ship in the early hours of 13 June having seen no sign of the missing party. Collinson was starting to become seriously alarmed about Parkes and his men, surmising that they might have been brought to a halt or, worse still, marooned, by leads in the ice. Nonetheless, the normal affairs of the ship had to be seen to. On the 14th the two men who had got drunk at Princess Royal Islands were flogged, although Collinson does not specify the number of strokes of the cat-of-nine-tails. Then, on the 16th, since the ice around the tide gauge had become dangerously rotten, it was moved to a safer spot. A few days later, still concerned about the missing sledge party, Collinson sent Lt. Jago out to the west to leave a depot of provisions on the north shore midway between Pemmican Point and the ship in case Parkes and his men had had to abandon the ice in favour of an overland route. To supplement the rations, hunting parties were sent to outlying camps: Phayre and Jago took it in turn, week about, to maintain hunting camps over on Minto Inlet or on the outer part of Walker Bay, and two men were sent out to hunt to the west. With the game they all brought in, plus what was shot by Dr. Anderson and Mr. Adams near the ship, the cook was able to serve two meals of fresh meat per week. Caribou were numerous but very wary.

By this time Collinson was anticipating that he might have to send a search party as far north as the Princess Royal Islands. The men had even come aft as a body to volunteer to go searching for the missing party, but Collinson had declined their offer, in light of the wide leads Jago had observed in the ice. But then, on 29 June, Collinson heard his men cheering and, going on deck, saw Parkes and his men coming round the point.

Having parted from Collinson and his sledge party at Peel Point on 5 May, Lt. Parkes and his men set off north across M'Clure Strait, heading for Melville Island, with provisions for 18 days and orders to be back at Peel Point by the 22nd. For the first three-and-a-half days they encountered relatively smooth ice and made good progress, about 15 miles per day. But then they ran into very rough, hummocky ice, and after searching in vain for a feasible sledging route, Parkes decided to leave the sledge and carry everything on their backs from there on. Among the items they left behind was the tent, so from then on they were sleeping in the open, in their blanket bags and a raccoon-skin bag. Since the latter would accommodate only four men, only half the group could sleep at any one time.

On the 11th one of the men, Thomas O'Bryan. started complaining of problems with his legs and difficulty in walking. By midday on the 12th he was unable to continue. "Dug a hole in a snow drift for him, and gave him the raccoon skin and blankets, and made him some hot grog."[52] While he rested, the rest of the group walked about the area to keep warm. By 8 PM Parkes decided to push on again; O'Bryan would have to make an effort to keep up. That evening they sighted Melville Island ahead, but it wasn't until the early hours of the 16th that they reached land; they had been delayed by several cases of snow blindness and one case of frostbite (William Cooper). Their landfall was Cape Providence.

Here Parkes decided to leave Cooper and the snow-blind men and to push on east to Winter Harbour[53] with James Rich and William French. Soon after starting, however, Parkes spotted tracks of a sledge and three men heading east towards Point Hearne, but was unable to determine if they had been made by Inuit or by Europeans. Shortly after that (still on the 16th), he spotted more sledge tracks, heading in the opposite direction. These were, in fact, the tracks of a sledge party under

Captain Robert M'Clure that had left *Investigator* at her winter quarters in Mercy Bay, northern Banks Island, on 11 April, had reached Winter Harbour on 28 April, and was back at Mercy Bay by 11 May.[54] In other words the sledge tracks heading west were not more than about two weeks old!

After sleeping for a few hours, Parkes and his men got under way again, and by 6 PM were within about four miles of Point Hearne when they had another surprise:

> Heard the howling of Esquimaux dogs, as if being put into harness. Having no arms, and being so far from the people, I was not in a fit condition to have any communication with the natives. Although very loth to do so I was obliged to turn back.[55]

It is highly unlikely, though not impossible, that there were any Inuit on Melville Island at this time. One wonders whether Parkes and his men had heard a wolf pack howling.

Returning to where he had left the rest of his party, Parkes built a cairn, scratched *Enterprise*'s name on the large rock on which the cairn was built, and left a message in a cylinder. Point Hearne was clearly visible to the east.

They started back west to Cape Providence in the early hours of the 17th and left the land to head back across M'Clure Strait that evening. By the evening of the 19th three of the men, Rich, Cooper, and O'Bryan, had frostbitten feet. They got back to where they had left the sledge and tent on the morning of 21 May and rested there for a day. On checking the sledge, they found that the foxes had eaten all the hide lashings. They started south again on the evening of the 23rd, heading for Banks Island, in the hope of finding driftwood and of shooting something, since they had only eight lbs. of meat and some cocoa left. They reached land in the early hours of the 25th and managed to shoot three ptarmigan and to find some driftwood. The ptarmigan and the last tin of meat formed the basis of soup. When they pushed on again, later in the morning, O'Bryan was riding on the sledge, unable to walk.

Next evening (26th) Parkes estimated that they were only about 12 miles from the depot on Peel Point and sent Rich and two other men ahead to get some provisions. On later hearing this, Collinson calculated that Rich and his party had reached the depot just 24 hours after he had left it. And indeed, Rich found the message that Collinson had left, dated the 26th. But, perhaps more importantly, Rich brought back some supplies from the depot, and Parkes and his men shot a hare and eight ptarmigan. The party started again late on the evening of the 28th but, encountering fog and snow, took until the late afternoon of 31 May to reach the depot.

Getting under way again early next morning, they headed south along Prince of Wales Strait, with O'Bryan riding on the sledge for much of the way. By the morning of 5 June they were within sight of the Princess Royal Islands, and Rich and a party were sent ahead for provisions from the depot there. But, due to blizzard conditions, it was not until the evening of the 9th that the main party reached the islands; by then three men were incapacitated, and Parkes decided to rest for a day. They got under way again early on the 11th but made only slow progress. They all appear to have been suffering from food poisoning from the supplies picked up on Princess Royal Islands: "Since having our provisions all hands have been loose in the inside, and felt very sick."[56] The problem persisted for three days.

As they headed south along Prince of Wales Strait they encountered gales, heavy drifting snow, and fog. The temperature was rising, however, and on the afternoon of the 21st they had to contend with heavy rain. By now all the snow had melted off the sea ice, and the ice surface was covered by melt-pools six inches or more in depth. On the afternoon of the 22nd, therefore, Parkes headed for land, and they spent the rest of the day trying to dry their wet clothes and bedding. Next afternoon they got under way again and found themselves wading through knee-deep water on the ice for most of the time. On the 24th they also had to contend with deep snow with water beneath it for long distances. On the evening of the 26th, morale was raised somewhat when they came across the depot left by Jago, and even more so when they reached the depot (of bread, potatoes, and meat) that Collinson had left off Bear Island Point. Finally, on the morning of the 29th, they reached the ship.

On examining the invalids, Dr. Anderson reported that he would probably have to amputate most, if not all of O'Bryan's frostbitten foot; in the case of Cooper he could not tell as yet how much he would have to remove. All the other frostbite cases would recover fairly quickly, however.

From now on various preparations were put in hand for going to sea. In early July the flagstaff was brought back aboard and the sails were bent. Since a shore lead had developed, getting ashore posed problems. The solution was to station a dinghy there that could ferry people ashore when not picking up driftwood or hunting ducks. On the 18th the tide-gauge pole was retrieved, since the ice around it was now too rotten to visit it safely.

On the 16th, a crucial event occurred: the ship moved out of the ice-cradle in which she had lain all winter, although it was not until the 19th that she could be manoeuvred at all. Even then the ice still kept her imprisoned in Winter Cove.

Mr. Phayre, who was ashore on the isthmus, sent word on the 21st that the ice on Isthmus Lake had disappeared and that he had seen many fish rising; he thought that with a seine net and the Halkett boats he could catch plenty of fish. Next morning Lt. Jago took two Halkett boats and a 45-fathom seine net ashore to Isthmus Lake where the net was set; thereafter a party went ashore to the lake every day. The fishing was very successful, and fish was issued in lieu of meat to the whole crew at the rate of three lbs of fish for one lb. of meat. Sorrel (*Oxyria digyna*) also began to appear, and parties were sent to pick the fresh leaves, this being an excellent antiscorbutic. Dr. Anderson and Mr. Adams, having assembled a fairly complete collection of bird skins, now turned their attention to the plants and amassed a surprisingly varied collection of specimens. They also collected numbers of butter-flies, spiders, and other insects. Unfortunately, one species of insect, namely the mosquito, became much too numerous and a major nuisance.

Towards the end of the month, the ice in Winter Cove had broken up completely, but outside in Walker Bay the ice cover remained solid. Nonetheless, in anticipation of it too breaking up, on 1 August Collinson ordered the topgallant yards sent up. At about the same time, the carpenter made what Collinson described as "an outline sketch of a human skeleton," which was placed on Driver's grave, in the hope that this would deter the Inuit from disturbing it. The Inuit paid their last visit to the ship on 3 August, and on that occasion, in recognition of the game and fish they had supplied and the various items of clothing and equipment they had traded, Collinson made them a parting gift of one of the small spars he had acquired at Sitka.

As officers and men prepared for the imminent navigation season, they must have had mixed feelings about the winter that they had just experienced. A consid-erable amount of effort had been expended on man-hauled sledge journeys, but to little real purpose. On his trip along the southwest coasts of Victoria Island, Lieu-tenant Jago had found that one of *Investigator*'s search parties had been there before him at every turn. And on his much longer trip northwards with Lieutenant Parkes, Collinson had achieved very little; his contribution to knowledge of the geography of the area was confined to his short foray eastwards along the north coast of Victoria Island as far as Glenelg Bay (now Wynniatt Bay). And none of the sledge parties had discovered any trace of the missing Franklin expedition.

Even more troubling was the fact that relations between Collinson and his officers had clearly deteriorated during the wintering. The captain's prohibition of gambling on 11 January (and the officers' vehement reaction to that prohibition) had shown which way the wind was blowing. And whatever fears the officers may have had concerning their captain's behaviour were fully confirmed by his placing the Second Master, Francis Skead, under open arrest for what can only be described as a very trivial offence; indeed, no rational person would have considered it an offence at all. The captain was clearly out of control, and all the officers, even including the First Officer, Lieutenant Phayre, who had been instrumental in getting Skead arrested, must have dreaded what the future had in store for them. ●

FARTHEST EAST

Early ON THE MORNING OF 5 AUGUST Collinson climbed to the top of Flagstaff Hill and decided that the ice had opened up sufficiently to allow the ship to leave the bay. The dogs were brought aboard and the fishing party recalled from Isthmus Lake. *Enterprise* got under way at 9:30 AM. The winds were light and baffling, however, and it was not until 8 AM on the 6th that she reached open water, only to find a wide expanse of ice to seaward. However, it allowed the ship to round Cape M'Clure and to stand to the south towards Point Wollaston. She reached a shore lead along the south side of Minto Inlet about six miles east of Point Wollaston on the morning of the 7th. At 7:30 Collinson sent Lt. Phayre ashore with two boats to collect driftwood and to see if there was any open water to the southwest. The boats returned at noon with large loads of wood, but with the disappointing news that the ice towards Point Wollaston was still solid. In view of this, after the boats had brought two more loads of wood, in the evening Collinson steered north across the mouth of Minto Inlet and, finding a promising-looking bay on the south side of Mt. Phayre, by towing with the boats, he got the ship into it; by 1 AM on 8 August *Enterprise* was lying quietly at anchor. The bay was named Fish Bay.

That day, being a Sunday, was spent fairly quietly. As usual the crew mustered at divisions and Collinson held the usual church service. Thereafter the men aired their bedding while Collinson took a walk on the hills above the harbour. He discovered a large lake only a short distance inland, which offered an excellent source of water. In the evening a boat was sent ashore for water.[1] Next day, while the off-duty watch washed their clothes, Collinson went ashore in the first whaler to examine the coast to the east; he discovered that they were only about two miles from the mouth of Boot Inlet, which they had frequently visited overland from Winter Cove. Parkes went along the shore westwards, surveying and wooding in the cutter, while the third whaler and the dinghy searched the shores of Fish Bay for driftwood. Lt. Jago, meanwhile, was put ashore with the Halkett boats and the seine net to try the fishing in the lake; he was encouragingly successful.

Ice drove into the bay during the morning, putting great strain on the anchor cable, until the ice fetched up against the shore. This posed quite a problem for the various parties trying to get back to the ship, since the ice was too broken to allow them to walk easily across it, but too close to allow a boat to force its way through.

On the 10th the ice drifted in and out of the bay with the wind, but it was still close to seaward. A fishing party was again sent to the lake on the 11th, while another party collected four tonnes of rock ballast from the beach, as the ship was now quite light since a considerable amount of provisions had been consumed over the winter; the ballast was distributed between the stream cable locker and the fore peak. On the 12th the fishing party was particularly successful, catching 560 lbs. of fish, some weighing 30 lbs.

In the hope that the ship might get out of the bay on the 13th, Lt. Jago went ashore in the early hours of the morning to retrieve the fishing gear. But the ice turned out to be too close to allow the ship to escape from the harbour. It was not until the evening of the 14th that the ice drifted out of the bay and *Enterprise* was able to stand out to sea under topsails and foresail.[2]

The ship spent the next five days working through ice in the mouth of Minto Inlet, trying to get to Point Wollaston and further south, but it was not until the morning of the 19th that she managed to get into a shore lead about two miles south of the point and headed south along it. Soon afterwards her southerly progress was blocked again, about five-and-a-half miles south of the point. Collinson sent Mr. Arbuthnott and Lt. Phayre ashore with boats, in part to get driftwood and in part to erect a cairn on a conspicuous conical mound. Arbuthnott got a good view of the ice to the south; it was close and heavy, and prospects for further progress in that direction were clearly not encouraging. Two boats were sent ashore for wood again next morning, and then in the afternoon the ship got under way, trying to move south, sailing where possible, warping with ice anchors where necessary. The ship made ten miles that afternoon, but then she became beset. Throughout the 22nd the current carried the ice (and the ship) back northwards, and by noon on the 23rd, she was abeam of Point Wollaston again. Collinson therefore decided to try to find open water to the north, and by further warping and blasting the ice with gunpowder managed to get into sailing ice again by the evening of the 24th and headed west. By 9 PM on the 25th *Enterprise* was lying only two miles off the coast of Banks Island, about 12 miles east of Nelson Head, near the mouth of the Nelson River; here Arbuthnott went ashore to leave a message and to check on ice conditions to the west.[3]

His report was far from encouraging, so Collinson decided to head back east. The ice was drifting northwards, forcing him to swing well north into the mouth of Prince of Wales Strait. By the evening of the 27th the ship was lying off Bear (Ramsay) Island again. Lt. Phayre was sent ashore to leave a message on the island; after he was gone two caribou were seen on the island and a party was sent ashore in the third whaler to try to cut them off, but without success. The ice to the south opened somewhat on the morning of the 28th, and by noon *Enterprise* was halfway across the mouth of Minto Inlet, continuing to work her way south, in relatively open ice. Soon she was south of Point Wollaston, but was then blocked again, drifting back north to within five miles of the point. Phayre went ashore for another load of driftwood.

Thereafter, however, the ice progressively slackened, and by noon on 5 September Holman Island was in sight. By this stage, however, there were about four hours of darkness every night, forcing Collinson to heave-to for that period every night; moreover new ice up to 1" thick was forming on the leads every night. Fortunately, however, the shore lead opened progressively farther south every day, and by the morning of the 8th the ship was off Investigator Island. Lt. Phayre went ashore to leave a message in Lt. Haswell's cairn (which Lt. Jago had found earlier) and brought a boatload of wood on his return. From there the ship headed south across the mouth of Prince Albert Sound. Reaching the south shore of the inlet, somewhere in the vicinity of Cape Back or Cape Baring, on the morning of the 9th, Lt. Phayre and Mr. Arbuthnott took two boats ashore to check a cairn; it turned out to be an *inuksuk*, however, built by the Inuit.

On the 10th a confusing and baffling situation developed. The sky was overcast, and the compasses were totally useless. [4] Nonetheless, all on board were convinced that they were heading east, working to windward. But when the sky cleared some-what on the evening of the 10th, the sight of a sunset dead ahead, followed by some star sights later, demonstrated that they had, in fact, been heading west! [5] No doubt Skead, whose opinion would naturally not have been solicited, found this situation quite amusing. Rectifying the situation, Collinson headed east along the north shore of Prince Albert Sound throughout the 11th.

Next morning an island was spotted ahead (George Island). Collinson headed down the channel to the left (north) of it, only to discover almost immediately that this appeared to be the head of Prince Albert Sound. The channel south of the island appeared to end after an even shorter distance. Lt. Phayre was sent in a boat to confirm this rather disappointing situation and to try to find an anchorage. He returned at about 4:00 having found nowhere safe to anchor, and Collinson began beating back west, off what was potentially a very dangerous lee shore. To add to this rather tense situation, the ship ran aground. As Richard Shingleton, the gunroom steward, reported, "She rubbed over the ground a short time and gave some heavy plunges but by the exertions of the Capt. and all hands we soon got her off again." [6]

Having at least the consolation that he had demonstrated that Wollaston, Prince Albert, and Victoria lands (now Wollaston, Diamond Jenness, and Prince Albert peninsulas) were all connected, that is, that they were peninsulas of Victoria Island, Collinson now had to decide where he should make for next. He knew that Dolphin and Union Strait, leading to Coronation Gulf, had been explored by Dr. John Richardson on Franklin's second expedition in 1826, and Coronation Gulf and Dease Strait by Franklin in the summer of 1821 and by Dease and Simpson in the summers of 1838 and 1839. From the information he had obtained at Honolulu in 1850, he also knew that in 1848–49 Drs. Richardson and Rae had searched the mainland coast from the Mackenzie Delta to the mouth of the Coppermine. As far as he was aware, however, the coasts farther east had not been searched for traces of the missing Franklin expedition. He therefore decided to make this his next search area.

Enterprise now began beating back west down Prince Albert Sound. Around 9 AM on 13 September, while Lt. Phayre took a boat to examine an inlet, the captain and Mr. Arbuthnott went ashore and climbed a hill about 300 feet high, where he erected a cairn. He determined the position to be 70° 22'N; 112° 3'W, and named the site Point George, after Arbuthnott's son, whose birthday it was.

By mid-afternoon the ship was back abreast of Investigator Island. Mr. Arbuthnott was sent ashore with another message to be left in the cylinder in the cairn on that island,[7] then the ship continued out of the Inlet. By 3 PM next day she was off Cape Baring, the most westerly point of Wollaston Peninsula, and, heading south, by 9 AM next morning was off Cape Ernest Kendall. Heading almost due south across the entrance to Dolphin and Union Strait, Collinson raised Cape Bexley on the mainland coast on the evening of the 19th and swung east into the straits.

When daylight dawned on the 20th, two islands lay in sight ahead, Sutton and Liston Islands, but due to light winds, by 11 AM they were still five miles away. Lt. Phayre was sent ashore on Liston Island to build a cairn and leave a message. The boat returned at 5:30, bringing some driftwood and a seal Dr. Anderson had shot. Shingleton reported that

> The hind quarters of these animals are very good eating but the flesh is dark having so much blood in them but when boiled in salt water very much usable meat on them. The flippers make very good soup and the livers equal to pig's to my taste.[8]

On the 21st *Enterprise* ran south through the narrowest part of Dolphin and Union Strait and, rounding the west and south sides of Douglas Island, headed east along the south coast of Point Becher (now Lady Franklin Point) and on along the south coast of Victoria Island. Having anchored for the night because of darkness, on the 22nd Collinson ran through the Duke of York Archipelago between Kellett (now Murray) and Bate islands, and on along the coasts of the Richardson Islands. He described this coast as follows:

> This range, to which I gave the name of Sir J. Richardson, continues along the coast for 20 miles, presenting several fine bays, three of which will, I think, be found excellent harbours. The grassy slopes (on which several deer were seen) afforded a pleasing contrast to the low barren ridges we had hitherto seen.[9]

Having anchored for the night again, Collinson pushed on east in thick, snowy weather, with the spray thrown over the bows freezing wherever it landed; the result, as reported by Shingleton, was that "everything was in one cake of ice having the appearance and [illegible] of a Twelfth cake iced over."[10] By mid-afternoon Cape Franklin on Kent Peninsula was in sight, but Collinson now held over for the Victoria Island shore as he entered Dease Strait and continued sailing all night, despite the darkness. He was soon to regret this decision. Shingleton reported the result as follows:

> 2.20 saw what was thought the land and the next minute she was on shore. Luckily the wind had shifted and gave us a weather shore[11] so that we did not go very heavy on it. Turned the hands up to get the ship off again, which thank God we succeeded in doing by 5.30 a.m.[12]

No doubt Skead was again enjoying some degree of *Schadenfreude* at Collinson's discomfiture, although he was probably relieved that the ship was refloated without too much difficulty. The location of this grounding was in Byron Bay. The details as entered in the log are as follows:

> 2.20 Ship grounded in 2 fms. Shortened & furled sails. Down boats. Laid out kedge astern. 3.15 Obsd. the land ahead and on both bows about 200 yards from the beach. 4.00 Ship swung stern to the shore. Sent stream anchor[13] ahead. Hove off. 6.00 Ship floats. Hoisted up boats. Stowed anchors and made all plain sail on port tack.[14]

Collinson had clearly been lucky, but he realized from the fact that new ice was making along the shores wherever the water was calm that it was already time to find a wintering site.

For the rest of the day *Enterprise* ran east through Dease Strait and across the mouth of Wellington Bay, the wind freshening to a gale so that by sundown she was running under close-reefed topsails and becoming heavily encrusted in ice. Next morning, as the captain recorded, "it took us the greater part of the forenoon to clear our decks and sponsons of ice."[15] After anchoring for the night, next morning (26th) officers and men were treated to quite a remarkable sight: as Shingleton described the scene: "The sea for a long distance out covered with young Ice heaving and rolling something like quicksilver and appearing to be quite pliant."[16] In the afternoon the ship ran through between the Finlayson Islands and anchored just in their

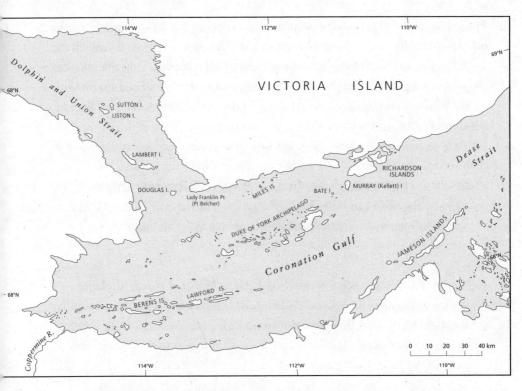

Dolphin and Union Strait and Coronation Gulf: the challenging waters negotiated
by HMS *Enterprise* in 1852 and 1853.

lee a mile off the Victoria Island shore. Everyone was glad to be in such a sheltered
anchorage since a gale blew all night. Since it did not let up next day, Collinson
decided to remain at anchor.

By noon next day the wind had slackened somewhat and the ship got under
way, heading east for Cambridge Bay, about 20 miles away, where Collinson hoped
to find a sheltered wintering site. As the ship stormed along just after noon under
double-reefed topsails at about 7 knots with the wind right aft, she touched bottom:
"fortunately it was merely a graze, and hauling to the south, we soon deepened our
water."[17] But then, at 2 PM, Shingleton described the ship as

> running 7 Knots took the ground before there was time to trim the sails. The
> leadsman called out 4½ fathoms; the next minute we could feel her grinding
> on the shoal right off a point that forms the small cove we intend to winter
> in and about 1 Mile from the anchorage.[18]

The sails were furled immediately and the stream anchor was laid out, to try to haul her off, but this operation was greatly complicated by the thick layer of slush on the surface of the sea, which made boat-handling extremely difficult. The same problem was encountered when the pinnace and other boats were lowered and loaded with the deck-load of provisions to haul it ashore. Once again, Skead was probably experiencing a mixture of emotions.

At 4 AM next morning (29th) the work of moving stores and heavy items ashore continued. Then the best bower anchor was lowered into the pinnace and led out astern to try to haul her off, but without success. Collinson now ordered the stone ballast to be discharged and the fore hold emptied. The slush was now getting very thick and was proving a serious impediment; watching from the ship, Collinson reported,

> the boats sometimes being within half a cable's length of the ship, and not getting on board for an hour.... Unless...the boats entered it with way upon them and a free wind, they were often brought to a standstill. I saw the cutter in one instance remain stationary half an hour, although there was as much wind as the mast would stand.[19]

On the 30th the slush was so thick that the boats were useless and were hoisted aboard. While it would not support a man's weight, the dogs were able to make their way to shore across it. Most of the day the men were employed moving coal from the forward hold aft to the coal bunkers.[20] Next day, with a clear sky, the temperature had dropped noticeably; nonetheless, the ice would still not bear a man's weight, so the crew was kept busy getting saws, ice chisels, and similar equipment ready for cutting the ship loose.

A day later a man could safely venture onto the ice (the temperature had dropped to 3° F at 5 AM). During the morning the men were cutting a channel astern of the ship, in anticipation of trying to heave her astern in the afternoon; but the ship refused to budge. Thereafter the crew was ordered to run across the deck from port to starboard and back to try to roll the ship and loosen the ice, but this still did not help. All the boats were then lowered to the ice, along with the chain cables and another anchor, while the stores from the boatswain's and carpenter's store-rooms and provisions from the forward hold were moved aft to the captain's cabin.

A further attempt to heave her off at high tide on the 3rd was no more successful, and since the spring tides were now clearly past, Collinson decided to desist from the struggle to get afloat for the moment. Some excitement was provided in the early afternoon by the appearance of a group of Inuit; Shingleton recorded that he

> saw some people rising above the hill close to the ship which we found to be natives, 5 of them. They seemed to be quite astonished at seeing a ship for we all think they had never seen one before. They stood on the hill for a long time, when two of our people and the Doctor went to meet them, persuaded them the best manner they could to come on board, but only one would venture, a very old man. They appeared to be out hunting having their Bows and Arrows with them and several of their arrows were covered with Blood. They were headed with Bone, Iron, Copper and one with Brass, and some stone.[21]

These were members of the Eqalugtormiut, another sub-group of the Copper Inuit.[22]

On that particular day, Lieutenant Parkes (and no doubt most of the rest of the officers) had other concerns on their minds, since Parkes became the next officer to earn his Captain's wrath for an unspecified offence. An entry in the captain's Night Order Book reads as follows:

> October 3rd. /52
>
> Having had occasion severely to reprimand Lt. Parkes & that officer instead of submitting to the reproof having chosen to quarrel with his Superior & still refusing to acknowledge his error, I am under the necessity of suspending him from duty until an opportunity offers of bringing him to Court Martial; but as that period is likely to be distant he is (so long as he conducts himself with propriety) permitted to frequent the Gunroom between the hours of 8 AM & 10 PM. The port side of the Quarter Deck is allotted as a place for him to take the necessary exercise for the preservation of his health & I have particularly to caution him while he is there not to enter into conversation with the officer of the watch or in any way to interfere with the duty that may be going forward.
>
> RD. COLLINSON.[23]

Thus two officers were now under open arrest.

Next day some of the officers and men went out hunting and returned with seven ptarmigan. Meanwhile the rest of the crew were occupied erecting a flagstaff on a hill nearby, while others were hauling the boats up on shore and stowing all the equipment and provisions that had been moved ashore to lighten the ship.

On 5 October Lt. Jago was sent off with a travelling party to follow the coast eastwards; at Cape Colborne (the eastern entrance cape of Cambridge Bay) he was to build a cairn and leave a message with directions as to how to reach the ship. Three balloons, with the usual messages attached to their slow-match tails, were also inflated and released to spread the message about the ship's whereabouts more widely.[24] Next day Collinson himself set off with three men to climb Mt. Pelly, lying about 12 km east of the eastern shore of Cambridge Bay. The captain had hoped to be able to do some surveying from its summit and had taken a theodolite with him for that purpose, but was foiled by a "white misty haze, peculiar to Arctic regions." Hence he confined himself to building a cairn before returning to the ship.

On 7 October Edward Adams found himself in trouble with the captain again. On that date a memo to Lt. Phayre appeared in the Captain's Night Order Book to the effect that "You are required to give me in writing an account of the circumstances which took place on your ordering the Assistant Surgeon to take charge of the shooting party yesterday morning."[25] No doubt Phayre had already given the captain a verbal report on Adams's alleged misdemeanour. Phayre's written report reads as follows:

> I beg to inform you that on the morning of the 6th Inst. I sent Jos. Page, G.M.[26] to acquaint Mr. Adams, Asst. Surgeon, that he would again have to take charge of the shooting party for the day. The answer returned to me was that he could not go out with the party; his reply was "I do not wish to go." I then said to him "Are you aware it is Capt. Collinson's orders that you have charge of the men." He said he was, that I might tell him that he did not wish to go with them."[27]

It is hard to believe that this is a true reporting of what occurred, that Adams had calmly disobeyed a direct order relayed to him from his captain. That there is more to the story than is revealed here is suggested by the leniency of the punishment as revealed in the Night Order Book for the following night: "The Assistant Surgeon's leave is stopped for one month from this date. R. Collinson."[28]

On the 7th the captain started surveying the bay, the men chopping holes in the ice (now 12.5 cm thick) to take soundings. The crew was gathering rocks for ballast and cutting peat for fuel. Very large numbers of caribou were seen, some of them approaching quite close to the work parties; nonetheless, a hunting party brought back only nine ptarmigan.[29] The following day was spent similarly; again up to 100 caribou were seen, but none were killed. What *Enterprise*'s men were observing was the seasonal phenomenon of large herds of caribou which, having spent the summer on Victoria Island, were congregating in the area of Cambridge Bay, waiting to cross Dease Strait to Kent Peninsula once the ice had formed. In the spring they would return to the island.

This was confirmed by Lt. Jago, who returned with his party on the morning of the 9th. He had followed the coast round past Cape Colborne and Point Back as far as Anderson Bay, then straight overland back to the ship. He reported that

> The deer had accumulated in large herds on the peninsula, waiting for the ice to form a bridge for their passage to the continent; on their trail were several wolves, and a party of natives were hanging about them, from whom he purchased a couple of very good dogs.[30]

Caribou were now wandering across the ice within gunshot of the ship, and Collinson ordered the ship's two twelve-pounder cannon cleared away and made ready, with the intent of firing shrapnel shells at them. There is no mention of whether this plan was ever put into practice.

A group of Inuit, probably the same group Jago had seen, appeared near the ship later in the day and also on the following morning (10th), as Shingleton reported:

> 11 am some few Natives were seen on the flagstaff hill but did not venture on board till some men went on shore to entice them, and after some persua-sion they ventured. After they were on board they seemed perfectly easy. They had their Bows and Arrows beside spears for catching game and a few pairs of Mocassins. They parted with their articles very freely taking Brass buttons and beads for them. Their arrows were the best I ever saw amongst the Natives of these regions; many of them had been broken in several places and fixed equal or better than a European could do it. I bought some arrows of theirs, some with stone heads others with iron and some Bone. We hope they will be here again finding us friendly so that they might bring some

game, for I believe they can catch it when they want it and that without much trouble. They were tolerably clean and had the same kind of dress on as those we saw at Winter Cove.[31]

With the next spring tide approaching, further efforts were made to lighten the ship by emptying the main and after holds. A channel was cut in the ice astern of the ship, and on successive days attempts were made to haul her off, on the first few occasions without success. On the 14th, a 6-inch whale line had been led from one of the quarter bollards to a block secured to an ice anchor embedded in the ice and back to the capstan, but when the men threw all their weight against the capstan bars, the fluke of the ice-anchor broke. But next day, as Shingleton recorded in his journal, the tide rose about 3" higher just before noon: "The people had not been long heaving when she made a move and the old ship slipped off very easy."[32] The day, already noteworthy for the ship thus being refloated, was also memorable for another reason. During the morning, about 20 Inuit came aboard to trade, offering especially skin clothing and *kamiks*; one of them offered "a large piece of Composition Metal for a spear head with the appearance of a broad Arrow on it."[33] The broad arrow was the Navy's distinguishing mark, and hence there was a strong possibility that this item had derived from Franklin's ships, *Erebus* or *Terror*, although, as Shingleton discussed in his journal, it might also have come from Captain William Parry's ship, *Fury*, which he had abandoned at Fury Beach on the east side of Somerset Island in 1825. This find must have given rise to hopes that more clues to the fate of the missing expedition would be found in the future.

While the ship was now afloat, she was not in a particularly safe position, and for the next ten days the crew was kept busy cutting the ice astern of the ship and hauling her astern, bit by bit, until she was in what Collinson deemed the optimal position for spending the winter, with 17 feet of water under her bows and 24 under her stern. She was still exposed to winds from southeast to southwest, but Collinson counted on being able to move her into a sheltered cove in the spring, before the pack began driving to and fro.

Over the next few days all the equipment and provisions that had been temporarily stacked on the ice or on shore to lighten the ship were now moved back aboard. The main deck housing was erected on the 28th and the quarter deck housing on the 29th. Meanwhile, others of the crew were banking up the sides of the ship with snow. Groups of Inuit visited the ship regularly throughout this period. For example, on the 29th Shingleton reported,

A party of Natives visited us this morning but they did not bring what we expected although every one had either some fish or pieces of venison all frozen as hard as mahogany. They parted with what articles they had and staid on board till past Noon. Some of the Men brought them up some part of their dinner which was preserved Meat and potatoes. They at first would not touch it till they saw the Men eat it then they eat [sic] as fast as our Men and seemed to enjoy it and they appeared also very fond of biscuit the first I suppose they ever eat [sic] in their lives. They were cruising all over the decks but not the least sign of stealing amongst them. The women here are marked [i. e. tattooed] similar to those at Point Barrow but by no means good looking.[34]

At 7:30 AM on 1 November Captain Collinson set off with a sledge, pulled by seven men, for Cape Alexander on Kent Peninsula, with a view to looking for cairns and leaving cairns with messages about where the ship was wintering.[35] Having camped near the largest of the Finlayson Islands, next day he sent two men, Henry Hester and John Charters, southwestwards to Cape Alexander, while he with the rest of the party cut straight south for Trap Point. About a mile from the islets off that cape, the ice became so thin that Collinson was afraid the sledge would break through and decided to camp there for the night. While he and some of the men walked ashore to Trap Point, built a cairn there and left a message, two of the men, William Gowan and William French, were sent along the coast to the southeast until it got dark to look for cairns and to leave messages. Thus cairns and messages were distributed along about 25 miles of the mainland coast. The party started back north across the strait next morning and was back at the ship by noon on 4 November. With a vague hope that the cairns and messages might guide survivors of the Franklin expedition to their ship, the officers and men of HMS *Enterprise* settled down for their second arctic wintering.

Collinson and his officers could now be proud of what they had achieved. To manage to take a ship the size of *Enterprise* as far east as Cambridge Bay, through the uncharted, hazard-strewn waters of Dolphin and Union Strait, Coronation Gulf, and Dease Strait, a feat never previously attempted, was certainly cause for self-congratulation. It had not been a trouble-free achievement, however. The ship had run aground three times, and on the last occasion, in Cambridge Bay, she had grounded heavily, and it had taken a great deal of effort to get her afloat again.

On the other hand, the tensions on board, with regard to conflicts between captain and officers, had multiplied. While the disagreement between the captain and Edward Adams was evidently relatively minor, the case of Lieutenant Parkes clearly must have been (at least in Collinson's view) much more serious, in that he felt that it merited this officer being put under open arrest. With two executive offices under arrest, only two (Lieutenants Phayre and Jago) were available to help run the ship. Tensions on board must have been growing steadily, and there can have been little prospect of a happy wintering. ●

9
WINTERING
AT CAMBRIDGE BAY

Next DAY (5 NOVEMBER), wintering preparations continued. A layer of snow one foot thick was spread on the upper deck, then a layer of gravel on top of that. The Fifth of November, Guy Fawkes night, was properly celebrated, as Shingleton nostalgically recalled:

> Some of our lads has not forgotten old times of their boyhood. They stuffed a guy up and loaded him with combustibles to blow him up, Rockets, blue and red lights and crackers besides powder. It put us all in mind of our young days, besides we must have something for change of scene as well as to talk of.[1]

Confined to the ship by a severe blizzard, on the 8th the carpenters prepared the tables for the classes planned for the winter, while some of the men were making and mending clothes or the costumes intended for the theatre. The boats (the pinnace, cutter, two whaleboats, and a dinghy), stowed on the ice, were covered with snow, while a large porch was built at the entry-port on the 10th; within it a hole was chopped in the ice and kept open both as a water source in case of fire and also to accommodate a tide gauge. From Shingleton's description, this porch was quite impressive:

> A very natty affair it will be for it is built of large blocks of frozen snow, very hard and cut square similar to stones, besides a flight of imitation stone steps to get on board by, cut out of thick pieces of Ice almost 18 Inches thick.[2]

Meanwhile, another group of men was building a snow-block observatory on shore, while yet another was building a skittle alley, roofed with ice blocks, near the bows, and a third was cutting peat for burning in the Sylvester stove, thus saving 20–30 lbs of coal per day.

At noon on the 28th an unusual phenomenon was observed. The sun was clearing the horizon to the south, just as the full moon was setting to the north. The sun, or at least its upper half, was seen for the last time on the 30th. This was also a memorable day for another reason: the skittle alley was finished, and the men took full advantage of it that evening.

The evening of 2 December saw the winter's first performance of the Royal Victoria Theatre; the theatrical manager was Vincent Bulkely, the captain's steward. The first production was *Othello*, followed by a few songs and ending with a comedy, *Old Honesty*. These theatricals were held every two weeks throughout the winter. About this time, too, work began on a billiard room, built of snow blocks and roofed with planks, with large squares of clear ice for windows, on the ice beside the ship.

There had been no sign of the Inuit for a month, but then on the morning of 9 December Shingleton spotted three Inuit men approaching:

> As we had not seen them for a long time we were surprised, thinking they had left this land and gone to the Main, but while they were on board it began to blow again and a thick drift blowing past, so that they were forced to remain on board. They were looking remarkable well, very fat since we saw them last, and their faces put one in mind of a full moon but not quite so bright as they are naturally of a brown colour. Today was the first time they were allowed between decks. They made themselves quite at home, eating whatever was given to them, but Tobacco and grog they do not like. Lime juice they are very fond of. In the afternoon as the weather was worse they were shown where they could sleep and perfectly understood what it

meant. In the evening we had the fiddle and drum playing and they were quite overjoyed. It is a great thing to have these poor people friendly with us, for they may be able to serve us, if not us perhaps other Europeans that might come here.[3]

But next morning,

before 8 our guests left us very precipitately. The men were getting their arms down to clean as usual on Friday mornings. As soon as the Natives saw that they started on deck and left the ship although it was blowing very hard and the wind in their faces. They do not like the idea of firearms, the first no doubt they had ever seen, but they have seen the execution they do and I suppose they cannot make it out. They will not touch them on board.[4]

The evening of 16 December was enlivened by a spectacular paraselene: three false moons, with one on either side of and a third above the moon, all joined by a halo. The second theatrical performance of the winter was also held that evening: *The Beggar's Opera* followed by *All the World's a Stage*. Collinson clearly was very encouraging of these endeavours, as Shingleton recorded:

Some of the female dresses are got up in fine style; nothing but white, black and yellow Satin will do, there being plenty of it on board and Capt. Collinson spares nothing, even his own clothes if required to wear, and even gives his Cabin up for the Actresses to dress.[5]

On 22 December the billiard table was completed and, as Shingleton noted, immediately became very popular:

We have got some very good pastime now the Billiard table is finished and the Officers that are Judges of such pastime say that it is as good or nearly so as most in England. The table stands about 3½ feet from the bottom; the Top is as smooth and level as Marble, being nothing more or less than a shield of fresh-water Ice; the cushions and pockets are made of Walrus hide, the former stuffed round. The balls are made of Lignum vitia [sic] by the Carpenter and excellent substitutes they are for bone or Ivory. We have lots of the best Ivory on board, the Walrus tusk, but there is no turning lathe.

The cues are very good, made from boarding pikes. Most of the people on board never saw the game before, which is a thing not to be wondered at as in England it is above their sphere, but I expect before the Winter is over we shall be all [first] class players. Every one appears very fond of it, for the table being so large they can keep themselves much warmer than at skittles. Some are at it till 11 or 12 at night.[6]

A group of a dozen Inuit came aboard at noon next day and were allowed below, where they were fed preserved beef and rice; it was explained to them that there was not room for such a large group to spend the night. For the first time they were detected stealing various items; some were recovered before they left, but Shingleton lost two items: the glass stopper from a decanter and an oil feeder. Because of this, and because of the strong smell when they became overheated in the relative warmth of the ship's interior, Collinson decided that they would be barred from below decks in future except for special occasions.

On Christmas Day, after church service, the men were treated to special rations for their dinner: a pound-and-a-half of caribou meat per man in addition to their usual meat ration, as well as currants, flour, and suet to make a pudding, along with preserved potatoes. The Captain contributed a gallon of beer to each mess and an extra allowance of grog.

The Warrant Officers and the Ice Mates were invited to join the officers in the gunroom, where Shingleton served a rather splendid Christmas dinner, of which he was rightly very proud:

We had a fine Salmon 16 lbs weight caught by the Natives, a fine leg of venison 16 lbs and a large ham with Pease, Parsnips, and preserved Potatoes, a Plum pudding, Mince Pies, the meat of which I made 18 months before, and a Gooseberry Pie, Cheese, plenty of Beer and sweet Chinese preserves, scotch Biscuits and a Currant Cake with Wine, Brandy and Whiskey.... [7]

On Boxing Day (26th) a party of Inuit again came aboard but were not allowed below decks. Nonetheless, one of them could not resist temptation, as a sharp-eyed Shingleton noticed:

Today one of them had a shovel concealed up his Coat, the end of it reaching his throat while the handle was exposed below the bottom of his smock, but he had his hand over it as well as he could to cover it, so that he assuredly knew that he was doing wrong. However it was taken from him.[8]

There would normally have been a regular theatrical performance on 30 December, but it was postponed for a week since all the actors had allegedly forgotten their parts. Shingleton, however, surmised that "the good cheer of Christmas day" was probably responsible. On the same date the gunner's mate and two marines were engaged in making shot cartridges, since in the New Year the men would be allowed to hunt for themselves, two men out of each of two of the messes to be permitted to go hunting daily.

Another spectacular paraselene was visible on the night of 2 January 1853, while some splendid auroral displays were visible most nights when the sky was clear. School classes started again on the morning of the 4th, and on the evening of the 6th the postponed theatrical performance occurred: a play called *George Barnwell* and a pantomime. Shingleton noted "that they did not come off with such applause as usual for I think that having three weeks to learn they had forgotten."[9]

A large group of Inuit (40) arrived on 7 January; they had nothing to trade, and it appeared that their objective was to pick up whatever they could. A candlestick was lifted from the observatory, and, according to Shingleton, they even had their eyes on one of the anchors. Collinson was in the habit of carrying some beads, buttons, and halfpence in a coat pocket to give to the Inuit children, and one of the young Inuit men tried to help himself from this pocket:

> one of them had his hand in Capt. Collinson's pocket whilst with the other
> he tried to take off his cuff from his wrist but the Capt. stopped him shortly.
> He struck him on the nose which made it bleed and he walked off.[10]

Collinson reported that he gave the man a ring before he departed. Shingleton expressed fears that they might expect some violence in the long run, and that he would "be sorry to see any of them hurt, but if it comes to the push, harsh measures must be taken."

Over the next few days varying numbers of Inuit came aboard, their apparent objective being to steal whatever they could get away with. To prevent this, some of the men were ordered to stay on deck, and to be on the alert whenever any Inuit were on board.

On 8 January the upper edge of the sun reappeared, after an absence of 39 days; thereafter the period when the sun was above the horizon rapidly lengthened. On the 21st another theatrical evening was staged. *The Beggar's Opera* was performed again "and much better than on the last performance of the piece."[11] This was followed by *The Quaker*, and the evening wound up with a pantomime.

By the 25th the sun was above the horizon for four hours. On that date a group of seven Inuit came aboard but did not show much inclination to steal. This was undoubtedly in part because several men were detailed to be on deck or near the ship, armed with cutlasses. If one of them pulled his weapon from its scabbard, his action provoked an immediate fearful reaction from the Inuit.

On the evening of 28 January another theatrical evening was held, the plays performed being *The Heir-at-Law* and *Le Diable à Quatre*. One of the players particularly impressed Shingleton:

> One of the men that had not taken a female's part before astonished every one,
> his dress which was of black Satin and ringlets down by cheeks of Jet black
> and his voice which he could alter well made him appear more like a female
> than any one I ever saw of the male sex; he went through his parts first rate.[12]

There had been complaints that the roof of the billiard room was too low, and hence on 1 February this was rectified; the walls were raised five feet, and at the same time panes of ice were inserted in the walls and roof, to give enough light to play without the need of artificial light.

Starting on 8 February, a survey of the canned meat, vegetables, and soup was made. It was found that in total 12% of the cans of meat (almost 3000 lbs) had to be condemned. Fortunately there was still a surplus in hand. Fortunately, too, with the increased hours of sunshine (8 hours on 9 February), shooting parties could be sent out again. On the 11th Lt. Phayre brought in a hare and three ptarmigan, of which Shingleton heartily approved:

> They are fine birds and better flavoured than any thing we have had in this
> country; there is every appearance of having plenty of them here, for they
> are collecting fast 30 or 40 together, but very wild.[13]

That evening the plays *Cymbeline* and *The Quaker* were performed, and on the 17th *Three Weeks after Marriage* and *High Life below Stairs*.

On 21 February the temperature in the sun was +19°F, although still only –25° in the shade; for the first time snow was seen to be melting on the black bulwarks. Two days later the deadlight was removed from the gunroom skylight, giving daylight in the gunroom for about six hours. The result appears to have taken everyone, especially Shingleton, by surprise:

> When we came to look at things in daylight they all have the appearance of a
> Collier's forecastle, coated from the smoke of so many lamps between decks.
> The Oil being bad, the atmosphere we breathed was thick and I expect if we
> had kept so a few months longer, we should all of us have been smoke dried.
> Even our bedding is as black as a coal bag, although everything was clean
> washed last summer.[14]

The plays performed on the evening of the 24th were *Miss in her Teens* and *Le Diable à Quatre* again.

On the 26th a single Inuk appeared, the first for several weeks; he traded a suit of caribou-skin clothes and a dog. The usual theatrical performance was staged on the evening of 4 March, the plays being *Two Strings to the Bow* and *The Jew and the Doctor*. One of the able-bodied seamen, Joseph Wiggins, shone as usual, impressing Shingleton:

> He can humour himself to anything: in the first piece he was the principal
> actor, being a servant under two Masters, and [in] the last piece he took the
> character of the Jew, which he performed first rate and would make some of
> the actors in the better London Theatres blush; in fact he is the star of our
> Royal Theatre.[15]

A week later the plays were *The Watermen* and *The Heir-at-Law* again. Throughout this period the crew was mainly employed in hauling rock ballast from shore and piling it on the ice in preparation for ballasting the ship—this despite some severe temperatures, such as a daily mean of –45°F on 10 March.

On 14th the quarterdeck housing was removed and a skylight fitted in the main hatchway. This latter may have been a little premature, however, since the frost built up on it so badly that it was barely translucent.

Since late February work had been going ahead at digging a pit on a small island (known as Simpson Rock) about a mile south of the ship, in which a cache of provisions was to be left. These provisions were placed in cache on 16 March: 100 lbs of biscuit, 320 lbs of pork, 2 bushels of oatmeal, 30 lbs of sugar, 5 lbs of tea, 20 lbs of chocolate, 30 lbs of rice, plus ammunition and some presents.[16]

On 21 March Lt. Jago set off with two sledges overland towards Point Back. His mandate was to establish a depot for the main spring travelling parties, and also to select the easiest route for them for this initial stage of their journey. The crew meanwhile was hauling ballast down through the forward hold to the bilges. It was a particularly pleasant, sunny day with a shade temperature of +20°F, and Shingleton was tempted to dry some laundry outdoors:

> For the first time for the last 5 months or nearly six, I dried my clothes and
> a large table cloth in the open air. It was a great treat to smell them when I
> took them down—so much difference in drying against hot pipes and fires,
> and the open air.[17]

On the 22nd the programme of filling and releasing hydrogen balloons with messages was started again. Jago and his sledge parties returned to the ship on the 23rd. They had seen numerous ptarmigan and the first raven of the year; while crossing a lake with a snowfree ice surface, they had also spotted the intriguing sight of a large salmon embedded in the ice about four feet below the surface. Then, on the 24th, the captain, accompanied by two men, hiked to Cape Colborne to take a round of angles and to build a cairn. On his return he reported finding a bed of sea shells some considerable distance from the shore. This is a common feature of the arctic islands; due to glacio-isostatic uplift, the sea has receded from large areas that were submerged in immediate postglacial time, and sea shells and other marine fossils, such as whale bones, are commonly found at great distances from the shore and at surprisingly high elevations.

The final theatrical performance of the season was held on the evening of the 26th, the plays performed being *Macbeth* and *Hobb in the Well*. Wiggins again excelled, playing Macduff in the first play and the young lad who gets dropped down the well in the second. Collinson was very satisfied with the effect that the theatrical performances had had on morale:

> seldom, I believe, were more ends got from the simple means we had for the
> purpose, as no preparations had been made either in England or Hongkong.
> The occupation and enjoyment which it gave were both productive of good,
> without, I am glad to say, any counter-check.[18]

On the morning of the 28th three sledges started eastwards to lay depots for the main travelling party, George Fowler in charge of two of them. They were hauling provisions to be cached four days' travel beyond the depot Jago had already established. Collinson commanded the third sledge, which was to add its load to the depot already laid by Jago. The captain and his men returned on the 30th, despite a fresh wind with heavy drifting snow that reduced visibility to less than 100 yards.

On the intervening day (29th March), Shingleton had had to cope with a rather unusual problem:

> a large tablecloth that I had hung up to dry very soon got hard frozen, but as soon as the breeze sprang up and had got inside the cloth, it being hung up double, split it clean down beginning at the bight first. It was done as clean as a piece of firewood.[19]

Collinson set off again on 2 April for the Finlayson Islands, to survey that group. He got there on the following day, but unfortunately the weather did not cooperate; for several days visibility was greatly reduced by drifting and blowing snow, so he managed to get only one round of angles. He had hoped to find some Inuit there too, but was disappointed. On the other hand, he did see four caribou crossing from the mainland to Victoria Island, the first caribou seen this spring. He and his men got back to the ship at 5 PM on the 7th, to be followed by Jago and his party half an hour later. There had been real concern about all three parties since they were due back on the 6th. Indeed, Lt. Phayre had even sent another sledge with provisions to meet Jago and his party, since they must have been running low on supplies.

Having placed two of his executive officers under arrest, Collinson's options were undoubtedly constrained when it came to plans for the main spring sledge trip. Lt. Phayre was left in command of the ship, along with the two surgeons and the two ice mates. The three sledge teams that took the field were led by Collinson himself, Lt. Jago, and the Quartermaster, George Fowler.[20] Collinson claimed that he had considered sending at least one team across Victoria Strait to search its eastern side, that is, the west coast of King William Island, but abandoned the idea on finding the ice too rough. Or possibly it was because he could not trust either of the other two leaders to operate independently that he kept all three sledges together, all three searching the southeastern coasts of Victoria Island. Had he sent one party east across Victoria Strait to King William Island, only some 50 km away, it would have discovered the traces of the Franklin expedition (a boat, sledges, skeletons, and abandoned equipment) that Captain Leopold McClintock and Lieutenant Hobson were to discover in 1859. It might even have found the only message giving details of the final fate of the Franklin expedition that Hobson found at Victory Point.[21] Collinson would then have become famous as the man who solved the Franklin mystery. As it was, through no fault of his own, since he had had no contact with the outside world since the spring of 1851, he was now about to search a coast already searched by Dr. John Rae in the summer of 1851.[22]

It should be noted, however, that Collinson had been given a rather strong hint that he ought to search to the eastward. As his editor (and brother), Thomas Collinson, noted,

> he [Richard Collinson] says in his journal that if they (in the *Enterprise*) had possessed the means of understanding the natives in Cambridge Bay (the interpreter of the expedition, Mr. Miertsching, had been accidentally left on board the *Investigator*), they would have got a clue from them which would have induced him to pass over to Boothia and examine its western face instead of examining the east coast of Victoria Island. But, although the natives at Cambridge Bay apparently wished them to understand that there were ships to the east of them fast in the ice, and drew a chart to illustrate it with the usual cleverness of their race, as this chart turned out to be incorrect, a doubt was thrown on the whole story, and no further thought given to it.[23]

But if Collinson gave no further thought to it, his officers did. In his later annotations to his copy of Collinson's book, Skead wrote,

> It was the common belief with the officers, the captain excepted, that Back's River ought to have been searched.[24]

He further comments:

> Instead of taking 3 officers and 21 men with 3 sledges in one direction—why not have sent 2 to the Nd. & 2 to Back's River?[25]

The significance of the references to the Back River is that it debouches into Chantrey Inlet, just southeast of King William Island, and indeed the survivors from the Franklin expedition headed for that river after abandoning their ships.

Several of the clauses in the orders that Collinson left for Lieutenant Phayre before starting on his sledge journey are most revealing:

5. From you I expect that all persons (whether officers or others) be corrected, or their conduct properly represented, who shall be disobedient to the Printed instructions or the orders I have deemed it necessary to issue, or who by their conduct or conversation shall endeavour to render any Officer or other person dissatisfied with his situation or with the service on which he is employed....

7. So long as Lt. Parkes and Mr. Skead conform themselves strictly to my general orders as well as to the particular ones relative to themselves you will grant them from time to time permission to take such exercise as may be good for their health but the fact that they are Prisoners at large is never to be lost sight of....

9. By the Queen's Regulations the military command of the ship during your temporary absence devolves in succession upon the following officers: Mr. Atkinson, Ice Mate; Mr. Arbuthnott, Ice Mate; Mr. Woodward, Boatswain; Mr. Waldron, Carpenter.[26]

It is clear from the content of Clause 5 that Collinson was seriously worried about the possibility of the disaffected officers "contaminating" the others. One wonders if he was even afraid of a mutiny in his absence. He had every reason to be. And one suspects that the period of the Captain's absence was a very tense period for Lieutenant Phayre, since he cannot have been popular with his brother-officers.

The main spring sledge party set off on the morning of 12 April. It consisted of three sledges, commanded by Captain Collinson, Lt. Jago, and quartermaster George Fowler respectively. The latter was in charge of a support party, which would turn back after about 11 days. Each sledge was pulled by seven men and three dogs. Two of the sledges, *Enterprise* and *Victoria*, had been made at Woolwich, while the third, *Royal Albert*, had been made on board over the winter; its runners had been made from an ice saw.

An innovation in the sledging equipment was the use of "fire balls" for fuel. These consisted of six-inch lengths of junk[27] soaked in a mixture of oil, saltpetre, and resin, then rolled up in old bread bags. In a trial it was found that one of these fireballs, "with the thermometer at −30°, thawed and boiled 8 pints of water in half an hour, the material only weighing ¾ of a pound."[28] Fireballs weighing three lbs, along with a barrel stave, provided enough heat to cook two meals per day for one of the sledge crews. Collinson admitted that there were some minor drawbacks, however:

> the only inconvenience was that it required more attention from the cook; and that the smoke and soot, as we could seldom afford water for washing more than once a week, dirtied our blanket bags.[29]

Provisions and equipment were taken for 40 days; this meant a load of 1904 lbs on each sledge, comprising the following:

> Bread, 320 lbs; pork, 160 lbs; pemmican, 160 lbs; potatoes, 10 lbs; rum, 12 pints; tea, 40 lbs; sugar, 160 lbs; dogs' meat, 160 lbs; fuel, 160 lbs; 3 kettles; 1 stove; 3 muskets; ...tent, floor-cloth, racoon skin; buffalo robes; 5 boarding pikes; 8 blanket bags, axe, saw, men's clothes; and ammunition.[30]

It took the three sledges two days (travelling over nine hours each day) to reach the depot just short of Anderson Bay (which Collinson called Rae Inlet). Since Collinson does not indicate in his journal the daily distance covered or mention any place names, it is extremely difficult to follow his progress in detail from that source. Fortunately, however, his track chart has survived and has been reproduced by McKenzie.[31] It is clear that, after reaching Anderson Bay, Collinson's route was along the sea ice parallel to the south shore of Victoria Island. By the early afternoon of the 17th, the party was heading into the strait between Jenny Lind Island and Victoria Island, although Collinson took it for a bay rather than a strait. The ice here was evidently particularly rough, because he was forced to head back to the south-west and around Jenny Lind Island, not recognizing it as a separate island: "hauled out of bight at 3.30; ice becoming packed; low land to the E.S.E. ; connection not visible."[32] The visibility must have been poor, since on his boat trip along this same coast in August 1851, John Rae had seen Jenny Lind Island from Macready Point, and from the coast east of Stromness Bay had recognized it as an island and sailed through the strait.[33]

On the evening of the 19th Collinson and his men pitched camp off Clestrain Point, the southern tip of Jenny Lind Island, and next day headed north parallel to that island's east coast. A major depot was cached on the east coast of Jenny Lind Island on the evening of 21 April. This came from the load on Fowler's sledge, *Royal Albert*. He also transferred five days' supplies to each of the other two sledges.

Collinson exchanged one of his men, John Charters, for one of Fowler's, Charles Elmore, since Charters had a sprain.

Next morning Collinson set off at 7:30 with Fowler's men, helping the other two sledges through rubbly ice near the shore. Then at 8 AM Fowler started back for the ship with *Royal Albert* while Collinson pushed on to the northeast with the other two sledges. An hour later, however, one of the runners of the captain's sledge, *Enterprise*, broke. William Murray was sent back to overtake Fowler's sledge, while *Enterprise* was unloaded and the broken runner fished (spliced). The captain's coxswain, Henry Hester, was then sent back with the empty, repaired sledge, to exchange it for *Royal Albert*. He returned with it at noon, and soon after 1 PM the two sledges were under way again heading northeastwards.

In the early afternoon of the 23rd, they ran into problems:

came up to the junction of the new and old ice at 2.30; camped and sent out four parties who returned in the evening, reporting the ice impracticable for sleighs from E. to W. by N. , forming a similar barrier to our progress as was experienced last year by the Resolution, between Banks Land and Melville Island. Here there was scarcely such a thing as a level spot to be seen, but a most confused jumble of angular pieces, many of which were upwards of 20 feet high, while the snow between them laid so loose that we frequently sank up to the middle, and only extricated ourselves by our hands.[34]

Next morning, since further northward progress was clearly impossible, Collinson backtracked towards the southwest-by-south, heading for the northeast coast of Jenny Lind Island. Even then the men were forced to unload the sledges and carry half their loads at a time across a zone of pressure ice a cable-length[35] in width. And to reach the shore they had to offload half the loads to cross a zone of tortured ice near the coast, then return for the offloaded items and camp.

On the following morning (25 April), they had travelled north for only two hours when they reached a conspicuous low shingle point on the northeast corner of Jenny Lind Island, where they were brought to a halt by blizzard conditions. They remained weather-bound all next day, and got under way again on the morning of the 27th. The going was quite good, although occasionally both crews had to combine their forces to move each sledge forward. That night they camped on the north coast of Jenny Lind Island and were again weather-bound the following day. Shortly after starting on the morning of the 29th, they reached the northern point

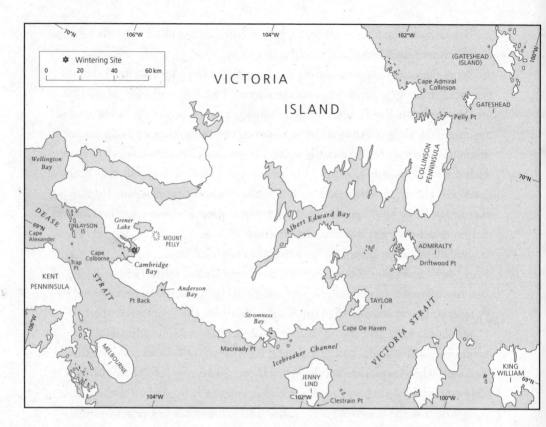

Southeastern Victoria Island, showing Collinson's wintering site and search areas, spring 1854.

of Jenny Lind Island, "on which were five *caches*, circles of stones showing summer encampment, and a small piece of drift wood; land trending to the S.W...."[36]

Striking north from here across smoother ice in the afternoon, Collinson was again crossing the strait between Jenny Lind and Victoria islands, although he had still not realized that he had been coasting around a separate island for the past 12 days. At 4 o'clock next morning, at their camp on the ice southwest of Cape De Haven, one of the men, William Jefferson, spotted a bear within 400 m of the tents; the dogs raced off after it, but soon returned except for Daddy. He had still not returned by the time the party got under way at 7:30 AM. In the early afternoon they reached Cape De Haven, "a low point on which large stones were pressed up by the ice, much old ice off it,"[37] and at 5 o'clock camped halfway to the southern tip of Taylor Island (which Collinson again assumed was part of Victoria Island). To everyone's delight, Daddy returned at 10 that evening.

Pushing on next morning (1 May), they reached a cliffed headland at the southern tip of Taylor Island. Here Collinson decide to leave another cache containing "... 32 lbs. of pork, 32 lbs. of pemmican, 64 lbs. of bread, 32 lbs. of potatoes, 2 lbs. of tea, 8 lbs. of sugar, rum 3 gallons 2 pints, 4 packages of fuel, 8 tins of dogs' meat...."[38]

For the rest of the day they coasted along the east coast of Taylor Island, camped for the night, then continued to the north end of that island till noon next day, when they struck north across the southern entrance of Albert Edward Bay. Next morning (3 May) they reached a low islet at 10:30; here Collinson made an interesting comment: "no other land visible."[39] The comment is interesting because the islet lies only 11 km from the southern tip of Admiralty Island, 15 km from the northern end of Taylor Island, and 16 km east of Cape Adelaide on Victoria Island. Clearly the visibility must have been very poor. By noon, however, land (Admiralty Island) was visible to the east, and Collinson now headed for it. There is no indication in his journal (and only a suggestion on his track chart), that he realized that Admiralty Island was separate from Victoria Island.

Next morning at 9 AM the party reached (and crossed) a headland, which Collinson named Driftwood Point, since here he found four pieces of driftwood, "one of which was 3 feet 6 inches long, and part of a stump 8 inches in diameter."[40] This was almost certainly not the Driftwood Point now marked on the map, but a point nearer to the south end of Admiralty Island. The present Driftwood Point is probably the "bluff 150 feet high" the party reached at 11:00.

Continuing north along the east coast of Admiralty Island, after camping for the night, the party got under way at 7:30 (their usual starting time) on the morning of the 5th, travelling "along a low shore." At the northwest point of Admiralty Island they left another depot, containing four days' provisions, then struck north across the northern entrance to Alfred Edward Bay, camping about halfway across it. This time Collinson at least suspected that he was crossing back to Victoria Island since he remarked in his journal, "Land [i. e. Victoria Island] from N. by E. to N.W., then a gap of 3 points, and continuous to depot point."[41]

On the morning of the 6th a bear was spotted, and Lt. Jago and two men went after it, but it managed to outrun them. During the afternoon three cairns were seen at different spots on the low coastline, but they "found nothing in their vicinity to indicate by whom they were built."[42]After an uneventful day of travel on the 7th, on the afternoon of the 8th they came to a cairn that contained what must have been a profoundly disappointing message:

A party of 10 men and 2 officers of the Hudson's Bay Company descended the Coppermine river in the latter end of June, in two boats. Found a channel of open water along shore on the 5th of July. Came along the coast eastward as far as Cape Alexander; were detained there some days as the ice in the strait was still unbroken. Then crossed over by the Finlayson islands to Victoria land, which was found to run nearly E. to long. 102° 40', when it turned up to the north. There is a deep and irregular shaped bay between lat. 69° 15; and 69° 40'N, in long 102° 3'. The boats were arrested by ice in lat. 69° 43' and 101° 24' (?) W. long. A walking party traced the coast 35 miles further nearly due north. The only particular worthy of notice was an island seen about 5 miles long, and 4 miles from the shore. Much of the ice was still unbroken and was pressed close to the shore by a continuance of northeasterly winds, which will probably make our return difficult. As far as regards the object of the expedition, a search for Sir John Franklin and party, we were quite unsuccessful.

> JOHN RAE. CHIEF FACTOR. H. B. CO.
> Commanding the Expedition

Lat 70° 2' 30" N. , long. 101° 18' (?) W.
13th August 1851.
Note. Tomorrow I return to the boats. J. R.[43]

Determined to make the best of this frustrating situation, Collinson decided to push on northwards; he had eight days' supplies left and he hoped to use them to cover a further 70 miles. After a few more hours, Collinson and his men camped and, next morning, by 10:30 had reached Pelly Point, the farthest point seen by Rae and his men. From it Collinson spotted an island (or point) to the northeast and headed for it. The going was very bad, with rough ice, some open water, and soft snow. Having camped once again, they reached the land at 9:15 on 10 May. Here Collinson cached a depot of four days' provisions, then headed north again, until 2:30 PM,

> when on ascending a hill it became evident that we were upon an island, with no land in sight, except in the direction we had come from. The appear-ance of the pack to the N.E., N., and N.W. forbid all hope of penetrating even with our light load through it, so building a cairn, which our observa-

tions eventually placed in lat. 70° 26'N and long. 100° 47'W, and depositing information, we retraced our steps to the southeastward.... [44]

Collinson named the island Gateshead Island, after the town where he had spent his childhood. McKenzie has argued very convincingly that this was not the Gateshead Island now so named on the map but much too far from Victoria Island for Collinson to have seen it from Pelly Point or to have reached in the time he took.[45] Rather, his Gateshead Island is the much smaller island, unnamed on the modern map, about 17 km northeast of Pelly Point.

Collinson started back south on the morning of the 11th, reaching the depot at the south end of the island at 10 AM. From there he struck west to avoid the area of difficult ice he had encountered on the way north and reached the coast of Victoria Island some distance west of Pelly Point at 9 next morning. Here he left another cache of four days' provisions "at a large boulder of granite (9 feet cube)." Continuing along the coast to the west to a headland rising about 60 feet above sea level and seeing land to the west-northwest, the party headed towards it across the ice; after 90 minutes they came to a low spit. Here they spotted a bear, loosed the dogs, which brought it to bay, and shot it. They camped on the spit to skin the bear while it was still warm.

One might assume from the fact that a cape on this coast has been named Cape Admiral Collinson, that this was the spit on which the party was now encamped. However, to reach it on a west-northwesterly bearing would have involved a journey across the ice of some 18 km, an impossible distance for a man-hauling party to cover in 90 minutes. The low spit they had now reached, which was Collinson's farthest, must have been the long, narrow headland, aligned northwest-southeast, about 15 km west of Pelly Point.

His supplies exhausted, Collinson stayed in camp next day to take magnetic observations, but sent small parties off in different directions. Lt. Jago and two men headed west-northwest to an island where they built a cairn, before turning back. From that island another small island was visible beyond, and land was visible beyond it, namely Cape Admiral Collinson. Meanwhile the captain's coxswain, Henry Hester, with two men headed southwest along the coast, reaching a cliffed headland, beyond which the coast continued its southwesterly trend. Hester also built a cairn at his farthest point. Collinson determined the camp to be at 70° 12'N; 101° 40'W.

The party started on their homeward trip at 8:10 PM on the 14th, deliberately travelling by night when the lower temperatures ought to improve the snow conditions. By 10:15 PM on the 15th they were back at Rae's cairn, where Collinson left a message.

From time to time on the southward trip they travelled along the land, as offering easier sledging than the sea ice. By 5:20 AM on the 17th they were back at the depot at the north end of Admiralty Island, and by 3 AM on the 20th at the depot at the south end of Taylor Island, only to find that a bear had ransacked part of it:

> found *Victoria's* packing case broken open by a bear, who had helped himself to the pork and sugar, and destroyed the bread and potatoes; fortu-nately our provisions [i. e. *Enterprise's*] were in a cask, which bore the marks of his claws, and a 32-lb. pemmican tin escaped his notice. He had, however, extracted a bung from a beaker of spirits and capsized it; being concentrated and intended as a reserve supply of fuel, this might have proved a serious loss had not our fireballs done their duty.[46]

When they reached the depot on the east coast of Jenny Lind Island at 6:15 AM on 22 May, Collinson was relieved to find it intact, as he thought that, as far south as this, it might have been discovered (and rifled) by the Inuit; this would have been a serious situation, in light of the bear's depredations at the depot farther north.

Swinging around the south end of Jenny Lind Island, they headed west along the south coast of Victoria Island, although poor visibility greatly hampered naviga-tion. On the early morning of 28 May they spotted a tent and pitched camp beside it. Its occupants were quartermaster George Fowler and a support party who, by prearrangement, had brought provisions for the captain's party.

At 3:15 AM the combined party camped in a ravine at the head of Rae Inlet (Anderson Bay); having thus a good opportunity to examine the inlet, Collinson assessed it as the best possible wintering site in the area. They were back on board ship by 6:10 AM on 31 May, "all our party being hale, although many of us were much fagged."[47] While recognizing the difficulties resulting from rough ice and poor visibility, any assessment of Collinson's sledge trip must conclude that his track chart and his journal provide an incomplete picture of the east coast of Victoria Island. He had failed to establish the insularity of Jenny Lind, Taylor, and Admiralty Islands, and his track chart gives no indication at all of the existence of the large and complex embayment of Albert Edward Bay. Fortunately, all of these features had been mapped, at least provisionally, by John Rae almost two years previously. To be fair, however, had one to rely solely on Rae's work, one would have no concept of the size and eastern extent of the three islands.

In the sledging party's absence, the usual signs of spring had been recorded in succession and the usual related activities had been attended to. On 18 April the men began clearing the main hold of all the casks and tanks to get access to the coal stowed below them, with a view to replacing it with stone ballast. The first snow buntings were seen around the ship on the 19th. Meanwhile the snow was starting to melt everywhere, and there were four inches of water in the skittle alley alongside.

On the 24th the layer of snow insulating the upper deck was removed, and on the following day the main deck housing was removed so that, in Shingleton's words, "we begin to look like a ship once more."[48]

George Fowler's party, which had set off in support of the captain's party, returned to the ship on 2 May. However, they were, as Shingleton sympathetically noted,

> not all in the best condition; one poor fellow had the soles of his feet so galled
> and blistered that it was horrible to look at them. How he managed to walk
> I cannot surmise. Although his feet were wrapt in blanket, he must have
> suffered very much; besides his face was very much frostbitten. One came on
> board stone blind, and another, that was of Capt. Collinson's party returned
> with them, having injured his knee by slipping down a hummock of ice.[49]

On the following day even more of the party were suffering the painful effects of snow blindness. The crew that day was busy sending up the topgallant masts, the mizzen topsail yard, and the crow's nest. Shingleton proudly recorded in his journal, "We are now nearly ready for sea." On the 5th the porch sheltering the entry-port was dismantled, and on the 6th the housing on the forecastle was removed: "we are now a ship once more and can see over the sides all round."[50]

On the 12th Shingleton was moved to do some personal spring-cleaning:

> I have had two days' work in clearing the winter's smoke and dirt of the
> paintwork of my berth which was nearly as black as the Soot itself; it now
> looks wholesome and habitable.[51]

A few Inuit had appeared on 8 May, and then on the 12th a group of six turned up with three large trout, which were purchased for two small files worth about 2d each.

At this point, as Shingleton reveals, Captain Collinson had established new rules about acquiring game from the Inuit and about shooting game:

> Everything that is purchased from them by either Officer or Man is strictly ordered to be given over for the use of the ship at large, and everything shot likewise, so that people have but very little encouragement to take a Gun out. Last season the first Deer that was shot belonged to the man that shot it; the second shot one-half belonged to the Man; any afterwards were delivered over to the Purser. With Game [i.e. birds and hares] the 6th of everything belonged to the Man that shot it, which was very good encouragement to go out and was the means of having a great deal more than we otherwise would have had.[52]

Next day a large balloon and two small ones were released while another group of Inuit was on board; they appeared to be baffled by the balloons getting gradually bigger as they were filled with hydrogen, and were even more so when they rose into the air. As Shingleton conjectured, they almost certainly had never seen anything like them before. The other noteworthy event that day was that the first caribou were seen on the ice on the bay, having crossed Dease Strait from the mainland. Increasing numbers were seen over the next few days, and on the 20th Dr. Anderson took a tent and set off inland to camp at what he thought would be a suitable spot for intercepting them.

On the 25th George Fowler and his party set off to meet the Captain's returning sledge party. Later that morning the first snow goose was seen flying north. The four men who had gone with Fowler's group to help them on the overland route to Anderson Bay (Rae Inlet) returned on the 28th, one of them completely blind, and the rest with some degree of snow blindness. On their way back they had run across a tented Inuit encampment.

Almost immediately on his return, Collinson identified some further misdemeanour on Skead's part. In his Night Order Book on 2 June Collinson decreed that "The second Master's leave is stopped from one month from this date."[53] Skead's offence appears to have been that, failing to comply with the Printed Instructions, he had been guilty of not "passing the Gunroom Victualling Account at each period when the quarterly accounts were brought to me for signature."[54] Given that Skead was still a "prisoner at large," it is unclear as to what this latest penalty signified.

After the return of the captain's sledge party (on 31 May), signs of spring's approach became increasingly frequent. More geese were seen on 2 June, as well as the first plovers and the first gull. On the 4th the first swans and the first oldsquaws were seen. On the evening of the 5th Lt. Phayre set off with a party of men, heading across the strait to Cape Alexander, intending then to head east to Trap Point. His objective was to leave messages about the depot that Collinson had left on Simpson Rock in mid-March, as well as to hunt whatever game he encountered. Then, on the evening of the 7th, four men were sent off to Mt. Pelly with camping gear, also with the purpose of shooting as much game as they could. Collinson was well aware of the importance of getting as much fresh meat as possible, as there were five cases of scurvy on board, four of them men who had been with him on his major sledge trip. Even Collinson himself had been temporarily afflicted by scurvy:

> I found immediately on my return, that the black marks (together with pains in the joints), which had shown themselves slightly on my person at the commencement of last winter, had again made their appearance; by, however, taking my established allowance of limejuice regularly, they disappeared in the course of a week.[55]

He had taken no limejuice with him on the sledge trip, counting on finding game, but in fact little had been shot. As in his own case, all the scurvy patients recovered within two weeks in response to the "surgeon's remedies," presumably limejuice and fresh meat.

On the 10th one of Lt. Phayre's party reached the ship; he had been sent to get more ammunition and a further week's provisions. Phayre and his men were at Trap Point and were having some success at hunting (4 hares and 6 ptarmigan); they hoped to get even more game in the future. The gunner's mate, Joshua Page, returned with the messenger in order to bring back the game Phayre and his men had shot.

Despite all the signs of spring, however, winter was reluctant to loosen its grip; on the night of the 10th /11th there was a heavy fall of snow, as Shingleton recorded: "There was about 8 inches of Snow on our deck, but in some places on the Ice and shore it was several feet where the wind had drifted it."[56] Probably discouraged by this weather, the shooting party from Mt. Pelly returned on the evening of the 11th, having shot nothing. To compensate for this, however, on the 12th Lt. Jago came back aboard with five hares and four ptarmigan.

This blast of winter did not last long, however. On 15 June Shingleton reported,

> The snow is sinking fast and flowers on shore are coming out in blossom;
> it is very pleasant the first thing in the morning when all is still to hear the
> birds on shore singing.[57]

Some of the Inuit, now camped about six miles north of the ship, came to the ship almost daily. Collinson had bought a kayak at Port Clarence that was greatly admired by the local Inuit, and the captain had indicated he would sell it for five caribou. Apparently misunderstanding this message, however, on the 15th a group of them turned up with a very well-made kayak of their own and proposed swapping it for the Port Clarence model,

> which I was glad to do, in order to get a specimen of their work, where
> wood is so scarce: both were calculated to hold only one man; but ours was
> much larger, weighing 60 lbs., while theirs was only 26. In shape, too, they
> were somewhat different; ours, however, was slightly damaged; I therefore
> threw in an ash paddle, made of a broken oar, which sent them away highly
> pleased with the exchange.[58]

At midnight on the night of the 15th /16th a dense fog rolled in. Since there were a number of men out shooting, Collinson ordered that a gun be fired at regular intervals to help them locate the ship. The result of the fog next morning was quite magical, with all the rigging encased in hoarfrost.

From now on the amount of game harvested increased in quite a spectacular fashion: on the 16th Dr. Anderson bagged seven ducks and a loon (probably a Pacific loon or a Yellow-billed loon), the first of the season. On the 18th the two surgeons shot 21 ducks and three geese, while a party that had gone back to Mt. Pelly on the 16th returned on the 18th with seven ducks, three geese, and some fish. Then, in the early hours of the 19th, Lt. Phayre and his party arrived from Trap Point across the strait with 39 ducks. In total, by the 21st, 250 ducks had been shot, 60 of them on the 20th alone, mainly by the surgeons (see illustration p. 264). On the 22nd Lt. Jago, who had set out for a shooting camp on the 19th, sent back an impressive 67 ducks. He and his party returned on the morning of the 26th, having shot 160 ducks, four geese, and three ptarmigan over the course of a week!

As a by-product of all this game coming aboard, Shingleton acquired a new hobby:

This is a fine time for me in the skinning line for it is an art I am particularly fond of; several fine specimens of Ducks and Gull and small birds I have skinned.[59]

However, he gives no indication as to the ultimate fate of these skins.

In memos dated 20 and 23 June 1853, some 15 months after Skead was placed under arrest, Collinson was still badgering him for his accounts relating to the Gunroom Victualling stores, Paymaster's stores, purser's stores, and so on, up until the date on which he was arrested, along with explanations of why he had not submitted these earlier. [60] While one can understand why Skead was proving less than cooperative, this was probably not the most diplomatic course of action (or inaction).

It was around this time that some visiting Inuit were asked to demonstrate their skill with their bows and arrows; specifically, they were asked to try to hit the wind vane at the mast head from the deck. The result was quite impressive, three or four of their arrows hitting the wind vane, although it was moving with the wind.

Despite strong winds and heavy rain, Captain Collinson set off to survey the Finlayson Islands, but was forced to turn back within a few hours. Later the weather improved somewhat, and Lt. Jago again set off for another week at the shooting camp near Mt. Pelly.

On the evening of the 29th an event occurred that clearly distressed Shingleton and must have cast a shadow over the ship:

At 7.30 PM we had a most awful visitation of God: one of our Marines, Mr. Cheeseman, fell down on the forecastle and never spoke more; he turned quite black in the Mouth. The Surgeons were on the spot immediately and tried restoratives but of no avail. He was gone. The poor fellow had been sitting at his Mess-table mending a pair of stockings not 5 minutes before; he had complained of a pain in his back during the afternoon but did not think it sufficient to go to the Surgeon. The poor fellow was well beliked on board, for he was a good hard-working man and willing to do anything for his shipmates.[61]

The surgeons' diagnosis was that he was suffering from an enlargement of the heart.

In what may well have seemed a callous decision to his officers and men, "the melancholy event which had just occurred having banished sleep,"[62] Collinson and party set off for his postponed trip to the Finlayson Islands at midnight. In the meantime, on the morning of the 30th a party went ashore to dig a grave, while the carpenters started making a coffin. Since the ground was frozen it took them until some time on 2 July to finish the grave, and even then it was only four feet deep.

Captain Collinson returned from his surveying trip that afternoon (as did Lt. Jago from his shooting camp). Soon after leaving the ship, Collinson's party had run into dense fog; he had tried to maintain his course by sending a man half a cable behind the sledge, while he himself walked half a cable ahead, but without much success. After five hours he and his men pitched camp on a low, sandy point on Victoria Island, having first experienced some difficulty in getting from the ice to the land across a shore lead. The fog cleared off by noon next day, and the party now headed across to the Finlayson Islands, which they reached at 6:00, having had to wade through melt pools up to two feet deep for most of the distance. Collinson obtained a round of angles that evening and observed correctly that these islands represent the higher parts of a lava ridge extending from Trap Point right across Dease Strait to Victoria Island.

The captain's coxswain found some gulls' nests and collected over 50 eggs, but unfortunately the embryos were too well developed for them to be edible. Another more exciting find was also made on the Finlayson Islands, as Collinson reported:

> Another of the crew picked up at high-water mark, on the east side of the island, a piece of wood, which being almost the only article we have met with which could have belonged to the missing ships, demands a description; other pieces of drift-wood were picked up at the same time; I do not think, therefore, that it was brought there by the natives, more especially as it is better suited for making arrows than the drift-wood we have seen in this neighbourhood, and they would not have left the copper hasp, screws and nails in it; moreover, they have no means of getting to the Finlayson Islands until the sea is frozen over, at which period sufficient snow has fallen to cover all sea wrack. It is composed of two pieces of fir nailed together, the largest piece being 51 inches long by 3¾ in its broadest part, and ¾ of an inch thick; both ends are broken and worn, apparently by being washed against the rocks. The back has been painted lead colour, and then black; and 13 inches from one end is a copper hasp for securing the latch of a door, fastened on by three screws, and with the Queen's mark ^ on it; the edge next the hasp has been painted, while the irregularity of the other shows it has been split from a broader piece. On the inside, 3 inches from the end, is a batten, 24

inches long, 2 wide, ¾ thick, chamfered at both ends, secured to the larger piece by copper nails, but with the marks of one or two iron ones; the batten is painted white, as is part of the lower side of the larger piece, which has originally had a coat of light green. I cannot think that it formed part of any fittings to a boat, but is either part of a companion hatch or the lintel post to an observatory. It may have formed part of the stock of fuel which Dr. Rae had with him; but then I cannot account for the broad arrow appearing upon it; if it has not been left there by him, it must have been thrown up by the sea since, as it could scarcely have escaped his observation.[63]

Collinson and his men started back to Victoria Island at 4 AM and, on reaching Sandy Point at 9, spent the rest of the day taking bearings from there. Getting under way again at 7 PM , they crossed the narrow neck to the western end of the inner part of Cambridge Bay and camped on its shores at midnight.

Next morning they headed up its outlet river to Greiner Lake, and from a hilltop Collinson got a good view of it, still ice-covered and dotted with islets. Returning downstream to the bay, and seeing what looked like a good fishing pool at the river mouth, some of the men were sent back to the lake for a sanpan or punt and a seine net that had been taken there earlier. When they hauled the net, they were amazed to find that it contained 1237 fish (probably arctic char; see illustration p. 264), averaging four lbs. each. Shingleton later remarked that if the Inuit had seen this they would have been totally amazed, since their only fishing equipment was hooks and lines.[64]

Next morning Collinson sent the sledge with the dogs and two men, with some of the fish for immediate consumption on board, to recruit help to haul the remainder back to the ship. By 5 PM he and all his party were back on board, and the fish were issued in lieu of salt meat for the next three days.

In the captain's absence another problem had been festering, namely a dispute between John Atkinson, one of the ice mates, and Lieutenant Phayre. As the latter reported the matter to Collinson in a letter of 29 June,

On requesting Mr. Atkinson, Ice Mate, this forenoon to read your order to the Senior, 2nd Lieut. & himself respecting the Survey on a portion of damaged canvass, he without doing so threw the book on the lower deck & said in a most contemptuous manner he knew more about it than myself. Repairing on deck shortly afterwards where the said canvass was ready for his inspection, he again (in the presence of Mr. Woodward, Boatsn., Jo. Wood, Sail Maker) when asked by me to give his opinion of the state of it, & what it was fit for, said it was condemnable & that he knew better than me what it was fit for, adding that I was a mere Thief & Jew in the ship & if he had me on shore abreast of her would let me know who he was. I told him that was not language to use to me, his Superior Officer. His answer was "You my Superior Officer. I consider you as the snot from my nose," suiting the action to the word. In fact his language was outrageous & although requested by me several times to cease it. I considered it my duty to report such disgraceful conduct to you.[65]

Not surprisingly, Collinson's immediate reaction was to suspend Atkinson "from further duty until I have enquired into a complaint lodged against him."[66] In response to a request for further clarification of the incident, on 4 July Phayre wrote,

Sir,

In obedience to your order that I should put in writing what I have to complain of with regard to Mr. Atkinson's conduct on the 28th Ult. I have only to repeat what I have already communicated to you, namely that Mr. Atkinson (in the presence of witnesses whose evidences were not heard by you this forenoon) applied to me the language of the most outrageous & insulting kind & threatening me with personal violence. You appear, Sir, to be determined to support Mr. Atkinson & to be deaf to all I have to urge against him. You have not only written an apology for Mr. Atkinson, but attempted to force it upon me against my will. His conduct in this matter is not to be set right by an apology; the outrage against me has been far too gross for that, & it has now come to this that Mr. Atkinson & I can no longer do duty together, & that it rests with you to choose between us.

Insult & injury have been heaped upon me of late to an incredible extent & I can no longer submit to the degradation from which any man of common spirit must recoil.[67]

Atkinson's apology, which Phayre claimed was written by Collinson and was forced on him "against his will," reads as follows:

Sir,

I am extremely sorry that on Wednesday morning last I made use of improper & unbecoming language to the Senior Lieutenant for which I beg that Officer's pardon. And I assure you, Sir, that if you will permit me to return to my duty I will be more careful to govern my temper in future & endeavour by my conduct to show respect to those who are placed in authority over me. John Atkinson, Ice Mate.[68]

The remarkable outcome of this confrontation is contained in two General Orders, both dated 4 July:

Mr. Atkinson (Ice Mate) is directed to return to his duty.

RD. COLLINSON, CAPTAIN.[69]

The other states:

Lieutenant Phayre is suspended from duty until further orders, he is directed to deliver to me as early as possible the Watch Bills, Station bills, accounts of the stowage of the holds, sailrooms etc. & other Documents connected with the routines of duty as at present carried on.

RD. COLLINSON, CAPTAIN.[70]

Of the regular officers, this left only Lieutenant Jago and the two surgeons not relieved of their duties. While one is inclined to feel that Phayre was getting only his just deserts for his despicable behavior of reporting every little misdemeanour of his fellow officers to the captain, one can also detect here a potentially very damaging tendency on Collinson's part, namely to take the part of the "auxiliaries" such as the ice masters over that of any of his regular officers.

The funeral for Cheeseman, as reported by Shingleton, was held next afternoon (3 July):

At 4.30 PM the remains of our late shipmate, William Cheeseman, were taken on shore to his last resting place. The whole of the ship's company followed with the Officers. Three volleys were fired over him, as is usual with military men. The poor fellow is much regretted on board. There were no traces of the grave left on account of the Natives, for it is quite likely they would disturb or rob the coffin after we leave, but a marked stone will be placed there to indicate his place of interment in case any Europeans calling here.[71]

Preparations for the upcoming navigation season were now put in hand. For example, the task of filling the ship's water tanks was completed on 10 July. On the 13th the flagpole was brought back aboard from the nearby island. By this time there were few ducks and geese around any more, and the shooting parties were having little luck. In contrast, fishing became a major activity. Thus, on the evening of 14 July, 16 men went ashore to Lake Greiner to try their luck with the seine net. They caught 300 fish overnight and a further 100 on the following day, and hauls of a similar size were made regularly until the 23rd. Over the preceding week almost 1000 fish, averaging four lbs each in weight, had been brought aboard. Some 1200 fish were salted or dried "as a reserve in case we should get kept another winter—which I trust in God will not be the case."[72]

On the morning of the 18th the crew bent sails; Shingleton's comment that "everything ready for sea now," was rather premature, however. There was no sign of movement in the ice, although many of the melt pools had melted right through and walking across the ice could be quite hazardous. At the same time, the narrow stretch of water along the shore had widened to the point that one of the whalers was placed in it to facilitate getting to and from the land. [73]

During a gale in the early hours of 28 July the ice began to break up. The crew began sawing and blasting the ice, and by 5 PM the ship had reached the polynya that had opened. Having picked up all her anchors, some of which had been down all winter, the ship then got under way and sailed about half a mile along leads to a safer position, between Simpson Rock and Flagstaff Island, in case the ice began closing again.

The next two weeks were very frustrating. Several times the ship had to move a short distance since it was being threatened by driving ice. The stocks of two anchors were broken at different times and had to be repaired. As Shingleton feelingly noted, "It is very awkward to be without Anchors in this place, for the water is shoal in so many places."[74] To add to the frustration, there appeared to be open water out in Dease Strait; it was only within Cambridge Bay that the ice was so persistent.

From time to time parties were sent ashore with seine nets to fish either in bays or in nearby lakes. One party on 5 August was particularly successful, taking 45 fish.

On other occasions, groups of men were sent ashore to get some exercise and to gather sorrel (*Oxyria dygna*) as an antiscorbutic, although it was found to be very sparse whereas, as Shingleton noted, "In last winter's quarters it was very plentiful and fine large leaves too. I made several pies of it and found it equally as good as rhubarb."[75]

Finally, in the early hours of 10 August, Collinson was tempted to try, despite a foul wind, to work his way along a narrow channel between the ice and a reef, in order to reach open water to the west. But with wind and current against him, after several narrow escapes from running aground, he was forced to return to the anchorage around 9 AM. But when the wind swung into the north in the afternoon, Collinson tried again, and this time got clear of the ice as Shingleton feelingly noted: "...by 8 PM, thank God, we were outside of our second winter's quarters, and we all strongly hope the last in these regions—10 months and 12 days in this last barren place."[76]

Arguing that the ship was short of fuel (for heating and cooking purposes), Collinson now started back westward, despite the fact that the part of a wooden door frame that he had found on the Finlayson Islands, which he himself admitted could have come from the missing ships, must have drifted from somewhere farther east, since other signs of wreckage must have been spotted if Franklin's ships had been wrecked farther west. Skead felt that the alleged shortage of fuel was a feeble excuse, and that they should be trying to push farther east. He pointed out that in early June they still had 21 tonnes of coal, by Collinson's own admission, a full year's supply. Hence such annotations in Skead's copy of Collinson's book as "The fuel excuse is all fudge; other fire was deficient"[77] and "Lies only! Fabricated to excuse our running away to the West!"[78]

Due to a combination of circumstances, the results of HMS *Enterprise's* second arctic wintering were quite limited. With regard to the results of Collinson's spring sledge trip, once again he found that almost the entire stretch of coast where he was searching for traces of the missing Franklin expedition had already been searched, in this case by Dr. John Rae on his boat trip in the summer of 1851.

What the ship's officers, and even Collinson himself, must have found particularly frustrating in later life was the decision, taken back in the Strait of Magellan years previously, that Johannes Miertsching, the Inuktitut interpreter, should stay on board *Investigator*—a decision that had a profoundly negative result. Had he been on board *Enterprise*, as had been the original plan, Collinson would have been able to elicit a much clearer idea of what the Inuit at Cambridge Bay were trying to tell him when they appeared to talk of ships beset in the ice somewhere to the east. And had that matter been clarified, he would, one must hope, have sent at least one sledge east across Victoria Strait to King William Island. There he would have discovered the traces of the missing Franklin expedition (boats, clothing, skeletons, etc.) and possibly the only written record indicating the fate of the missing expedition, later found by Lt. William Hobson while searching the coast of that island during McClintock's expedition in 1859.

In terms of relations between Collinson and his officers, the situation had deteriorated further during this second wintering. The First Lieutenant, George Phayre, who had previously been Collinson's most reliable supporter (apparently at least), had been suspended from duty, leaving Lieutenant Jago as the only executive officer still available for duty. Quite apart from the mechanics of running the ship, this was clearly having a very negative effect on the atmosphere and discipline on board, as revealed by the altercation between Lieutenant Phayre and John Atkinson, the ice-mate, an altercation in which Captain Collinson took the part of the ice mate, a decision that probably exacerbated an already tense situation. •

10

RETREAT TO THE WEST

To EVERYONE'S PLEASANT SURPRISE, as *Enterprise* started back west Dease Strait appeared to be clear of ice, but now the weather became less than cooperative. By 6 PM on the 11th the weather, as Shingleton noted, was "looking very dirty with missling rain";[1] despite this, by 4 AM on the 12th the ship had worked up to the Finlayson Islands.[2] But then, once the ship had worked through that chain, on the morning of the 12th, the wind died, so that the ship was becalmed in dense fog, and with a strong current setting to the northeast *Enterprise* drifted steadily eastwards again. This was an anxious time since it was known that there were numerous reefs around the Finlaysons.

Fortunately the wind picked up again, dispersing the fog; Collinson steered over to the mainland coast, and by 1 AM on the 13th had rounded Cape Alexander. He then hauled across the strait for the Victoria Island shore, and by 8 AM had passed Byron Bay.

Thereafter progress was slow, however. But then, on the morning of the 16th, conditions greatly improved, to Shingleton's delight:

a most beautiful morning, the Sun quite warm. 8 AM a light air sprang up
from SE and gradually freshened all day. Set the studding sails alow and
aloft on both sides. We had a fine piece of canvas on her. The wind dead
aft all the afternoon, running from 4 to 7 knots per hour between a group of
islands not down in the chart....[3]

The islands were the Miles Islands, *Enterprise* having slipped through the Duke of
York Archipelago by steering between Bate and Kellett Islands. But then the situation changed abruptly around 6 PM, to Shingleton's disappointment,

when some pieces of Ice passed us, and shortly afterwards we were in the
thick of it. Took all the studding sails in and pushed her through it. The
whole width of the Strait was covered, but all broken and very heavy pieces
too. However we kept on getting some heavy blows as we came in contact
with a large piece and soon shivered it.[4]

By late in the evening *Enterprise* was off Douglas Island, but here her progress was
blocked by close ice. She lay hove-to in the ice in fog and rain all next morning, but
when the fog cleared around noon she got under way again. Initially Collinson tried
to work south, anticipating that the water pouring out of the Coppermine might
have cleared the ice along that coast. Finding that this was not the case, he steered
north for the Victoria Island coast, working through ice, as Shingleton describes:

Made sail with the wind nearly dead on east and lots of ice, but all detached
pieces. We gave the old ship some heavy thumps; had she been an ordinary
vessel [she] would have gone to pieces in quick time.[5]

Collinson's objective was a coastal polynya extending all along the Victoria Island
shore of Dolphin and Union Strait. *Enterprise* had reached this open polynya, but
around 5 PM, just after the successive casts of the lead gave 13 fathoms with no
bottom, followed by five fathoms, the ship ran aground about two miles from shore,
with only two fathoms under her bows, 3½ fathoms under the main chains,[6] and
four fathoms aft.[7] Fortunately she had not struck very heavily, and although the
first anchor, a kedge anchor, "came home," that is, failed to get a hold, the second
anchor, a stream anchor laid out over the stern, held, and with the men heaving on
the capstan and a strong wind from right ahead, she slid off quite easily.

This was only the beginning of a very stressful week as Collinson tried to fight his way north and northwest through an ice-choked Dolphin and Union Strait. Passing the end of Lady Franklin Point, Collinson found the channel between it and Douglas Island blocked by ice. Initially the ship made some headway through the ice, although at some cost, as Shingleton noted: "Our old craft has stood some heavy thumps from it, so much so as nearly to take a person off his legs."[8] But in the early hours of the 20th it fell calm. Collinson grappled to a floe, and with it *Enterprise* drifted steadily to the southeast; several close calls from grounding on reefs or being driven onto islands made for some very tense moments. At one point, on 21 August, the ship was only about 15 miles from the mouth of the Coppermine.

Thereafter the ice slackened somewhat, and she managed to work her way back north; thus by 6 PM on the 23rd she managed to reach open water about four miles off Cape Krusenstern, and with all sails set, including studding sails, she forged northwards. When it got dark around 10 PM, however, Collinson hove-to for the night. In the morning the situation did not look promising. The entire area from the low series of reefs that run between Lambert and Douglas islands east to Victoria Island was choked with ice, and soon *Enterprise* found the ice driving down on her where she lay at anchor. The outcome was that several hawsers broke in succession, and she lost three anchors and about 180 fathoms of chain. Boats were lowered to try to recover the anchors, but in thick fog, it was a near-hopeless task; Collinson even had to order guns fired to guide the boats back to the ship. When the fog cleared on the morning of the 25th, Collinson reluctantly decided to take advantage of a fair wind and, abandoning two bower anchors and 130 fathoms of chain, set a course to the northwest. By 10:30 the ship was passing Sutton and Liston Islands, but it was again foggy, and with the compass still useless and no sign of the sun, the ship strayed north almost to the Victoria Island shore, amidst moderate ice. Discovering his mistake when the sun came out, Collinson headed back south through sailing ice, and emerged into open water near the mainland shore in the evening. It fell calm again around 8 PM , but at least there was the consolation that the hazards of Dolphin and Union Strait were now astern.

Getting under way on the morning of the 26th, *Enterprise* made good progress despite some sailing ice and quite thick fog for most of the day. When it cleared around 3 PM, the coast of Wollaston Peninsula was in sight, somewhere in the vicinity of Caen Point or Williams Point. Meanwhile, the carpenters were busy putting a new stock on a spare bower anchor, and by the afternoon of the 27th "we had the satisfaction of seeing two serviceable anchors at our bows."[9] By then *Enter-*

prise was storming to the northwest across Amundsen Gulf, in open water and with studding sails alow and aloft.

On the morning of the 28th the compasses began to traverse again, making navigation much simpler. When the wind swung into the west, Collinson made a long tack to the north, so that by evening the ship was within 30 miles of Nelson Head, just visible to the north. After tacking to the south again, by next morning Cape Parry was in sight to windward, but when it fell calm in the afternoon, the ship was carried by a current well south into Darnley Bay. With a freshening south wind, however, *Enterprise* headed back north, and by 10 PM was abeam of the More Islands, just east of Cape Parry. Here Shingleton made an interesting observation:

> Saw one solitary loom fly past the ship; those birds have not been near us this summer. They inhabit high cliffs and capes, but I should like to fall in with them for they are good eating, I fancy better than the ducks, for they eat very fishy, especially when the salt water opens.[10]

The bird he had seen was a Thick-billed murre (*Uria lomvia*), and he was correct in thinking that he had not seen any that summer, farther to the east; the cliffs at Cape Parry were the site of the only nesting colony in the Canadian Western Arctic.[11]

By midnight *Enterprise* was passing Cape Parry, and here encountered the first ice since leaving Dolphin and Union Strait. Soon it became apparent that Franklin Bay was almost completely choked with ice, except for a coastal polynya along its western side. Collinson thereafter worked his way across the bay to take advantage of this open water.

Before the ship left the ice a bear was spotted, as Shingleton excitedly recorded:

> 6 AM observed a Bear laying asleep on the Ice, but he soon woke and took the water. Lowered a boat down and the Gunner's mate took a Rifle, but the beast swam for his life. However, the boat reached him and the man fired. He never moved afterwards; they then towed him on board. He was an enormous beast, weighing at the time he was shot between 9 and 10 cwt.[12] I have taken one of his feet to cure and bring home so as to give an idea of what an enormous animal he was... the Bear shot this morning had three Arrow heads in him all under the right shoulder; one was bone, buried abut 3 inches in the shoulder, the other 2 were iron, completely

buried. The poor beast must have been in great pain, for it appears by the wounds they had been in some time.[13]

Several whales were also sighted in Franklin Bay. *Enterprise* reached the coastal polynya around 4 PM on the 31st and swung north within two miles of the shore. Here both Collinson and Shingleton noted and commented on the phenomenon of the Smoking Hills, where, at numerous points along the cliffs north of the mouth of the Horton River, plumes of smoke billow constantly from the ground and roll out across the sea or west across the tundra depending on wind direction. They were first reported by Dr. John Richardson, while travelling along the coast leading part of Sir John Franklin's second expedition in 1826. Collinson was not completely sure that he was seeing smoke: "In several of the ravines a column very like smoke was seen, but it may have been mist thrown up by the eddy wind under the high cliffs."[14] Shingleton, on the other hand, was sure he was seeing smoke, but his guess as to its source was a little wide of the mark: "Observed three volcanic eruptions issuing from a cliff; there was no fire but volumes of smoke."[15] The spontaneous combustion is in fact the result of oxidation of very fine-grained pyrite and organics, encouraged by periodic slumps and minor landslides that continually expose more combustible material.[16] Nonetheless, Shingleton's guess that the combustion was somehow due to volcanic activity is certainly understandable.

As *Enterprise* rounded Cape Bathurst that evening, an Inuit encampment of several tents was seen on the low spit, and soon an *umiak* was seen coming off, which tried to overtake the ship. Having a fair easterly wind, however, Collinson decided not to stop, since he wanted to round the Baillie Islands before dark. This he achieved, but then hove-to till daylight. There was a lot of ice in the mouth of Liverpool Bay, but, once through it, *Enterprise* stormed westwards past the Mackenzie Delta, "the ship running 8 knots—the first good run since we left Cambridge Bay."[17]

But then, on 2 September, the ship was working through ice again, "heavier than we have yet seen it."Some of the pieces as high as the main yard," to quote Shingleton.[18] The morning of the 3rd was calm, with a thick fog, but when it cleared in the afternoon the ship began working her way west through the ice again: "the breeze blowing very steady right aft but the heavy ice occasionally giving us a thump that would shake an ordinary ship to pieces but the old craft stands it all."[19]

By noon on the 4th Herschel Island was visible on the port bow, but by 8 PM it did not appear to be much closer. There now began a period of intense frustration. Although a surface current was running to the west, it appeared that beneath it, at a depth less than the ship's draught, a strong east-flowing current was running, carrying the ship with it; quite dense fog made the situation appear even more bizarre. When the fog cleared at noon on the 5th, the ship was again abeam of Herschel Island, about ten miles north of the island. But around midnight the ship encountered close ice and was forced to retreat. Collinson tried to work into open water closer inshore, but the wind was very light and variable, and the strong east-flowing current carried the ship steadily eastwards. By 8 PM on the 6th, she was back where she had been on the 4th.

On the 7th, unable to make any westward progress, *Enterprise* moored to a floe with ice anchors. There were large melt pools on the ice, and hence a pump was landed on the floe, hoses rigged, and the water tanks filled, "and delicious water it was, pure melted snow," as Shingleon delightedly reported.[20] When the fog cleared on the 8th, it revealed that the ship was now abeam of Point Kay: she had been carried back 40 miles since midnight on the 5th.[21] The ship was still among ice and, despite attempts at warping and blasting, made very little progress during the day.

In the midst of this activity some Inuit came off from Point Kay, four men in kayaks and a number of women in an *umiak*. To quote Shingleton,

> These poor people are not like our old neighbours [at Cambridge Bay]; they are very dirty and badly clothed. The men have the mouth ornament [labrets] and the cartilage of the nose drilled. They understand Towac meaning tobacco; the women was a little neater dressed, and their hair, I believe, if it was loose would trail the ground. Some 2 or 3 feet of it was fast at the back of the head—something like a large wisp of straw. They were also tattooed on the skin.[22]

Despite attempts at persuading the Inuit that the explosions associated with blasting the ice were innocuous, they evidently found them alarming and left the ship.

On the morning of the 9th, by blasting and warping, the crew finally managed to get their ship into open water and, with a fine east wind, she started running westwards again, with studding sails set. There was a tense moment when the lead suddenly indicated only 2¾ fathoms (16½ feet), since the ship drew 15 feet, but fortunately she cleared this shoal without touching. By 4 PM she was in totally ice-free water and storming westwards with a fair wind right aft; at 6:30 she was again abeam of Herschel Island, where she had been on the 5th. Several times she had encountered the strange east-flowing eddies and had been brought almost to a standstill, but this phenomenon was not encountered west of Herschel Island. Some Inuit were spotted on Herschel Island and several whales blowing in the waters around the island.

In the open water *Enterprise* ran west under easy sail all night, but around 5:30, in fog, she found herself pressed against the edge of a large floe and took several hours to get clear of it. By noon on the 10th she was off one of the long, narrow offshore bars just east of Point Manning, but then she ran into ice again. All afternoon the ship continued running west amongst this sailing ice, taking some hefty impacts against floes. But around 5 PM she encountered much heavier ice and was brought to a standstill. By 8 PM all efforts to extricate her had failed and the ship lay-to against a floe for the night, the rudder having been unshipped to prevent damage to it if the ship were nipped.

When the ice slackened next morning (11th), *Enterprise* got under way again, and made about a further eight miles to the west. The wind was quite strong, and two reefs were taken in the topsails to reduce her speed somewhat so as to lessen the impact of the inevitably frequent collisions with floes. When the depths in the only available open channel ahead became too shoal, soon after noon the ship was made fast to a grounded floe in a gale-force wind and driving snow.

By noon on the 12th the gale had slackened considerably, but the route west was completely blocked by heavy ice. In the afternoon two boats were sent to a nearby offshore shingle bar to gather driftwood, since vast amounts of driftwood lined the top of the beach; six loads were brought aboard, and then the boats were hoisted up, in hopes of getting under way again next morning.

As there was no improvement in the situation next morning, the boats were again sent to the offshore bar for firewood. One tree trunk was found, large enough for a topmast, but when it was trimmed it was found to be rotten on its lower side; nonetheless it provided a very fine long plank. In total 21 loads of wood were brought aboard, totalling 34 tonnes. Lt. Phayre had gone ashore to hunt ducks and had taken his dog Neptune with him to retrieve, but the outcome, as noted by Shingleton, was very unfortunate:

> The old dog Neptune was on shore with his master to fetch ducks out of the water after being shot. He was very fond of the sport. He brought two ducks out and was running about for some time afterwards; when his master fired at some birds, the dog started to run to him but at about 100 yards off he fell down, gave 2 or 3 kicks and died instantly.... The poor brute was buried on the reef by his master and one of the men.[23]

Next morning, since the ice had slackened, *Enterprise* got under way and, reaching open water, was soon sailing west across Camden Bay. Unfortunately it was foggy, and hence only light sail was carried and her speed kept to about 4 knots. But in the late afternoon the sun came out, and by 6 PM Flaxman Island was in sight. After coming within an ace of running aground, Collinson decided to moor to a grounded floe for the night.

Next morning (15 September), Lt. Jago was sent with a boat to sound the narrow channel between the pack to the north and Flaxman Island, but even the whaleboat ran aground several times. Meanwhile an easterly wind was packing ice into the western end of Camden Bay, threatening to block the ship in completely. During the morning, two bears were seen swimming towards the ship, but they swam back to the ice when they saw boats being lowered, then raced off across the ice.

There was little change over the next couple of days, except that more and more ice was being packed against the shore, jamming the ship ever more firmly. On the 16th, the floe to which the ship was moored split in two, producing a natural ice dock, and Collinson ordered the ship warped into this secure position.

There was little change in the situation over the next few days, the strong east wind persisting. The only excitement was provided, on two separate occasions, by bears. On the 18th a large bear was spotted lying on the floes about 300 yards from the ship: "He looked as silly as anything I ever saw, lolling his enormous head from one side to the other."[24] Some men headed towards it with guns and one of the dogs, but it took to the water as soon as it spotted the dog. Then, next day, what appeared to be a young bear came within range on the ice, but no guns were loaded and it ran off before any guns could be made ready.

The wind finally died on the 22nd, but the ship was now blocked in by ice, although Collinson took the opportunity to move the ship to a safer spot within the "dock." In the early evening, a ptarmigan flew out from the land and landed on one of the yards; it was shot from the yard with a shotgun.

It snowed steadily on the 23rd, the snow forming a steadily thickening sludge as it fell into the water of the "dock." By the 26th the ship was surrounded by new ice, and Collinson was forced to face the fact that the expedition's third arctic wintering had begun. In recognition of this he ordered some minor reductions in rations; tea and sugar were reduced by one sixth, and the daily rum ration was reduced to half a gill. Since this was the normal Royal Navy ration, this was not too great a hardship. There were adequate amounts of all other provisions. On the 29th a crack appeared in the young ice of the ship's "dock," and Collinson was afraid that the ship might experience some pressure, but the ice settled down again and the crack froze over. The third arctic wintering had definitely begun. Everyone on board must have been extremely disappointed, but for the officers under arrest, namely Skead, Parkes, and Phayre, the prospect of having to wait an additional year before they could present their cases to the Lords of the Admiralty must have been truly depressing.

On the other hand, they must have been relieved that they had managed to extricate the ship from the hazards of the narrow waters of Dease Strait, Coronation Gulf, and Dolphin and Union Strait relatively unscathed. The ship had grounded twice, certainly, but they had managed to refloat her with relative ease, and at the cost of only two anchors abandoned. And the officers must have been somewhat relieved that no more of their number had fallen foul of the captain's unpredictable moods, although that was to change before long. ●

11

WINTERING
AT CAMDEN BAY

The NIGHT OF 30 SEPTEMBER, the first night of the ship's third arctic wintering, was clear and sufficiently dark that the first splendid display of the aurora was visible. The next morning was calm and sunny with excellent visibility, the Romanzof Mountains clearly visible to the south: "they looked magnificent with the Sun on them and being white withal."[1] The usual preparations for wintering and the usual winter tasks began immediately. The men were set to cutting blocks of snow and ice for banking up the ship, and on 1 October the first balloon of the winter was filled and released; it floated off to the southwest.

On 3 October, since the ice was now bearing, Captain Collinson set off with three men to walk to the mainland to investigate the driftwood situation. After struggling through very rough ice for an hour, they came to smooth, new ice and soon reached the shore about five miles from the ship. To Collinson's relief the beach here, too, was lined with great masses of driftwood. Shingleton was also very relieved to hear this on the party's return:

So thank God we shall have lots of firing to warm us during the winter; a good fire and short provisions are to my fancy much preferable than a full allowance and perishing with cold—especially in this country.[2]

Next day Lt. Jago was sent ashore with two sledges to fetch driftwood, although it was bitterly cold and blowing hard. He and his party returned at 11:30, with one sledge-load of wood and one of the men riding on the other sledge. He had collapsed of exhaustion about four miles from the ship. Another party was sent for wood in the afternoon but barely managed to get back before nightfall.

At 8:30 on the morning of the 5th Captain Collinson set off eastwards with a party of men, with provisions for eight days, two sledges, a tent, sleeping gear, and cooking utensils, hoping to reach Barter Island and to trade with the Inuit. The remainder of the crew went ashore to fetch driftwood. In his journal entry for this date, Shingleton makes the first reference to the fact that one man, William Green-away, A.B., was seriously ill and had been confined to his cot for three months.

For the next few days work parties hauled driftwood from shore every day. Along their route there and back they picked up numbers of dead ducks and a loon; Shingleton surmised that these were young birds that had been caught by the freeze-up before they had learned to fly.

Collinson and his party returned to the ship at 2 PM on 12 October, the men exhausted. They had reached land at noon on the first day and had headed east. They saw several foxes and a wolf hunting ducks and found six or eight birds with their heads bitten off but otherwise untouched. In the afternoon they also encountered a strange ice feature: a heap of ice about 15 feet high, but consisting of layers of ice only about four inches thick piled on top of each other. Collinson's quite reasonable conjecture was that this was the result of a short-lived flood in a river that had already frozen to some thickness. Since they were in the delta of the Canning River, this event might have occurred on one of its distributaries.[3]

The next day (6th) was clear, and they again had a good view of the Romanzof Mountains to the south. They came across two groups of Inuit huts during the day, in one case clearly occupied quite recently judging by the footprints and wood chips. Before camping they crossed another shallow river, possibly another distributary of the Canning, or possibly the Katukturuk River.

On the 7th there was a strong easterly wind and driving snow, and conditions deteriorated over the course of the morning. Some of the men developed frostbite on their faces, and Collinson therefore stopped to camp at noon. They remained weather-bound throughout the following day (8th). At some time during the day, the dogs found the pork bag and demolished four days' rations. In the light of this, having sat in the tent for yet another day, on 10 October Collinson decided to start back to the ship, despite the fact that it was still blowing and drifting.

That evening they camped at the first group of Inuit huts they had encountered. One of the houses was substantially larger than the others, and the presence in it of two drum frames indicated that it was probably a dance house. Leaving some pres- ents in exchange, Collinson took the drum frames with him. The weather remained foul on the 11th, and although the party reached the shore as early as 2:30 PM, since he had no idea of the precise direction in which the ship lay, Collinson decided to camp for one more night, despite being so close to the ship.

At 4 AM the two men at the door of the tent woke everyone; they found themselves lying in six inches of water! The tent door was snowed up, and while breakfast was being cooked some of the men had to dig it out. The weather was foggy, but when it cleared somewhat, Collinson discovered that they were not at the seashore, but on the banks of one of the Canning distributaries. Heading north over about two miles of snow-covered tundra and a few frozen lakes, they reached the coast. As they headed out across the sea ice, the fog fortunately lifted around 11:00, allowing them to spot the ship.

It was a somewhat fruitless trip, in that they had not reached Barter Island, and due to poor visibility Collinson had been unable to survey the features along his route. Everyone was slightly frostbitten, but otherwise there were no ill effects from the trip.[4]

Immediately after the captain's return, things came to a head between him and his officers concerning his stipulations as to the obligations when going ashore to hunt or to get exercise, as laid out in an order he had issued on 5 October, the day he left on his trip to the east. In other words, the matter had been festering for the entire period of his absence. The problem had arisen directly from the fact that he had relieved so many of his officers of their duties. The aggrieved officers had conferred on the matter and had "volunteered" Lieutenant Jago, as the only commis- sioned officer still on duty, to present their concerns to the Captain; this he did, first verbally, then in writing:

Sir,

As you this morning peremptorily refused to listen to the representations which the Officers requested me to make to you relative to the orders you have lately issued about leave to go on shore, and ordered me to convey what I had to say in writing, I have now the honor to obey your commands.

You have ordered that the Officers must obtain your permission and that of the Commanding Officer before they can leave the ship. In my absence the commanding officers are by your rules Mr. Atkinson and Mr. Arbuthnott (Ice Mates). To ask permission to go on shore of those individuals the officers deem a degradation to which they dare not on any account submit.

You have also ordered that the Officers before they leave the ship, and on their return to the ship, are to make certain reports touching their intended and past proceedings to the Officer of the watch, who is either a Petty Officer or seaman. This also the Officers deem a degradation not to be borne.

You have ordered the Officers of the watch to inform you if the Officers should happen to return separately. This the Officers conceive to be an intolerable espionage, insulting to them; equally foreign to the Spirit and Practice of Her Majesty's Service; subversive to all the established relations between Officers and Men and only calculated to depress the former from their proper position and make them objects of compassion or contempt to their inferiors.

The Officers entertain the same sentiments in connection with their being mixed up in the liberty book on an equal footing with the Crew.

Though your order applies to "Every person" in the Ship the Officers are fully convinced that it had been framed for their peculiar annoyance.

They also remark how strange it is that permission to walk on shore, the single recreation this country affords, should be considered as a high personal favour and indulgence, flowing from your bounty alone, and to which they have no claim that does not centre in your goodness and condescension. The paragraph in your instructions which counsels care for the cheerfulness and comforts of those placed under your command have long ago convinced the officers that the Lords Commissioners of the Admiralty entertain sentiments of a very different character. The Officers desire to do nothing offensive or disrespectful to you, but they cannot deem themselves wrong in making you acquainted with what they smart under and view as a measure not only degrading to them but adopted for no other object but their degradation.

The above contains the substance of the representation I was requested to make to you and I have only to add that I fully agree with all that is there expressed.[5]

Collinson replied in writing two days later, deliberately misinterpreting the officers' complaints:

> To Lt Jago, Sir,
>
> I have to acknowledge receipt of your letter of the 13th inst. setting forth the four degradations to which yourself, the Surgeon and Assistant Surgeon are subject to in consequence of my order of the 5th inst. I can only regret that the measures which I have hitherto taken for the prevention and succour of distress & a trustworthy account of the game obtained should now be converted by you into an act of peculiar annoyance.
>
> In regard to the first paragraph I have on a former occasion pointed out to the surgeon that according to Chap. II, Art. 3 of the Queen's regulations, he is, in the absence of the Lieutenant and myself subject to the control of Officers otherwise of subordinate rank to him; and that it is his duty to make reports and to ask permission from the Officer in military command of the ship.
>
> With regard to the three last paragraphs, it will be observed in reference to my order book that they form part of the standing orders of the ship since April '52, under which date you will perceive that the Officers of the Watches are directed to enter the name of any person acting contrary to my orders in the log book, & the following paragraph occurs: "A liberty book will in future be filled up by the Officer of the watch after the following form & no person whatever is to go beyond a half mile circle round the ship without giving him the necessary information."
>
> The experience of a second winter convinces me of the utility of such a control. I forbear to make any comment on the style of your letter, simply assuring you that a factious opposition to your Captain can only end in your being removed from your present responsible situation.[6]

By this final sentence Collinson was threatening to relieve his last remaining executive officer of his duties. Despite this threat, as simply the spokesperson for his fellow officers Jago felt sufficiently strongly about the matter to respond in writing, refusing to knuckle under:

Sir,

I have the honor to acknowledge the receipt of your letter of the 15th Inst., and in reply beg leave to state that I did not willingly address you in writing on the subject of the complaints the Officers desired to make to you through me, the senior executive officer on duty. It was in obedience to your express order that I did so. If to represent the complaints which the Officers desired me to make to you be "factious opposition to my Captain," I must plead guilty to the charge you have made against me, otherwise I declare myself to be free from such an imputation. I stated in as clear a manner as I was able the complaints of the Gunroom officers, and then added that I fully agreed with all they had expressed. With regard to the style of my letter which you "forebear to remark upon" I can only say that I did not intend to make it otherwise than a clear statement of the particulars forming the grounds of the Officers' complaints.

I must point out to you that the complaint was made on behalf of the whole of the officers to whom your orders of the 6th Inst. was addressed, and not on behalf of the Surgeon, Assist. Surgeon and myself alone, as your letter states, and you will see by referring to my letter that the Officers' complaints regarding your orders on the subject of leave spring chiefly from the singular change of circumstances which have taken place since your orders of April /52 were issued. At that time three Lieutenants were doing duty, one of whom by your orders was always to be on board. It is now very different, when the Senior & Third Lieutenants, Surgeon, Second Master, and Assistant Surgeon are required in my absence to solicit permission from an inferior, before they can leave the ship.

So far from it being my desire or that of the Officers to make "factious opposition" to your orders, those very orders at the time of their issue caused much discontent, but the officers forbore to complain because you might not have any excuse for making the charge against them which you now make against me. A deep conviction that it is your object, still more to humiliate them, has now caused them to make the complaint which has given you so much offence.

If the second paragraph of your letter is intended to imply that your endeavours to obtain game for the use of the ship have been converted by me into "an act of peculiar annoyance" I am bound in justice to myself to state that you do me a grievous wrong. It is now, as it has always been, my great desire to procure the largest amount of game for the ship's use, but the Officers as well as myself have all along felt their efforts cramped by the numerous restrictions upon, and rules to be observed in obtaining leave of absence, yet notwithstanding this, you will permit me to remind you, that you have yourself expressed to me your satisfaction at the successful efforts made by the Officers in procuring by far the largest proportion of the whole of the game obtained by shooting parties.

I much regret, in common with the rest of the officers, that you deem it necessary to retain in force the present rules and restrictions regarding leave as they will effectually prevent any Officer's leaving the ship, for they cannot accept the humiliating conditions upon which, alone, leave of absence is to be obtained.[7]

And indeed, it would appear that, apart from Lieutenant Jago, when ordered to do so, none of the officers left the ship after this date.

The surgeon, Robert Anderson, also took exception to the specific reference to himself in Collinson's letter:

Sir,

Were I not to notice that paragraph of your letter to Mr. Jago which has special reference to me, you might justly conclude from my silence, that I admitted the accuracy of the statement made there and yielded assent to the conclusions to which the statement inevitably leads.

Far from doing this, I must positively affirm that you never once mentioned what was due from me to an officer in Military Command, of a rank otherwise subordinate to mine. A remonstrance from me was the immediate cause of what you said on the occasion to which you have called attention, and your statement clearly implies that I was either ignorant of my line of duty in the supposed case or [illegible word] to perform it. I beg to say that I was neither the one nor the other. In fact no such question arose nor, if we pause to consider it, could by any possibility have arisen at that time. Three Lieutenants were then all in good health and doing duty; by your orders these officers could never be absent from the ship all at the same time. Consequently there could not be any question as to my having to ask permission to go on shore from an officer in Command of inferior rank. Could I have seen into the remote future and foreseen that two Lieutenants would be suspended from duty and Mr. Atkinson raised to the Chief Military Command by some casual absence of the third. That was surely impossible.

The matter in dispute was of a very different character and, before stating what it, in reality, was, I beg to remark that if the business appeared to you altogether unimportant and only made a transient impression upon your mind, it was far different with me. It touched me home and all circumstances connected with it took firm root in my memory.

An order issued by you on the 30th of June led to the interview to which you refer in your letter. That order enjoined the Officers who wished to go on shore to obtain your permission, with that of the Commanding officer, and then to report themselves to the Officer of the watch before they left the ship as well as on their return. Only the latter part of the order was taken notice of by me. The ice-masters are keeping officers' watch. I deemed it humiliating to me to be compelled to carry reports to them; told you so and begged you to withdraw that part of your order. You refused, saying that what you had ordered was necessary for the good of the Service. I pressed my request and you again refused. Your very words were: "No one else has complained. I cannot legislate for you separately." And so the order remained as it was.

It was far from my mind to have revived in this manner the subject of an affair which, at the time it happened, gave me much annoyance and disgust, but the statement in your letter left me only the choice of acquiescing in the propriety of what I know to be altogether wrong, or of writing this letter.[8]

The captain's orders remained unchanged.

Hauling firewood from shore was the major activity over the next few weeks. Two sledge loads per day were brought until 21 October, and thereafter four sledge loads per day. When this activity ceased, on 7 November, 76 sledge loads of firewood had been cached at the edge of the smooth ice about 1 km from the ship. One log had a circumference of over 6 feet at its base, and weighed over 1 tonne.[9]

Other preparations for the wintering were also pushed ahead: an entranceway was built over the forward hatch to keep the lower decks warmer. The boats were lowered onto the ice on 14 October, and the main hold was cleared so that the men could sleep there and clothes could be dried there. Also, an emergency cache of provisions was stowed on deck. Due to a shortage of soap, a ration of one third of a cake of soap per man per month was instituted, and the frequency of laundry days was reduced.

One inconvenience that was experienced this winter but had not seemed to be such a problem in previous winters was condensation below decks. It was reduced to some degree by installing a ventilator over the main hatch, but nonetheless the deck beams had constantly to be wiped to avoid steady dripping. Sixteen men berthed in the orlop deck, somewhat drier than in the hold, and every day two of the men were allowed to dry their bedding behind the Sylvester stove.

On 28 October the men were banking up the ship's sides (see illustration p. 265) and cutting ice blocks for building steps up to the entranceway. On the morning of 4 November William Greenaway finally died from a combination of scurvy and dropsy (œdema). He had lost a great deal of weight but his stomach was greatly swollen. The night before he died, the surgeon had drained a large amount of fluid from his abdomen. Apart from Greenaway, however, the crew was in very good health. There was only one slight case of scurvy, that of Edward Adams, the Assistant Surgeon.

Greenaway was buried through the ice on the following afternoon. Collinson had considered burying him ashore, but apart from the distance involved (5 miles), he was concerned that a grave might be desecrated by bears, wolves, or the Inuit.

The major projects over the following few days were building a porch at the entranceway, a skittle alley from snow blocks, and a wooden observatory. Throughout this period there were spectacular auroral displays whenever the sky was clear; the effects on the night of 10/11 November were particularly impressive, as Shingleton noted:

> the Aurora Borealis shown with greater splendour than we ever witnessed before. It came down nearly to the Masthead of the ship; the colours at times were bright and of the hue of the rainbow but the predominant colour was red. At intervals it would disappear and then shoot out in broad flashes like lightning and at the same time appeared to make a rustling sound as of a woman's silk dress brushing past an object.[10]

A westerly gale blew for the following two days, making life for the watch keepers quite miserable, since the housings had not yet been set up. Indeed, on the night of the 13th/14th they were forced to stay below decks. The main and quarterdeck housings were set up on the following afternoon. Then, on the 15th, a wall of snow blocks was built across the quarterdeck, just ahead of the mizzenmast, to provide even better shelter.

The major project designed to keep the men occupied in the latter half of November was that of building a skittle alley alongside the ship, although it did not arouse the same excitement as in previous years since "that even is employment that loses all its interest having done so several times before."[11] To make matters worse, the partly finished walls blew down several times, and then on the 29th the ice beneath the skittle alley gave way due to its weight, and the wreckage had to be pulled down. Two days later (1 December), work began on a new skittle-alley, a billiard room, and the observatory on a grounded floe on the other side of the ship.

That evening the first theatrical performance was staged, the plays being *Hamlet* and *The Irish Widow*. Shingleton did not think *Hamlet* really appropriate, "as I think it is rather too high for our poor actors but, however, they done their best."[12] On the 3rd work proceeded on building the billiard room, as well as a covered passageway to it from the ship.

December was an extremely cold month; during the night of the 13th the temperature dropped to $-54°$F. Despite this, once the billiard room was finished on the 15th, it became a very popular place "and according to reports the table is far superior to last season's."[13] The evening of the 16th saw another theatrical performance, the piece being *The Mayor of Garret*. It was the only play offered since one of the actors for the other planned piece was sick. A concert was held in its stead. A week later (23 December), the plays staged were *The High Life above Stairs* and a repeat performance of *The Mayor of Garret*.

Since no caribou had been shot, the Christmas fare was not very exciting; each man got half a pound of pemmican, although a pint of sherry per man was perhaps seen as making good this deficiency.

Fetching wood from the depot about a kilometre away, then sawing and splitting it, represented the major activity of the crew throughout the winter, in terms of work, while the billiard room and the skittle alley were both very popular during off-duty hours.

In early January the Sylvester stove had to be shut down for three days while the armourer replaced part of the stovepipe. This provided a useful demonstration of just how beneficial the stove and its system of warm air pipes and vents were, particularly in keeping the condensation problem relatively under control. Fortunately, as compared to December especially, January was a fairly mild month. On 12 January the temperature rose to +22°F at noon, and the men were out on the ice playing rounders, the British equivalent of baseball.

By now the reserves of wood at the ship were almost exhausted, and what was left at the depot was frozen into the ice. Hence, on 17 January all hands set off with four sledges to retrieve a large tree trunk the captain had spotted on a shingle bar on his first trip ashore back in early October. It proved to be 94 feet long and 14" in circumference at its smallest end; cut up and split, it filled all four sledges.

On 7 February an attempt was made at recovering the wood from the depot that had become frozen into the ice by using explosives. Two canisters of gunpowder, each holding 10 lbs, were placed in holes in the ice beneath the wood and detonated, but they had no effect. By then the wood reserves were practically exhausted, and in light of the cold, stormy weather that allowed the men to go for wood on only four days in February, Collinson was obliged to give orders to use some of the limited coal stocks for heating.

In mid-February two minor accidents occurred, putting two men out of action for a while. Around the 10th William Murray, A.B., slipped and dislocated his knee while playing skittles. And then on the 12th William Simpkins, A.B., was carrying a large block of ice up the steps to the gangway when he fell; the block of ice fell on his hand, breaking some of the bones. In Shingleton's view the poor design of the steps was at least partly responsible for this accident.

A few days later, on 15 February, Shingleton gave vent in his journal to some of the few criticisms of any of the officers he allowed himself to commit to writing. The officers in question were Lt. Phayre and Lt. Jago, who found fault with what in their view was his extravagant use of candles issued to him:

> Consequently they were taken from me. At the same time I asked what I
> was to burn; my answer was, work in the dark. At the same time those two
> officers had a sufficient quantity of their own private candles to last them a
> long time.[14]

Next they accused him of wasteful consumption of the stores and provisions bought for the gunroom out of the officers' own pockets, rather than the general ship's stores. It had been anticipated that the stores bought at Hong Kong should last for 18 months or two years at the most, and yet Shingleton had managed to make them last almost three years. It must have been considerable consolation to him that he had the complete support of all the other officers:

At dinner the subject was broached and him [Lt. Phayre] and his confederate were totally defeated, for everyone in the mess were perfectly satisfied with my management and would not for one moment have a doubt of my strictly doing my duty. I would as soon have thought they would have charged me with drunkenness, for I have not tasted either spirits, beer or wine for nearly 4 years. The fact, I believe, is there is a misunderstanding between me and the first lieutenant, for I have seen a storm brewing for a very long time, but I little thought it was going to burst with such a treacherous accusation. The only benefit at present he has gained is the ill will of the rest of his messmates, but I have no doubt the both of them will try to do me an injury out of revenge, for a man that is capable of doing an action like that will not hesitate to go lower if possible.[15]

On 25 February, although the temperature averaged only −11°F in the shade, it rose to +29°F in the sun, and the snow on the ship's black hull was seen to be melting for the first time in 1854. Starting on the 24th, the trips ashore for firewood were begun again. Then on 1 March the crew was set to the task of removing the insulating layer of snow from the upper deck and the snow-block wall that had been built at the forward end of the quarter deck. Next day the curtains of the housing over the deck were taken down, and on the 9th the entire quarter-deck housing was removed.

From 13 March onwards the spring travelling parties began preparations for their planned trips.[16] The last theatrical performance of the season occurred on the evening of 16 March, the evening concluding with a rousing chorus of "God save the Queen."

On the 23rd the housing over the main deck was removed, but, as Shingleton recorded, the removal was evidently a little premature, "for last night the wind freshened from the W and blew strong so that the watch keepers were not able to keep the deck, there being not least shelter and the temperature down to −24°."[17] But over the next few days the temperature rose noticeably, and on the 27th Shingleton was able to dry some laundry outside for the first time: "It was a great pleasure to smell wind-dried clothes after so many months' drying between decks."[18] However, the fact that the removal of the housing was premature was further underlined by a three-day snowstorm at the end of March. The result was that the crew spent the morning of 1 April in clearing the deep drifts of snow from the deck.

Over the following few days the carpenters dismantled the captain's wooden observatory and modified it to function as a temporary dwelling for shooting parties, complete with a stove and a window. On 10 April two snow buntings were seen flying around the ship, the first of the season, true harbingers of spring. Good Friday (14 April) was designated a holiday, and since the temperature was 55°F in the sun, the men took full advantage of it, playing cricket on the ice, as well as the usual billiards, skittles, and cards. Streams of meltwater were running down the scuppers by the end of the afternoon.

On 17 April the re-configured observatory was moved ashore, and the carpenters stayed ashore to set it up as a shooting hut. They returned on the 21st, and three men moved ashore to the hut to spend some time shooting. Parties of men had been hiking ashore to shoot, but the round-trip across the ice of at least ten miles left little time for shooting; nonetheless, they had brought back a fair number of ptarmigan. Unfortunately, however, quite a number of men from these shooting parties, as well as from the wooding parties, were suffering from snow blindness from the sun's glare off the snow.

Having postponed his departure for several days, the captain set off with three sledges at 7:30 AM on 25 April. Two of the sledges were provisioned for 27 days, and the third, a support sledge, for just a week. They headed north, the captain's aim being to settle the question of whether there was an open sea to the north, at around 73°N. Shingleton, however, suggested a different objective, namely, that they might find land to the north, since many thousands of ducks had been flying in from seaward after the ship became frozen in the previous fall.[19] Whatever the objective, he was not very optimistic about their chances: "I think that the travelling will be heavy, for as far as the eye can search from the ship the ice is very hummocky."[20]

His prediction proved to be correct: the captain arrived back at the ship with one of the men at 11 AM on the 27th. Right from the start they had encountered extremely rough pressure ice:

> a confused mass of hummocks, from which the snow-drift, owing to the prevalence of easterly and westerly winds, lay in ridges directly across our path; so that our progress in either of those directions might have been practicable; but the difficulty of mounting the steep sides of the ridges, and the strain upon the sleighs in their descent, forbade all hope.[21]

He had therefore turned back at 10 AM on the second day. Soon afterwards one of the sledges collapsed and the loads had to be relayed with the other two sledges.

Worse still, one of the men had a bad fall and knocked himself unconscious. It was some time before he was missed, and he was still unconscious and suffering from the onset of hyperthermia when he was found. Immediately after the captain reached the ship, a party of four men was sent off with a spare sledge to help the party back to the ship. Most of the men from the sledge party suffered from severe snow blindness for the next two days.

Over the next couple of weeks the men were busy restowing the hold with the tanks from the ice alongside the ship, and with hawsers, ropes, sails, and so forth that had been stowed on deck for the winter. Wooding parties trudged steadily between shore and ship and back again, while shooting parties went ashore to the shooting hut for varying lengths of time. They brought back substantial numbers of ptarmigan, including 36 on 13 May. On the previous day one of the wooding parties had seen the first caribou of the season.

At 7 AM on 15 May Captain Collinson set off with a party of men, aiming to head up the Canning River and, if possible, to climb to the summit ridge of the Romanzof Mountains. It was an amazingly warm day, with the temperature reaching 48°F in the shade; melt pools were forming everywhere on the ice, and because of this and the deep, wet snow, high boots were required for any travel outside the ship. During the morning the first goose of the season was seen.

The captain and his party got back aboard on the afternoon of the 20th. They had started off eastwards, but had been unable to find the channel of the Canning because the snow was too deep. Hence, on the second day they had struck south, inland. In places the tundra was bare of snow, although it was still quite deep among the willows fringing the river channels. At one point they ran across the tracks of three caribou that a wolverine had been pursuing. Ptarmigan were plentiful, and they shot 30 during the day. The weather was foggy on the 17th, but when the land ahead started rising steeply in mid-afternoon, Collinson decided to camp for the night. According to his aneroid barometer, they were about 1000 feet above sea level. Next morning the fog had cleared, revealing the front of the Romanzof Mountains rising into the clouds ahead of them. Leaving the tent standing, with some of the men Collinson started up the mountainside, which rose at an angle of about 35° and was covered with sharp-edged sandstone talus. When they reached the cloud level, they halted on a narrow ledge at a height (by aneroid) of about 2250 feet, the only vegetation being moss and lichens. Occasional breaks in the cloud revealed mountains to the west and east, but Collinson was unable to get a clear view to the north, which had been one of the aims of the trip. Returning to the tent he moved camp to the northeast, hoping for a chance of another climb in clear weather next day but the fog did not clear, and he started back to the ship.[22] Their total bag of ptarmigan was 96 birds.

Next day (21 May) the few remaining invalids were discharged by the surgeon, which meant that there were no men on the sick list. That morning Lt. Jago set off with a party of four men with six days' provisions to set up a shooting camp about 16 miles from the ship. Two hours later three sledges set off to fetch firewood but returned empty-handed; they had been unable to get ashore since, with the melt-water flowing off the land, the ice was inundated for a distance of over three miles from shore. The wooding party reported seeing six ducks, the first of the season.

On the 27th, lightened by the amount of coal, provisions, and water consumed during the winter, the ship rose a foot, as she floated off the ice in which she had been embedded. In the afternoon Lt. Jago and his party returned with 247 ptarmigan. The lieutenant set off again on the 29th with eight men for the shooting camp, while two sledges went ashore for driftwood. They managed to get ashore this time, but on their return reported that the ice was getting very dangerous; they had been waist-deep in water in places.

Work to prepare the ship for sea had been going forward steadily, and on 30 May Shingleton was able to report,

> the ship is all ready for a start with the exception of bending sails, a few casks and a little lumber alongside which would take at most 2 hours and we should be ready. We look quite natty now, the masts and mastheads painted, all the ropes rove and everything ready for use.[23]

But, just as a precaution, the boats were being equipped and provisioned, in case the ship was not freed from the ice and the entire crew had to make their way westwards along shore leads in the boats. Provisions for such a contingency were packed in casks of a size convenient for handling in the boats. As a further preparation for putting to sea, the ship was watered from the meltwater pools on the ice alongside.

On 1 June the dinghy was hauled over the ice to the edge of the shore lead, to be left there for ferrying parties between the shore and the relatively dry fast ice. On the 3rd Lt. Jago and his men returned, with 184 ptarmigan and one swan. While the hunting was relatively easy, the tundra and the remains of the snow were so saturated by the melt that the hunters were wet most of the time. Nonetheless. the lieutenant and his party set off again next day. They and another shooting party returned on the 10th with a total of 215 ptarmigan, eight geese, and 24 ducks. They reported that the birds had started laying, some of the ptarmigan nests containing as many as ten eggs.

Early on the morning of 13 June a party of five men left for the offshore bar abeam of the ship since large numbers of ducks and geese had been seen on and near it. They took an inflatable Halkett boat with them for crossing the stretch of water along the shore, but unfortunately a fresh wind was raising quite a sea and the boat capsized. Fortunately the two men in it could swim, but they lost most of their provisions and all their ammunition. Three of the party came back to the ship to replenish their supplies. Lt. Jago went back with them next day to check that the others were all right and returned to the ship leaving the five men on the island. They returned on the 19th with 60 to 80 ducks and geese. Shingleton's assessment: "Considering the weather and the indifferent arms most of them had and being not the best shots, they did not do amiss."[24] On that same day the pinnace and cutter were hoisted aboard from the ice where they had spent the winter.

One of the shooting parties came back aboard on the 24th with 112 ducks, three geese, and 16 ptarmigan, while Lt. Jago and his group returned on the afternoon of the 25th with a total of 135 birds—ducks, geese, and ptarmigan. As Shingleton stressed, their return trip had not been easy: "the ice is now getting dangerous for [there are] large holes through in many places and they are not perceptible till a person is in them. In some places they had to wade nearly to the armpits."[25] Over the last few days of the month, however, there were frequent snow showers, and the water in the melt pools remained frozen all day. During this period the dinghy was sent ashore to recover everything from the shooting hut (the former observatory) except for its framework.[26]

On the last day of the month, Collinson made a decision that, while undoubtedly fiscally correct, probably appeared like petty-minded harassment, particularly since he had allowed the matter to lie dormant for four years. In a letter addressed to the Secretary of the Admiralty, Collinson announced,

> I have the honor to acquaint you that in accordance with an order from their Lordships dated Jany. 17th '50, having reference to the messing of Mr. Miertsching, Esquimaux Interpreter, I advanced from the public money the sum of 75£ sterling to the Gunroom Mess of this ship on the 29th of June 1850. And Mr. Miertsching not having joined I have caused the sum of £12 10s cash to be charged on the ship's books against the Officers named in the

margin. [Lt. Phayre, Lt. Jago, Mr. Skead, 2nd Master, Anderson, surgeon, Adams, Asst. surgn., Lt. Parkes].[27]

Late on the evening of 1 July about 40 Inuit were seen approaching from the east, but due to the state of the ice they did not reach the ship until the following morning. They were hauling three *umiaks*, which they used to cross pools and leads that were too wide to jump across. One of the young men had several buttons with a remarkably long message stamped on them: "Gone N. E. of Point Barrow *Investigator* August 1850, *Enterprise* August 1851, *Plover* at Port Clarence 1852, squadron with steamers searching N. and W. of Parry Islands 1852, depots of provision Refuge Inlet, Port Leopold and Admiralty Inlet, in Barrow Straits."[28] This was no doubt intended for the guidance of any survivors of the Franklin expedition that these Inuit should happen to meet and had presumably been given to them by Captain Rochfort Maguire of HMS *Plover*. One of the Inuit also had a printed notice from HMS *Plover*, dated 4 July 1853 at Point Barrow, to the effect that she had wintered there under Commander Maguire in 1852–53 and planned to spend a further winter there, indicating that she was still there at the time this notice reached *Enterprise*.[29] The notice further reported that there had been no word from HMS *Investigator*, and from this Collinson surmised (correctly) that she had become beset somewhere on the coast of Banks Island for one or probably even two winters. On the basis of all this information Collinson decided to send a boat west to Point Barrow to make contact with Maguire as soon as sufficient shore leads had developed.

Of the Inuit themselves Shingleton recorded,

The natives had come from the eastward—we suppose the Mackenzie—men, women and children were the most filthy looking wretches I ever saw, nothing to compare to those we had been used to on Victoria Land. They actually stink. Three of them had muskets with them and powder horns given, I suppose by some of the Hudson Bay officers in trade.[30]

The Inuit left while the Sunday church service was being held, but as he feared that they might make off with one of the shooting tents that was still on shore, Collinson sent a party of men after them. They caught up with them at the edge of the ice, just as they were loading the oars, mast, and sail from the dinghy into their *umiaks*, and managed to retrieve them. Fog rolled in soon after this, and the party of seamen was unable to keep an eye on them thereafter; when it cleared, however, they discovered that the Inuit had dismantled and removed the frame of the shooting hut.

Two days later Shingleton reported that everyone was ready to start on the journey home, either by ship or, if necessary, by boat:

> We are all ready for a start with the exception of bending the sails which will take but little time. The boats likewise are all ready and each man has 15 lbs. of clothing made up ready to take with him in the event of leaving the ship. The boats with all their gear and stores and provisions for 35 days will not admit of more clothing to go. For my own part I should be a very great loser for I have a great number of skins of different birds and animals for stuffing, Esquimaux clothing and implements for shooting and fishing, besides cannisters of their make, and Chinese work as well. But we trust in God we shall all get round [Point Barrow] safe in the ship.[31]

On that same day (4 July 1854), in a letter to Colonel John Barrow, Keeper of the Records at the Admiralty, Collinson made a brief acknowledgement of the problems on board, as he saw them:

> The men have done their work very well & with great cheerfulness.... I wish I could express the same satisfaction with regard to the officers, but I am sorry to say I have great cause of offence & that I fear one, if not more, court-martials will have to take place. It is a most lamentable thing that in expeditions of this description Men will not be at some pains to govern their tempers & overcome their selfishness but such is human nature. Nothing to do & therefore they must quarrel.[32]

It is noteworthy that the captain saw the problems on board as arising from dissension between the officers. Apart from the one reported case of the dispute between Lt. Phayre and John Atkinson, the ice mate, all the disputes had been between himself and his various officers. He was clearly in denial about the problem originating in any way with himself.

On the morning of 5 July, Captain Collinson went ashore with three men to choose a location for leaving a cairn and to take some readings on the height of the Romanzof Mountains since they were completely clear. There was a shooting party already at the tent on shore, and they had been signalled to bring the dinghy across from shore to the edge of the ice but failed to respond. For just such a situation the captain had taken a Halkett boat with him and, launching it from the ice, the men began paddling towards shore about a mile away. At this point, however, a wind got up, the Halkett boat sprang a leak and started to sink, and the captain found himself in the embarrassing situation of having to take refuge on a convenient floe. At this point, the dinghy came off from shore to rescue him and his party.

Even then, however, his troubles were not over. Where he tried to approach the land, the water was extremely shallow; he was forced to leave the dinghy and wade about three quarters of a mile to shore. Once on shore, however, he was able to clarify several features of the landscape. He found that what he had mistaken for the eastern end of Flaxman Island was a headland at the mouth of the Canning River, or at least of one of the distributaries that cross its delta. This channel was about half a mile wide, but on wading across it, he found it to be not more than two feet deep. He also determined, correctly, that the Staines River is simply the most westerly distributary of the Canning. On the tundra, he noted, "the flowers were out in all their beauty, and showed a variegated carpet of blue, purple and yellow."[33]

Throughout the evening of the 8th and the following night, a powerful thunderstorm rolled in, with thunder, lightning, a strong west wind, and pouring rain. It broke up the ice near shore, and by the morning of the 10th there appeared to be enough open water to the west for a boat to travel alongshore. Lt. Jago was ordered to take a party of six men and the first whaler and to try to reach HMS *Plover* at Point Barrow; they set off at noon, with provisions for a month.

On the 13th 16 Inuit arrived in kayaks and traded a few fish. One of them had a drum, and they gave a display of Inuit dancing and singing. In return, some of the ship's actors put on some of their costumes, to the great amusement of the Inuit. Collinson took the opportunity to obtain the Inuit names for about 15 locations from the mouth of the Mackenzie to Point Barrow.

On the 14th the boatswain was sent ashore with a party of men to try fishing in the mouth of the Canning with a seine net. He mistook the directions, however, and although he tried fishing in a lake, he was unsuccessful. On his way back, however, he struck the last of the tents that had been used by shooting parties, since the ship would be starting for home imminently.

This must have been an attractive prospect for all concerned. Although the ship had lain snugly in its wintering berth, unthreatened by ice pressures, the novelty of an arctic wintering had clearly worn off. The officers under arrest (Skead, Phayre, and Parkes) must have been especially happy to have survived the winter in their strange half-life, on board the ship, but not really part of the ship's normal routines and activities.

Even Lieutenant Jago, the only one of the ship's lieutenants not under arrest, had fallen foul of the captain for acting as spokesman for all the officers with regard to the contentious issue of Collinson's orders about officers going ashore. And even the surgeon, Dr. Anderson, had a run-in with the captain over the same issue. And the source of that dispute lay in the fact that so many of the officers were under arrest! By insisting that they must, before leaving the ship, get permission from the captain and the commanding officer (one of the ice-mates), and then must report to the officer of the watch on their return, the officers felt that they had been placed in a degrading situation, since the commanding officers and the officers of the watch (unless Lieutenant Jago was on duty) were men such as the ice-mates and some of the warrant officers. Predictably, Collinson refused to make any adjustments in the orders that he had issued with regard to officers leaving the ship. The tensions on board must have become increasingly intolerable. ●

12

HOMEWARD BOUND

*O*u THE AFTERNOON OF 15 JULY the ice, and *Enterprise* with it, began drifting eastwards; the men were ordered over the side with ice-saws and soon cut the ship clear of the floe in which she had spent the winter. By 6 PM she had drifted about two miles to the east. The ship was then moored with ice-anchors to a floe.[1]

Next morning *Enterprise* got under way, for the first time in 1854, no doubt to the intense relief of the arrested officers, Skead, Parkes, and Phayre, in particular; the ship made about ten miles to the west before being brought to a halt by ice again off Point Brownlow. A boat was sent ashore, but on its return the report was not very encouraging: while there was plenty of open water west of Flaxman Island, it was too shallow to float the ship. Next day the ship was surrounded by ice, which all began drifting westwards with a strong east wind. The floe to which the ship was moored fortunately grounded; the ice anchors were doubled, and the topgallant yards sent down.

On the 18th the ship continued to drive westwards, along with the ice. Three boats were sent ashore for wood from a shingle bar, which was liberally covered with driftwood. In the afternoon boats were sent ashore with a seine net and returned with 17 small arctic char.

A warm west wind on the evening of the 18th broke up the ice and produced a narrow shore lead, but the ship now drifted eastwards with the ice. At midnight Collinson made sail and clawed his way westwards, beating into the wind in short tacks between ice and shore. At noon, the ship was abeam of the spot where she had wintered and the garbage dump was spotted on the ice, only half a mile from where it had accumulated over the winter. Once again *Enterprise* moored to ice anchors.

On the 20th an easterly wind and increasing areas of open water promised the possibility of further westward progress. But warping into the open water took several hours. This was quite fortunate, in that before the ship got clear an *umiak* came off from shore; in addition to a number of Inuit, it contained a number of Gwich'in Indians (see illustration p. 266). One of them produced a message that read,

> The printed slips of paper delivered by the officers of HMS *Plover* on the 25th of April, 1854, to the Rat Indians, were received 27th of June 1854, at the H. B. [Hudson's Bay] Company's establishment, Fort Youcon; supposed Lat. 66° N. , Long. 7° 55'W (? 137°). The Rat Indians are in the habit of making periodical trading excursions to the Equimaux along the sea-coast. They are a harmless, inoffensive set of Indians, ever ready and willing to render every assistance they can to whites.
>
> WM. LUCAS HARDISTY,
> Clerk in Charge
> Fort Youcon, June 27th, 1854.[2]

The printed messages to which Hardisty referred had probably been delivered to Fort Yukon by the four Gwich'in Indians (not necessarily the same as those who now came aboard *Enterprise*) who were encountered by Captain Rochfort Maguire of HMS *Plover*, then wintering at Point Barrow, at Point Berens (now Okutok Point, at the east end of Harrison Bay) on 5 May 1854. They were then heading east, but may have been to Point Barrow or in contact with some of the Inuit from there. Maguire, too, was heading east, but, intimidated by the four Gwich'in (who were all armed with muskets) and the possibility that they might be members of a larger group, decided to head back to Point Barrow.[3] One must be impressed by the speed with which the Gwich'in had thus relayed information back and forth: from Point

Barrow on 25 April to Point Berens on 5 May, to Fort Yukon (at the confluence of the Porcupine and Yukon rivers) by 27 June, and back north to Flaxman Island by 20 July.

Collinson describes these Indians as follows:

These people were entirely different-featured from the Esquimaux, and were clad in blankets, and wore as necklaces and ornaments through the septum of the nose the eye e quaws (Dentalium), which are mentioned by Simpson in his narrative, and which form the currency on the N.W. coast of America. They were a quiet, well-behaved people, and I was sorry to turn them away somewhat unceremoniously; but the ship, having cleared the floe, began to move through the water at a rapid rate, which endangered the oomiak coming in contact with pieces of ice; and they at length shoved off, loaded with several useful presents, and a tin cylinder containing information. They appeared, like the natives of Sitka and Vancouver Island, to place a value on some papers of vermilion, while our friends the Esquimaux were much more intent on blue beads. It is no doubt from them, and most likely from the Youcon establishment, that the latter obtained the firearms, as each of the men who visited us on this occasion was armed with a musket.[4]

Shingleton's account adds some useful additional details: He noted that they were

the first and only Indians we have seen on the coast. It appears from a paper they had with them that they came from Fort Youcon, one of the H.B.C. forts. They trade along the sea coast yearly with the Esquimaux. We found by the paper which was written on 27th June 1854 that the Plover was still at Point Barrow on the coast. We hoped that Lt. Jago and his boat's crew reached her in safety for it is dangerous navigation for Boats amongst heavy ice. The Indians were a fine looking set of men, at least much more so than the Natives here on the coast. There were 2 females with them and nearly all had their faces painted in red streaks, besides a great profusion of Beads round their necks and wrists. They were very poorly clothed, principally worn-out European clothes but I am happy to say that they went away much better. They had 10 muskets with them and we gave them some Powder and shot.[5]

On 21 July, among mundane entries in the ship's log such as "2 four lb. tins of soup & 30 lbs. of carrots condemned," and "Set fore top mast & main top gt. Studding sails. Main Royal and mizzen top gt. Sail," there appears an eye-catching entry: "Placed Mr. Skead, 2nd master under close arrest for breach of 2nd Article of War."[6]

The Articles of War that then applied were those dating from 1749, as specified in *An Act for amending, explaining and reducing into one Act of Parliament, the Laws relating to the Government of His Majesty's Ships, Vessels and Forces by Sea (22° Geo. GG. C. 33, 1749)*. The text of Article II stated that

> All Flag officers, and all Persons in or belonging to His Majesty's Ships or Vessels of War, being guilty of profane Oaths, Cursings, Execrations, Drunkenness, Uncleanness, or other scandalous Actions, in Derogation of God's Honour, and Corruption of good Manners, shall incur such Punishment as a Court-martial shall then see fit to impose, and as the Nature and Degree of their Offence shall deserve.[7]

Next day (22 July) the following General Order appeared in the Captain's Night Order Book:

> Mr. Skead is placed under close arrest. The Officers are forbidden to communicate with him except by my permission.
>
> On reference to the Officer of the watch through Sergt. Jeffrey [Sergeant of Marines] he will be allowed to take what exercise is necessary for the good of his health on the port side in harbour & lee side at sea of the Quarter deck between the hours of 7 AM. & 8 PM., but on occasion of the hands being turned up or any particular duty going forward he is ordered below.[8]

Apparently Collinson had overheard Skead utter some (in his opinion) offensive remarks, although there appears to be no record of what they were, and Collinson evidently refused even to identify the precise remarks to Skead. Particularly since Collinson was now placing much more stringent restrictions on Skead, it is not surprising that he lodged a formal complaint in writing:

Sir,

I find it stated in the Ships' Log-book of 21st Inst. that I am placed under close arrest for a breach of the 2nd Article of War, & I further learn from the order book of 22nd that you have condemned me to solitary confinement, forbidding even my brother officers to hold Converse with me, thus aiming to mark me a man of deep but undefined infamy.

It is now, Sir, Two & a half years nearly that I have been in arrest, upon a charge which it was proved to you at the time it was made, to be unfounded, but you perverted the evidence that was given in my favour & made it appear as if spoken against me, & this you persevered in, notwithstanding the remonstrances of the Officers whose evidence you so misused. Since then you have made charges against me which you know to be unfounded, misrepresenting facts to my prejudice in the presence of all the Officers who knew them to be misrepresentations & upon these you condemned & punished me most iniquitously.

You now place me under close arrest, denying me access to the Gunroom, & forbidding the Officers from holding communication with me, upon the undefined charge of a breach of the 2nd Article of War, a charge which is, if possible, more unfounded than the others. You refused to make me acquainted with my particular offence, & have produced no evidence in support of a charge which you frame upon a private conversation you state to have overheard in the Gun Room about Noon on 21st inst. Whatever, Sir, you may have overheard while listening to my conversation which was not intended for your ear, I positively deny having used such language as that mentioned in the 2nd Article of War, but whatever it may be that you did overhear, I feel confident that I stated nothing that is untrue.

The deep & unrelenting animosity with which you have pursued me from the time of our quitting the ice in 1850 up to the present moment convinces me that I can look for neither justice nor even decent treatment at your hands. Yet I cannot rest satisfied without giving a distinct denial to an accusation so unfounded as the present one is, which is so calculated to blacken my moral character in the eyes of those unacquainted with the truth, and to protest against the felon-like treatment to which you have so arbitrarily & so unjustly condemned me.[9]

Collinson remained unmoved.

The following two weeks were extremely frustrating for all concerned. Prog-ress westwards was extremely slow, hampered by ice and fog; Collinson pushed westwards whenever he could and moored to ice anchors whenever the fog made it impossible to see where he was going. In case Lt. Jago should pass the ship in the fog, a gun was fired every half hour when it was foggy.

On the morning of 22 July the ice slackened enough to allow a boat to run in to the shore about two miles away; a pole was erected and a cylinder with a message for Lt. Jago was buried. On the 25th another pole was erected, and another cylinder with a message was buried, this time on John Franklin's Return Reef.

On the evening of the 27th two men, one of them the ship's cook, Richard Thomas, had a very narrow escape. They had been sent out onto the ice to recover the ice anchors when the floe they were standing on broke up and parts of it capsized. Neither man could swim, and although Thomas landed in the water, he was able to grab a rope thrown him from the ship and was hauled aboard; the other man was standing on another piece of the floe and managed to keep his balance.

Around noon on the 30th several kayaks and *umiaks* were seen working their way towards the ship through the ice from the west. They contained about 40 men, women and children, who came aboard; from their dress it was guessed that they were from Point Barrow. They handed over some printed messages from HMS *Plover*, dated 1 and 2 July, to the effect that she had been ordered south. On the back of one of them was a handwritten message from Lt. Jago:

> *July 17th, 2* AM Encamped on the ice not being able to get along, either in shore or off. The boat is greatly strained, and I think, if we get much more launching, we shall not be able to return till we fall in with some ship to repair her.
>
> C. T. JAGO, LIEUT.
> Drew Point, Enterprise boat. There are
> three tins of pemmican at Berens Point.[10]

The Inuit also handed over a major part of the *Illustrated London News* for May 1851, which contained an account of the opening of the Great Exhibition of 1851, as well as a fragment of another newspaper dated October 1852, which gave a glimpse of what had been happening in the outside world at that time. One of the Inuit could speak a few words of English and was able to convey the information that he had been to sea in *Plover* and had visited Port Clarence. The Inuit also traded a substantial amount of caribou meat, some geese, and a swan.

The frustrating struggle to get westwards continued until 6 August; the only difference was that there were numerous whale sightings during this time. On the 5th a boat was sent ashore to erect another pole and to leave another message for Lt. Jago. Finally, on the afternoon of the 6th *Enterprise* reached open water and was able to make all sail. By the following afternoon she was storming westwards with a wind right aft, making a steady 6 knots.

At 1 AM the house that Maguire had left at Point Barrow came into view and Collinson hove-to off it and fired a gun. Almost immediately Lt. Jago and his party came off in the whaleboat and clambered aboard. He reported that *Plover* had sailed on 20 July, just three days before he had arrived there. This was very unfortunate since Jago had been carrying mail which would now be much delayed in reaching England.

Jago and his men had had a very trying trip from *Enterprise*'s wintering site; it had taken them 25 days to reach Point Barrow. They had had to battle ice almost the entire distance, repeatedly hauling the boat over ice floes or across shingle banks to reach a lead or polynya that would allow them to gain a little more westing. In the process, the boat became so badly damaged that Jago had opted to stay and wait for *Enterprise* to arrive, rather than starting back to meet her.

Wasting no time, Collinson bore away as soon as the boat was hoisted aboard. By 4 AM *Enterprise* had rounded Point Barrow, which had for months been seen as the major obstacle to their progress homewards. By noon, the ship was abeam of the Seahorse Islands, and the last ice disappeared astern. By Collinson's calculation, 1164 days had passed since they had first sighted the ice on the way north in the summer of 1851, during which time there had been no ice in sight on only 38 days! By 6 PM that evening they had made a satisfying run of 100 miles from Point Barrow. There were walrus and whales in sight practically the entire day.

In the early hours of 9 August, a current swept the ship uncomfortably close to the shoals off Icy Cape, which on this occasion were not "signposted" by grounded floes. By midnight on the 9th they were off Cape Lisburne, but then the wind dropped and it was 8 PM on the 10th before they reached Point Hope. The ship was becalmed in fog throughout the 11th, but around 9 AM the lookout in the crow's nest spotted four sails. It had been three years and one month since the last ship had been sighted. These proved to be American whalers; *Enterprise* closed with the nearest one and a boat was sent aboard her. She proved to be *John*, out of New Bedford. The boat returned with some newspapers and with the rather vague information that HMS *Investigator* "had been reported upon the eastern side." A boat was next sent to *James Andrews* of New Bedford, whose captain, Benjamin Kelley, then came aboard, with a welcome gift of potatoes and pumpkins and more newspapers. His information about *Investigator* was a little more accurate, but still rather vague, namely that "she had communicated with the Eastern expeditions." Even this was a relief to Collinson. In fact, *Investigator* had been held prisoner by the ice in Mercy Bay on the north coast of Banks Island through the winters of 1851–2 and 1852–3. Lt. Bedford Pim had reached her in the very early spring of 1853 from Captain Henry Kellett's *Resolute*, wintering at Dealy Island on Melville Island, and *Investigator*'s officers and men had trekked across the ice to that ship.[11] Lt. Samuel Gurney Cresswell (of HMS *Investigator*), along with some of the sickest men, travelled east to the depot ship *North Star* later that same spring, and sailed home to England on board the supply ship *Phoenix* later that same year. This is how the news of *Investigator*'s fate had reached the United States.

The rest of *Investigator*'s officers and men were destined to spend a fourth winter in the Arctic, however. When the ice broke up, *Resolute* and her consort *Intrepid* had been able to get only as far east as Cape Cockburn on Bathurst Island, before becoming beset for a further winter. Then, in the spring of 1854, on orders from his superior officer, Captain Sir Edward Belcher, Captain Kellett abandoned his two ships, and he and his men, along with M'Clure and his men, hiked across the ice to Beechey Island. They travelled home to England on board *North Star*, *Phoenix*, and *Talbot* in the fall of 1854.[12]

Continuing southwards, *Enterprise* crossed the Arctic Circle at 2:30 PM on the 13th, and by 8 AM on the 14th was off Cape Prince of Wales, but, frustratingly, with a light wind dead ahead, so that progress could be made only by endless tacking. That afternoon a fleet of 42 *umiaks* was seen heading northwards; a few of them altered course to run alongside *Enterprise* to barter furs and walrus tusks. They wanted only rum and brandy in exchange.

There followed almost a week of vainly trying to beat round Cape Prince of Wales against persistent southerly winds. It was not until the morning of the 21st that *Enterprise* finally managed to double that cape and run east to Port Clarence. Even then, however, the running battle between Collinson and his officers continued. An entry in the ship's log at 10:30 that morning reads as follows: "Placed Lieut. Jago under close arrest for breach of 23 and 33 Articles of War."[13]

Article 23 reads as follows:

If any Person in the Fleet shall quarrel or fight with any other Person in the Fleet, or use reproachful or provoking Speeches or Gestures, tending to make any Quarrel or Disturbance, he shall upon being convicted thereof, suffer such Punishment as the Offence shall deserve, and a Court-martial shall impose.[14]

Article 33 reads:

If any Flag Officer, Captain or Commander, or Lieutenant belonging to the Fleet, shall be convicted before a Court-Martial of behaving in a scandalous, infamous, cruel, oppressive, or fraudulent Manner, unbecoming the Character of an Officer, he shall be dismissed from His Majesty's Service.[15]

A General Order pertaining to Lt. Jago's arrest and identical in wording to that pertaining to Skead's close arrest a month earlier appeared in the Captain's Night Order Book for 22 August.[16] While Lieutenant Jago may have protested verbally, he appears not to have lodged a written protest; certainly there is none in Collinson's In-Letter Book. Hence we are left in the dark as to the details of his alleged offence. But his arrest meant that the situation on board HMS *Enterprise* on her arrival at Port Clarence, as reported by Lieutenant Philip Sharpe of HMS *Rattlesnake*, a situation that he and his fellow officers found utterly bizarre and intolerable, was absolutely correct: all three Lieutenants and the Second Master were under arrest; only the Surgeon, the Assistant Surgeon, and the two ice mates were at liberty. The ice-mates, the quartermaster, and the carpenter were acting as watch officers.

As *Enterprise* approached Port Clarence, a ship could be seen lying at anchor; on reaching her she was found to be HMS *Rattlesnake*, Captain Henry Trollope. Collinson quickly learned that *Plover* had been here but had sailed again, bound back to Point Barrow only two days earlier; presumably *Enterprise* had missed her in the fog. Equally frustrating was the news that the supply ship *Trincomalee* (Captain Wallace Houston),had left for San Francisco only that morning. Collinson now decided that *Rattlesnake* should head south to San Francisco with his dispatches, while he took *Enterprise* back north to Point Barrow to recall *Plover*, since there was no longer any reason for her to winter there again; unfortunately, no message had been left at Point Barrow to the effect that *Enterprise* was leaving the Arctic Ocean—a major oversight.

Having loaded three-months' provisions from *Rattlesnake*, including 16 dozen bottles of porter, which were issued at a rate of half a bottle per man per day and, as Collinson noted, "proved highly acceptable,"[17] he put to sea again at 2 PM on 22 August. This time he had little problem in rounding Cape Prince of Wales, but in heavy weather and with high seas. At noon on the 23rd the martingale strop[18] parted and the jib boom carried away. By evening the carpenters had readied a replacement, but with the ship working heavily, it was not until 6 AM next morning that it could be mounted. A sail was in sight throughout the 23rd and 24th, but then it disappeared; it was thought to be a French whaler rather than *Plover*. But, just in case, blue lights were burned and rockets launched periodically during the night of 24/25 August—to no avail.

Enterprise passed Point Hope around 5 PM on the 25th. Another sail was spotted, but again it was not *Plover*. By midnight *Enterprise* was abeam of Cape Lisburne; the edge of the pack was reached on the 28th, and by 3 PM she was exchanging numbers with *Plover*, which was lying at anchor at Point Barrow. This was very fortunate; had Collinson, due to some accident, not been able to make contact with *Plover*, the latter would have spent another winter in the Arctic, to no purpose. Captain Maguire came aboard with mail and dispatches, including over 30 letters for Collinson from his mother. Maguire reported that he had arrived only that morning, and had learned from some whalers off Point Barrow that *Enterprise* had emerged safely from the Arctic.[19]

Not liking the look of the anchorage Collinson stood off-and-on all night, then, when the fog cleared at 8:00 next morning, headed south for Port Clarence again. *Plover* was to follow him south and they were to rendezvous again there. For the run back south to Bering Strait, *Enterprise* encountered either foul winds or just light, baffling breezes, and she did not reach Cape Prince of Wales until daylight on 8 September. She reached Port Clarence at 6 PM that evening.

Next morning *Plover* was seen working up towards the anchorage. Since the wind was ahead, involving a long beat to windward, Commander Maguire, along with his surgeon, Dr. Simpson, and his clerk-in-charge, Mr. Edwin Jago, took a whaleboat to *Enterprise*, reaching her after an hour's wet pull.

The two ships lay there until the morning of the 16th. During this period all the provisions that Maguire could spare were transferred to *Enterprise*, including six live pigs (just delivered by HMS *Trincomalee*) and some fresh potatoes. *Enterprise* also acquired caribou meat and fish from the Inuit, while the provisions that *Rattlesnake* had left at a house her men had built on shore were also embarked. Parties were also sent ashore to get firewood and water.

Shingleton was disappointed, even distressed, at the fact that the Inuit demanded liquor for anything they wished to trade, whereas they had not done so three years previously. Failing liquor, they asked for gunpowder, and Shingleton was particularly struck by the way prices had become inflated during the same period, specifically for some legs of caribou,

> weighing about 30 lbs. each which 3 years previous when we were down here I could have purchased for a string of Beads or a knife or a few Buttons each, but today I was forced to give them a 2 lb. Cannister of fine powder for each one I purchased which was 3. The meat certainly was cheap and most excellent but before they would have been content with a few trinkets of little or no value.[20]

On the evening of the 12th *Enterprise*'s crew put on a special theatrical performance for the officers and men of HMS *Plover*; the pieces performed were *The Birthday* and *The Beggar's Opera*. The audience was "all much pleased & gratified with the way in which they acquitted themselves."

The two captains went ashore on the evening of the 15th to examine the house built by *Rattlesnake*'s crew. The Inuit had already started to tear out the interior planking, and in an attempt to preserve the building for the use of any shipwrecked sailors, Collinson donated it to the Inuit "chief" Kaimoki. The latter was also put in charge of the decked pinnace *Owen* that had been left in Maguire's care by HMS *Herald*. She was hauled up on the beach, her gear, spars, and sails buried in casks under her bows, and a notice nailed to her side to the effect that she was also left for the use of any shipwrecked crew that might have need of her.

Both ships were ready to sail by the 14th, but gales and heavy seas delayed their departure until the morning of the 16th, when they both got under way. Collinson sent a bag of mail aboard *Plover*. The two ships kept company as far as King Island, but there they parted at midnight. For some time *Enterprise* was becalmed but then, with a fresh wind right aft and all sails including studding sails set, she stormed southwestwards at an impressive 9 knots. By noon on the 20th she was off the western tip of St. Lawrence Island, close enough to see large numbers of Inuit huts, but no people. On the 23rd she crossed the 180° meridian, and appropriately the date was changed to the 24th. On the 29th the ship rounded the west end of Attu Island, thus passing the western end of the Aleutian chain and leaving the Bering Sea for the last time.

A series of westerly and southwesterly gales slowed the ship's southward progress, but by 16 October, to the east of Honshu, she encountered the warm Kuro Shiwo current, with water temperatures as high as 68° and even 72°F and air temperatures around 72°F. On the 21st, they passed a small, densely wooded island, which Collinson refers to as South Island or Onosima (probably Mikura-jima or Inamba-jima), and on the following morning the ship was in sight of a larger, high island, called Fatsizio by Collinson (probably Hachijo-jima). Heading southwestwards, *Enterprise* on 27 October raised either Amami Oshima or Tokuno-shima, passing close enough to see patches of cultivated land, villages, and boats drawn up in the beach. Passing the south end of the island, she entered the East China Sea, then headed southwest through Taiwan Strait on the 29th. At midnight on the 31st she anchored off the entrance to Lei Yue Mun Passage. Next morning she ran up to the anchorage off Hong Kong and made her number[21] to Admiral Sir James Sterling's flagship, *Winchester*. Initially there was some confusion on board the latter ship since the signal books had been changed during *Enterprise*'s absence and the number she hoisted had been assigned to HMS *Endymion*. Once this had been cleared up, however, the Admiral sent the squadron's boats to tow *Enterprise* to her anchorage. All the ships of the squadron manned their rigging and cheered the new arrival and her crew.

While a gang of Chinese caulkers was at work on the ship, the ship's company was given 48 hours shore leave, half of the crew at a time, "the first run they have had in a civilized place for 3 years and 7 months...they all came off after enjoying themselves as Sailors generally do...."[22]

Two months later, a report of the ship's arrival at Hong Kong and, inevitably, of the bizarre situation on board, reached London, and was published in the *Illustrated London News*:

> Every one of the officers was suspended from duty or under arrest. One had been confined to his cabin for nearly three years; another for nearly the same period. A very unusual and a very deplorable state of things prevailed. The officers were not even allowed to go on shore at Hong-Kong when the men went. But, after some converse with the Admiral, they were liberated, but without any references to the questions at issue, which are of too grave a nature to be decided here....[23]

As this report suggests, Collinson submitted a request to Rear-Admiral Sir James Sterling, Commander-in-Chief of the China Squadron, that he convene courts-martial for all the officers whom he had placed under arrest. But Sterling, probably very wisely, declined.[24]

Enterprise remained at Hong Kong for two weeks and, as reported by Shingleton, was very well received by the British community there:

> They have been remarkably civil and are very much interested in the curios-ities we brought from the Polar Regions. We had two public days on board for all persons to see the ship and the different articles on board; those men that had anything in the shape of dresses, Bows, Spears, arrows or anything made of the Walrus tooth brought them on the quarter deck and were spread out for inspection. My part in this performance was to exhibit some of the specimens of birds and animal skins; those were ranged on one side of the Captain's Cabin to prevent their being damaged. Several Ladies and Gentlemen fell in love with some of them but as I had not collected them for sale I did not think proper to part with them.[25]

A regatta was held over the final few days of *Enterprise*'s stay, and on its final day a crew of ten from *Enterprise* provided great entertainment by giving a display of rowing and sailing one of the umiaks that Collinson had purchased, dressed in Inuit caribou skin parkas. In Shingleton's words, "they were cheered in all directions and going alongside the Steamer that was appointed Umpire a bottle of Rum was sent down to them to drink."[26]

In view of the fact that *Enterprise* was clearly short-handed in terms of compe-tent watch-officers, Sterling posted Mr. W.N. Wise as Acting Mate to the ship for the voyage home to England. Just before *Enterprise* put to sea again, twenty invalids came aboard, many of them suffering from dysentery; 19 were from the hospital ship *Minden*, and one from the flagship. A new clerk-in-charge, Mr. J. T. Turner, formerly in HMS *Encounter*, also joined the ship from *Minden* on 6 November, although he too was in poor health. For a while some nine members of *Enterprise*'s crew were also on the sick list as a result of their activities during their shore leave; as Collinson phrased it, "The relaxation and run on shore did our men more damage than all the exposure to the northward."[27]

Putting to sea at 5:30 AM on 18 November, *Enterprise* picked up the northwest monsoon and was soon scudding southwards across the South China Sea at speeds of 8 to 9 knots with all studding sails set, repeatedly making 200 miles per day. The mood on board was somewhat depressed, however, by a fairly steady succession of deaths and burials at sea. First to die, on 24 November, was one of the invalids from *Minden:* "the poor fellow was a perfect skeleton with scarcely a pound of flesh on his bones."[28] On the 28th, after a tropical squall that forced the officer of the watch to take in all the studding sails and reef the topsails, Mr. Turner died, having been confined to his bed only three or four days after joining the ship. The ship crossed the Equator that night and Turner was buried at sea next morning. Less than an hour later another man died, John Adams, a caulker from the depot ship *Styx:* "He was buried at 11 AM the same day the heat of the weather not permitting them to be kept any longer."[29] At midnight on 2 December the fourth death occurred: Corporal George Francis of the Royal Marine Artillery, also from the depot ship *Styx*, before being transferred to *Minden*.

Concurrently with this series of deaths, Collinson was embroiled in a fight with one of the few remaining officers on duty. On 28 November the following General Order appeared in the Captain's Night Order Book: "The leave of Mr. Adams, Assist. Surgeon, is stopped until further notice."[30] His offence was that he had called one of the men a "bloody fool!" Particularly since he knew that the ship would be calling at Banyuwangi or some other port in the Dutch East Indies in the near future, and that he would be prohibited from going ashore in light of the captain's punishment, Adams lodged a protest on the very same day:

Sir,

I beg to protest most strongly against the humiliating punishment you have now a second time, without cause, inflicted upon me, a cruel & tyrranous outrage upon a man of my age & profession, and one which I believe, has not for years been inflicted upon an Officer holding my position by anyone but yourself.

If I must submit to such indignities, which I believe you have no authority to impose upon me, to enable me to remain in H.M. Service, I have no desire to hold my commission one day longer.

The man Smith, whom you have supported and at whose instance you have stopped my leave is notoriously a troublesome character, & very often a malingerer. That he is so is known to yourself & to the officers, & he has been disrated for insolence to an officer.

I should have reported him yesterday many times before, but for the certainty that little redress was to be looked for.

I do not attempt to say that I was right in using harsh language, even under the strong provocation of his previous misconduct, but his repeated inattention under the same circumstances provoked me to the expression I used, which at the worst was merely asking the man if "he was such a bloody fool as not to know he ought to attend at the proper hour." For this my leave is stopped till further orders. As that is, I am prohibited from seeing places I have never seen & may never have the chance of seeing again, and this after having been cut off from the civilized world for nearly 5 years, four winters of which have successively been spent in the ice.

There is nothing very bad in the language I made use of, if the man's character in general and his conduct upon this particular occasion be considered. I have myself heard you use much worse language to the men when irritated & there must be something more than a simple desire to do justice when you, who defended & eulogized Mr. Atkinson, Ice Master, after having called the Senior Lieut. a Bugger, a thief & threatened to strike him, visit me with such a degrading punishment for so trifling an offence.

I again beg to protest against your decision in this affair. You heard the man's story and decided in the most summary manner, without allowing me to make my defence, or to produce the evidence I wished to bring to prove the great, unnecessary trouble he was in the habit of giving.

When it is decided by authority that my commission does not protect me from such outrage as this, I shall hasten to resign it, for on no account would I consent to such treatment as I have been obliged to submit to since I had the misfortune to come under your command.[31]

That a member of the crew would even consider bringing such a matter to the Captain's attention is a clear indication that the attitude of the men (or at least some of them) towards the officers had by this time been seriously poisoned, and that normal naval discipline had been completely undermined. Collinson responded to Adams' letter but, predictably, rather than helping to clear the air, his letter simply exacerbated the situation.

Sir,

I have to acknowledge the receipt of your letter wherein you protest against what you are pleased to call a cruel & tyrannous outrage upon a man of your age & profession. I have to observe that you have been convicted of acting in a manner unbecoming the character of an Officer & that as this is by no means the first time you have been brought before me for making use of opprobrious epithets I deem it necessary to put a stop by all means in my power to this unwarrantable use of violent & unbecoming language.

Whenever you behave as Mr. Atkinson has done (viz.), express sorrow for your offence & promise to be more guarded in future in your language I may permit you to go on shore but until I am assured that you see the impropriety of your conduct & that you will not again act so directly contrary to the twelfth article of the Surgeon's instructions, I shall show to the Officers and the ship's company that such conduct merits severe reprobation.

A copy of your letter shall be forwarded to their Lordships as well as the first Senior Officer we may fall in with.[32]

Replying in turn, Adams wrote:

Sir,

I have the honor to acknowledge receipt of your letter of this day's date in which you are pleased to assert that "this is by no means the first time" I have been brought before you for making use of opprobrious epithets. I most emphatically declare that this is the first time.

In June 1852 Mr. Phayre reported me to you for having used the word "cowardice" in conversation & which he chose to apply to himself. You took no notice of his report, but as I had nothing to conceal, and as I felt dissatisfied with the private nature of the transaction, I asked for an enquiry. The result was that you expressed yourself perfectly satisfied with my explanation, and cancelled your order with your own hand.

Upon one other occasion I was reported to you for, as Mr. Phayre asserted, refusing to go shooting when he ordered me. For that my leave was stopped for one month. These are the only occasions upon which I have been reported, to my knowledge.

I have never attempted to say that I was not wrong in using the words complained of to the man Smith. Had you allowed me to speak I would have acknowledged that & shewn what was true, that I spoke hotly and in provocation, a circumstance always taken into consideration elsewhere, and that it was a very unusual thing for me to speak to a man in that way.

As to apologizing to Smith, that at once I refuse to do. My idea of the relative positions of Officers and men will not allow me to do that.

If in referring to the 12th Article of the Surgeons' Instructions you mean to imply that I have been inattentive to it, I have no doubt that I shall be able to shew, by most ample evidence, that you have done me grievous wrong.

You conclude your letter with a kind of threat—that was quite unnecessary—for, fully convinced that the punishment you have inflicted upon me is unjust, excessive and at variance with usage, I had determined to appeal this, with other instances of ill treatment, to my Lords Commissioners of the Admiralty.[33]

Enterprise ran to the east of the Kepulauan Natuna (possibly Midai); Collinson intended running through Selat Gaspar (Gaspar Strait) and Selat Sunda (Sunda Strait), but with a succession of days of baffling winds, mainly westerlies, he was unable to get west of the island of Billiton (now Belitung) and hence ran through Selat Karimata (Karimata Strait) on its east side. All on board found the tropical heat and humidity extremely oppressive, especially when the ship was becalmed, as occurred quite often. For three days Collinson tried to beat westwards, still aiming for Selat Sunda, but was defeated by currents and the ragged condition of the ice-gouged copper on the ship's bottom. He therefore bore away for Selat Bali (Bali Strait) between Java and Bali. *Enterprise* passed the east end of Madura on 8 December, and on the 9th a water spout roared past the ship only about three miles off. Also on that date several large sea snakes four to five feet in length were seen swimming around the ship. Owing to light winds and strong currents, she did not reach the entrance to Selat Bali until 11 December. In the early hours of that morning a fifth invalid died, another Marine. On the morning of the 12th a pilot came aboard and, after beating through the narrows, the ship reached the port of Bango-Wangie (now Banyuwangi) at 8:30 that evening.

Here Collinson found a pleasant surprise awaiting him. By substituting letters for numbers from the Royal Navy signal book, he had devised a simple code for corresponding with his family. Using this code his family had placed a message in the *Times* on the 1st of every month since he had sailed from England. But Banyuwangi was the first port at which he had been able to find any copies of the *Times* with these encrypted private messages, and here he received four at once.[34]

Over the next couple of days the ship was watered, fresh fruit and other provisions, including some livestock, were loaded aboard, and at 11 AM on 17 December *Enterprise* put to sea again, bound across the Indian Ocean for the Cape of Good Hope. Just before she sailed, the Governor of Banyuwangi sent on board a mongoose and "a species of Tiger cat" to be taken to England, one assumes for London Zoo.

Almost immediately afterwards, on 19 December, the captain acceded to what at first sight appears a very strange request:

> Mr. Atkinson (Ice Mate) having requested to be relieved from further duty on board the Enterprise & as his services can be dispensed with without inconvenience to the service I have granted his request. The Military Command of the ship in the absence of Mr. Wise and myself will devolve upon the following officers in succession: Mr. Arbuthnott, Ice mate, Mr. Woodward, Boatswain, Mr. West, Boatswain. Rd. Collinson, Captain.[35]

While, clearly, Atkinson's experience in ice navigation would not be required on the remainder of the homeward voyage, it seems strange that Collinson would deprive himself of the services of an experienced watch officer, given the unusual situation on board his command. It seems probable that this special dispensation accorded to Atkinson is connected with a complaint lodged against him with the captain by Lt. Phayre on the same day:

> Sir,
>
> In obedience to your directions conveyed to me by Mr. Wise (Mate) that I should put in writing the complaint I made against Mr. Atkinson (Ice Mate) for twice saluting me with shouts of derisive laughter last evening, I beg to state that on two different occasions between the hours of 4 & 6 PM of he 18th Inst. , whilst I was passing his cabin he made use of the above-mentioned shouts of derisive laughter evidently, in my opinion, intended for the purpose of insulting me.[36]

One suspects that Atkinson, relieved of duty at his own request, and hence facing a stress-free voyage home, had simply been taunting Phayre, relieved of duty by the captain as a result of his confrontation with Atkinson over 18 months before. Unless occurring under the circumstances and in the atmosphere that prevailed on board HMS *Enterprise*, one would have thought that Phayre's complaint was of an utterly trivial nature, but under the circumstances it is symptomatic of the vicious undercurrents swirling around the ship.

The ship was then becalmed with almost unbearably high temperatures (up to 90°F in the shade) for over a week, but then on the 24th she picked up the South-east Trades. Hence the ship was making good progress on Christmas Day, the sixth Christmas since the ship was commissioned for this voyage. It was celebrated some-what more lavishly than in the previous years, to Shingleton's relief:

> We were all better provided, thank God, than we were last Christmas, every man on board enjoying himself, having plenty to eat and drink and make merry with Fiddling, dancing and Singing; were kept up till a late hour and in the morning were all able to go to their respective duties.[37]

On 3 January yet another death occurred: that of Robert Hamilton, formerly quar-termaster on board HMS *Winchester*, who "had wasted to a mere skeleton." Two days later *Enterprise* crossed the Tropic of Capricorn, still booming along at up to 200 miles per day. Soon afterwards, on 14 January, in one of the few entries in his journal that throws light, even obliquely, on the bizarre situation among the ships' officers, the gunroom steward, Richard Shingleton, noted,

> Mr. Phayre has raised another disturbance concerning me and has again accused me of wasting the provisions. I believe he cannot help it, for he is always prying into everybody's business as he has nothing else to do.[38]

On 16 January yet another invalid died, one of *Enterprise's* own crew, John Davidson, A.B. He had been suffering from "a pulmonary complaint" in the Arctic but had appeared to recover completely after the ship left the ice. At Hong Kong he was allowed to go ashore but only after being cautioned by the Captain and the surgeon about overdoing things but, to quote Collinson, "unable to withstand the tempta-tion, he fell into excess [i.e. got dead drunk], which weakened him so that he was unable to stand the change of climate."[39] His final illness began after leaving Banyu-wangi and, as Shingleton reported, for the last three or four days getting worse but we did not expect he was so near his end as he was. His speech was failing him yesterday and this morning he could scarcely speak at all and a little before 8 he breathed his last without a struggle.[40]

Shortly afterwards (on the 20th) yet another death occurred, that of William Simpkins, who had crushed his hand when a block of ice fell on it on 12 February. He had entirely recovered from that accident, but after leaving Banyuwangi he started displaying symptoms of dropsy. [41]

On 4 February the African coast was sighted, and on the 5th *Enterprise* was abeam of Cape Agulhas. Then the wind fell light, however, and on the morning of the 6th they were still only off Danger Point. Here Collinson communicated with a westbound steamer and heard for the first time that Dr. John Rae had returned to London the previous fall with an assortment of items (silverware, buttons, etc.) that clearly had belonged to members of the Franklin expedition and that he had acquired from Inuit at Pelly Bay and Repulse Bay. They had acquired them by trade from Inuit farther west, along with stories of numbers of white men having been seen hiking south along the shores of an island beyond the mouth of a large river (which, it turned out, was the Back River) and of large numbers of skeletons being later found on the mainland.[42]

Enterprise dropped anchor in Table Bay at 6 AM on 7 February. During the day Collinson travelled over Cape Peninsula to Simons Bay (near present-day Simon's Town) to report to Commodore Trotter. En route he visited the Observatory and compared his magnetic instruments with those of Mr. Maclear, the Astronomer Royal. The ship remained at Cape Town until the 18th, during which time the crew was allowed shore leave (half the crew at a time). They found that they were a source of great public interest, as Shingleton reported:

they have been very kind to us and the excitement was even greater than at Hong Kong. I cannot go into a house or come in the street but I am accosted and many questions asked about the Regions we have left; in fact I cannot answer to everything and many of them almost look upon us as beings of some other world, for in passing [in] the streets one will say to another that is one of the *Enterprise's*.[43]

After church service on the 11th visitors were allowed on board, and Shingleton again brought out his display of bird skins and Inuit tools and weapons.

The crew finished watering on 17 February, and six live bullocks were also hoisted aboard. The ship was also swung on that date. Shingleton found that sheep, poultry, and other foodstuffs he had hoped to purchase were in short supply, but he bought what he could. Next afternoon, with a light breeze, *Enterprise* weighed and made sail and had worked out of Table Bay by 5 PM.

She soon picked up the Southeast Trades and romped north "with Studding sails on both sides, at times rolling heavily."[44] She crossed the Tropic of Capricorn on the 25th. Two days later yet another death occurred on board, that of William Batson, a young lad who had been among the invalids who came aboard at Hong Kong. He had been on the mend, but had relapsed since leaving the Cape; Shingleton ascribed this to the abundant fruit he had consumed, which was so readily available at the Cape.

They reached St. Helena on 28 February. To his surprise Collinson learned that HMS *Sitka* had sailed from there only four days earlier; on board her was the crew of HMS *Plover*, which had been condemned at San Francisco as unseaworthy. *Enterprise* took on provisions and water, and the crew had another "run on shore." Although he was able to see something of the island, Shingleton experienced a disappointment here:

> I was very sorry that our stay was short here for I wished very much to visit Bonaparte's tomb but my time was too much taken up in getting a sea stock on Board for our Mess.[45]

Enterprise put to sea again on the afternoon of 3 March. On the following day yet another death occurred, that of Joseph Wiggins, A.B., which it appears to have particularly affected his shipmates, especially Shingleton:

> He is much lamented by all on board for a better shipmate never was on board any ship. He was the life and soul of the whole ship's company while on board, always joking and skylarking…and also the principal play actor on board during our long winter evenings.[46]

The next port of call was Ascension, which *Enterprise* reached in the early hours of 9 March. Here magnetic observations were made, eight live turtles were embarked, and once the ship had been swung to adjust the compass, the ship put to sea again at noon on the 10th. She crossed the Equator at 19° 30'W at 4 AM on the 15th and then languished through the Doldrums for several days, with light, variable winds, calms, occasional rain showers, and intense heat. On the 18th one of the turtles was killed and provided excellent turtle soup and delicious steaks. Also on that day *Enterprise* crossed her outward track, thus completing the circumnavigation.

Once she had picked up the Northeast Trades, the ship made excellent progress, often storming along with studding sails set, and making 150 or more miles per day. On 25 March one of the remaining turtles died, and as the remainder looked "very sickly," they were all killed, and presumably there was a turtle feast. On Easter Sunday (8 April) they passed Corvo, the northwesternmost of the Azores, about 12 miles off. Once she had lost the Trade Winds, however, *Enterprise* made only slow progress for the remainder of the homeward voyage; her copper sheathing was so badly gouged and torn from working through the ice that she could make very poor progress in beating to windward. Thus it was not until 5 May that the English coast was sighted, and two days later *Enterprise* reached Portsmouth. ●

13

RESULTS AND REACTIONS, THEN AND LATER

In TERMS OF ITS PRIMARY AIM, that of elucidating the fate of the members of Franklin's expedition, Collinson's expedition must be deemed almost a total failure. The only potential clues as to that fate were three artifacts he brought back that he felt might have originated with the missing expedition. The first of these was part of a door frame, with the catch for the latch of a door, which he had picked up on the Finlayson Islands in July 1853. He had also purchased two items from the Inuit at Cambridge Bay, "an iron implement" with a caribou-antler handle, the iron part of which appeared originally to have been a connecting rod from a steam engine, and a copper implement, also with a caribou-antler handle, the copper part "made, apparently from the copper bolts of a ship, having the Broad Arrow marked upon it."[1]

On *Enterprise*'s return to England, the first two items were sent to the Navy Yard at Woolwich for identification. With regard to the piece of door-frame, Mr. Reed, the Foreman Joiner, felt that it might have belonged to one of Franklin's ships since the doors of Winter Hoods of the 'Erebus' and 'Terror" were not framed, but made of ¾" Board and ledged similar to the fragment of Framing brought home by Captain Collinson, and that the Winter Hoods of other Vessels subsequently fitted out at this Yard on Searching Expeditions were framed in Panels in the usual manner.[2]

The piece of iron recycled by an unknown Inuit craftsman

> decidedly formed no part of the Machinery of either of the Vessels in question, but has evidently been part of the shank of a Boat's anchor. We are confirmed in this conclusion by the opinion formed by Dr. Rae who lately inspected these Relics & who informed us that three small anchors were left with Sir John Richardson's Boats on the Coast near the Copper Mine in 1848; it is there-fore more than probable that this piece of Iron is a portion of one of these especially as it has been galvanized, as were the three Anchors alluded to.[3]

The third item, made of copper, was sent to the Metal Mills at Chatham Dockyard for identification, but if a verdict as to its origin was reached it does not seem to have survived. It seems likely, however, that it too was derived from Richardson's boats, as Collinson himself suggested. [4]

Thus only one of the artifacts recovered by Collinson, namely the piece of door frame, came incontrovertibly from one of Franklin's ships. As suggested earlier, it must have drifted from farther east, and, one would have thought, should have represented a very strong argument for trying to push eastwards once the ice broke up at Cambridge Bay, freeing *Enterprise*, in the summer of 1853.

Perhaps the most unfortunate aspect of Collinson's expedition is that almost without exception the coasts he and his men travelled by ship or by sledge had already been explored either by parties from M'Clure's *Investigator* or by Dr. John Rae, trav-elling either by dog sledge or by boat. The only exception is the short stretch of the east coast of Victoria Island, north and west of Rae's farthest north at Pelly Point, to and including the small island that Collinson named Gateshead Island—this would amount to total of about 40 km of "new" coastline. It is perhaps ironic that the fairly large island now named Gateshead Island on the map was not seen by Collinson; his "Gateshead Island" is much smaller and farther south, closer to Victoria Island.

It is also worth mentioning that, had the map-makers been obliged to rely on Collinson's surveys, the resultant map would be seriously inaccurate in at least two areas. Both on his outward and homeward journeys along the southeast and east coasts of Victoria Island, he failed to realize that a fairly large island, named Jenny Lind Island by Rae, lies off Victoria Island. Collinson travelled around the east and south coasts of this island without noticing that a significant strait separates it from Victoria Island. In similar fashion, since his route, both going and coming, took him outside (i.e. east of) Taylor Island and Admiralty Island, he failed to survey, or even to detect, the large and complex embayment of Albert Edward Bay.

As we have seen, and as was alluded to in the report in the *Times*, when *Enterprise* returned to England, some news about the problems on board had already reached there from Hong Kong, presumably in part at least by telegraph:

> The only news the Enterprise has brought confirms the reports which have preceded her arrival as to the hostile relations between her captain and his officers. It is quite true that all the executive officers of the ship (Commander Phayre, Lieutenants Jago and Parks, and Mr. Skead, the master) are under arrest, and have been so for terms varying from three years to lesser periods. Mr. Skead has been under arrest over three years, and Mr. Parks more than two years and a half.... It now rests with the Lords of the Admiralty to try these officers by court-martial at the instance of Captain Collinson, and also to try that officer at the instance and demand of those who have been so long under confinement by his orders.[5]

A week later it was further reported in *The Times* that

> The "Enterprise" discovery ship, Captain Richard Collinson, C.B., has been taken into the lesser basin, Sheerness [at the mouth of the Thames], to be stripped and paid off. Nothing official has been communicated to her officers under arrest, who are now prisoners at large, as to whether any court-martial will be held to investigate the charges brought against them.[6]

The ship was paid off on 23 May. Already by then a formal preliminary investigation into Collinson's complaints against his officers had concluded:

> The inquiry into the charges preferred against her officers, who have been suspended from duty and placed under arrest for periods exceeding two years, has been, by order of the Lords of the Admiralty, intrusted to Vice-

Admiral the Hon. William Gordon. It appears that, after daily examinations of the different officers under arrest, which terminated on Wednesday week, the gallant Admiral, acting the part of a grand jury, has ignored the bills filed. The result is, that no courts-martial will take place on these officers. All the officers referred to have been granted Admiral's leave of absence, and two of them have been promoted.[7]

Nor were the officers' demands that Collinson be court-martialed granted. At this point the Royal Navy was embroiled in the Crimean War, which had broken out in March 1854. Apart from operations in the Black Sea, where Sevastopol had been under siege since September 1854, the Navy had also been engaged in operations in the Baltic, the White Sea, and the North Pacific. It was in light of this situation, and of his assessment of the strengths of the cases being made on each side, that Vice-Admiral Gordon reached his verdict, one which the Lords of the Admiralty were no doubt more than happy to approve. Only seven months previously the extensive press coveage of the courts-martial of four captains—Captain Sir Edward Belcher, Captain Henry Kellett, Captain Robert M'Clure, and Commander George Richards—for the abandonment of five seaworthy (but icebound) ships (HMS *Investigator*, *Assistance*, *Pioneer*, *Resolute*, and *Intrepid*) in the Arctic, had received extensive press coverage.[8] The acquittals of all four (except, perhaps, the bare acquittal in Belcher's case) had met with general public approval, but the entire matter had greatly embarrassed the Admiralty and the government. They wanted no further publicity of this kind.

As one might expect, Major-General Thomas Collinson, who edited Collinson's published narrative, in a footnote tried his best to absolve his brother in assessing blame for the frictions on board *Enterprise*. First he suggested that the unusual conditions on board a ship wintering in the Arctic might be responsible, even suggesting that it might be a by-product of scurvy, although there is no suggestion that scurvy was a particularly serious problem on the expedition:

The present Editor has no desire to raise the ghost of departed troubles, but it is impossible to give a true idea of the difficulties between the officers, and of the questions between them and the captain. Such troubles were, unhappily, not unknown in other Arctic vessels at that time. There appears to be something in that particular service—either the intense cold, or the poor feeding, or the close confinement between decks for several months without regular employment, or in all these together—that stirs up the bile and promotes bitter feelings comparatively unknown under the ordinary conditions of sea service. It might be supposed to be some form of that insidious Arctic enemy, the scurvy, which is known to affect the mind as well as the body of its victims.[9]

But the general gist of the Major-General's assessment is that the fault lay with the officers. Failing to mention that Collinson himself had no arctic experience he stated,

> Of the superior officers of the *Enterprise*, only one combatant officer and the two surgeons had been in the Arctic seas before; they were therefore untried as to their capacity for standing that service. It is unnecessary, and it would be wrong, to enter now into any particulars of the troubles that arose on this head. The fault and complaints, when laid in cold blood before officers in England in full health and spirit, doubtless seemed to them small, and sometimes even childish; but to the actors, as to children, they unfortunately appeared very real, and had a serious effect on the undertaking; and we must recollect that in all personal quarrels it is generally the manner, and not the matter, which gives the provocation. In all such cases the one officer in the ship on whose shoulders every such trouble really falls is the captain. He stands alone; he has the final adjudication of every case. He cannot escape from the responsibility, whatever occurs. It is he who is answerable for everything that goes on in the ship, for the duty to be done by every officer for every movement of the vessel. Now, in the case of the *Enterprise*, it unfortunately happened that, by the spring of 1853, at the end of the second winter—the second winter appears to be always the most trying one in the arctic seas—there were some of the officers suspended from duty; and the one lieutenant who had served in the arctic regions before [Lieutenant John Barnard] (and who by all accounts, was a very amiable fellow) was killed before they entered the ice. Thus the captain was deprived of the assistance of some of his superior officers for the last two seasons, and a very great additional labour and responsibility was therefore thrown upon him. It can hardly be supposed that any man would deprive himself of this help under such circumstances except from a feeling of dire necessity. This very difficult and trying position of a captain in such cases is not probably fully considered by the officers when these troubles occur; and, in the case of the

Enterprise it does not appear to have been fully considered by the authorities in England at the final adjudication. The captain of the *Enterprise* was a man of most tender heart and generous disposition, but his strong sense of duty to the service gave him a decided and somewhat severe manner; and the reserve that always enveloped the commander of a war-ship is necessarily increased under such circumstances. In a private letter from Hong Kong in 1854 expressing his sorrow at the condition of his officers, he says: "It has given me a warning that discipline is essential to comfort."

On the return of the ship to England he was induced, by the pressure of high authority, to compromise the matter. But, in answer to some remarks in one of the newspapers at the time, he said that if all the circumstances were known it would appear "that I only exercised the power entrusted to me when absolutely necessary." And in a private letter at the time he says he was drawn into the lamentable dissensions in an endeavour to settle amicably the disputes between the officers themselves.[10]

Skead's reaction to that last remark, in the form of a note in his own copy of Collinson's narrative was a vehement denial:

Not true. False! Had there been a Court Martial <u>he</u> would have been cashiered without doubt! He told <u>his own</u> story to their Lordships. The Admiralty <u>always</u> take the side of the Superior Officer <u>if possible</u>. In this case it was simply an impossibility. They actually sent copies of their disapproval to two Officers at least (I was one & the other was Capt. Phayre) of the Captain's subsequent conduct & gave a dispensing order for the Service Certificates, a Novel & unprecedented proceeding.[11]

It would appear that the point at which practically all the offices began to find fault with their captain and to scrutinize his every decision was when he rejected all advice and turned back from Point Barrow in 1850; the decision to winter in Hong Kong, rather than somewhere close to the action, can only have exacerbated the situation. Thereafter one gets the feeling that the officers, especially Skead, were extremely critical of every one of the captain's decisions, and some of the blame for the bizarre situation that developed must therefore lie with them.

As Collinson's brother pointed out (see his remarks above), by placing his officers under arrest Collinson was clearly reducing the ship's efficiency and taking an ever greater load on his own shoulders. The fact that he was able to take *Enterprise* through all the hazards of Dolphin and Union Strait, Coronation Gulf, and Dease Strait to reach Cambridge Bay, waters never before traversed by any ship, and safely to extricate his ship again the following year, emerges as an even more laudable feat, in the light of the load that the captain was himself carrying. At the same time, however, one must not forget that the two ice mates, Messrs. Atkinson and Arbuthnott, with vast experience of sailing arctic waters, were two of the watch-keeping officers.

On the basis of his own experience of taking the much smaller vessel *Gjøa* (47 tons) through Dease Strait, Coronation Gulf, and Dolphin and Union Strait in 1905, as part of the first transit of the Northwest Passage, and commenting purely on the navigational aspects of the expedition, Roald Amundsen was full of praise for Collinson for having taken his large vessel through these uncharted waters as far east as Cambridge Bay:

> Sir Richard Collinson appears to me to have been one of the most capable
> and enterprising sailors the world has ever produced. He guided his great,
> heavy vessel into waters that hardly afforded sufficient room for the tiny
> "Gjøa." But, better still, he brought her safely home.[12]

And with reference to Dease Strait: "Collinson's description of these waters was very helpful to us. He had throughout done excellent and reliable work."[13] Amundsen, however, would have had no knowledge of the ongoing battles between Collinson and his officers.

While it should be noted that few (if any) later commentators had consulted the archival sources on which this study is based, later opinion as to which side was in the right has been split. Historian Leslie Neatby comes down on Captain Collinson's side:

> The rejoicing over the safe arrival of the *Enterprise* in England in May 1855
> was soured by her captain's insistence that some of her officers should be
> court-martialled for the disorders of which they had been guilty. The Admi-
> ralty, sympathetic to the nervous strain of prolonged Arctic service, knew
> that the squabbles bound to arise among a small group of men penned up for
> months of darkness and discomfort, if aired in court, might make both pros-
> ecutor and accused appear ridiculous, and did its best to pacify him. When

Collinson consented to soften his charges, their Lordships absent-mindedly took them as withdrawn and, by immediate promotion of the offending officers, put judicial proceedings out of the question.... [Collinson's] severity to his officers arose less from malice than from his strict sense of discipline. He had the uncompromising morality of the North Countryman; and, it should be added, his sense of justice, if aggressive and unyielding, was wholly impartial.... Collinson's journal, plain and unvarnished as it is, reveals a man lacking neither in humour nor good nature; the expressive portrait contained in his brother's memoir suggests kindness more than stubbornness, though both characteristics are there.[14]

Compare this last assessment of Collinson's character, based on a photo (see illustration p. 251), with that of Lieutenant Sharpe, on seeing the man himself:

I had an opportunity of seeing this beau idéal of a captain, whose aspect is nearly as forbidding as our man's [Captain Trollope's]. He is a lean, spare, withered looking man, with a vinegar countenance & wears spectacles. He has not one good look about him.[15]

Clive Holland, too, has sided with Collinson:

On the voyage from Honolulu in 1850 Collinson's extreme caution had begun to exasperate some of his officers, who already showed signs of the indiscipline and unrest that were to embroil this expedition more than most. They were baffled by his course around the Aleutians. They queried his insistence on seeking a route directly across the Beaufort Sea towards Banks Island, instead of attempting an inshore route around Point Barrow. And some of them clearly resented his decision to return to Hong Kong rather than to winter near Point Barrow. They may have been justified in showing some frustration at the loss of a whole season, but instances of overt criticism and other signs of unrest recurred so frequently throughout the voyage that, on later occasions, Collinson was driven to placing officers under arrest in order to keep them in check.

In spite of his disciplinary problems and his rather limited discoveries, Collinson won high praise from both contemporary and later navigators, notably for his excellent seamanship in negotiating notoriously difficult channels and his perseverance throughout so long an expedition. But the acclaim of his colleagues was not matched at the Admiralty where he received a distinctly frosty reception. He annoyed them by electing to resurrect the matter of indiscipline aboard his ship and urging them to court-martial some of his officers. The Admiralty, taking a kinder view of the behaviour of men subjected to the stresses of such a testing voyage, preferred to let the matter rest—an attitude Collinson regarded as a personal affront...

It was not malice that drove him to seek courts martial for his officers so long after the events had occurred but a strict regard for discipline and justice which, he believed was "essential to comfort" on board ship.[16]

Overall, Pierre Berton has taken the opposite view, that Collinson was largely responsible for the bizarre situation on board *Enterprise*. He notes that on his return to England,

His reception was chilly... because he was at odds with his officers. At one time or another all had been under arrest. Collinson... demanded that they be court-martialled. The Lords of the Admiralty declined. They were used to this sort of problem. It was understandable that after more than four years cooped up on a crowded ship, even disciplined naval men would feel the tension. History has excused Collinson on these grounds.[17]

Then, having noted some of Collinson's brother's views on the matter, Berton continues:

This brotherly assessment scarcely absolves Collinson. For one thing, his bitterness did not dissipate on the return journey round Africa's southern tip, as might be expected, but lingered on after completion of the voyage. For another, too many of his officers were at loggerheads with their commander.[18]

There are some very striking apparent contradictions in Collinson's behaviour during the voyage. In terms of ship-handling and navigation, his approach to the challenge of rounding Point Barrow in the summer of 1850 was one of timidity and excessive caution, combined with a refusal to heed the advice of his ice-mates, let alone his executive officers. This is in striking contrast to the boldness with which he forged east through Dolphin and Union Strait, Coronation Gulf, and Dease Strait to Cambridge Bay in the summer of 1852. It was this feat of navigation, taking a sailing vessel of 530 tons through uncharted, ice-infested waters previously travelled only by canoes and small boats that earned Collinson the respect and admiration of such an experienced polar navigator as Roald Amundsen.

Even more striking is the contrast between Collinson's treatment of his men and of his officers. Towards his men he was, by the standards of Royal Navy captains in the mid-19th century, quite benign and solicitous. He took the side of the members of his crew who fell foul of the civil authorities in Honolulu and ended up in jail.[19] And during the various arctic winterings, his efforts to provide entertainment for his men in the form of a billiard room (complete with ice table) and a skittle-alley are in striking contrast to the regulations imposed by other Royal Navy captains of wintering ships, such as periods of obligatory exercise on the ice, no matter what the weather.

Moreover, Collinson was one of the most ardent supporters of the theatricals, staged by the men, that enlivened every one of the winterings, and even lent items of clothing from his own wardrobe[20] and made his cabin available as the dressing-room for the men playing female parts.

Contrast this with some of his more draconian orders directed at his officers: the prohibition of "gambling" in January 1852; or his allowing his officers to smoke only when the men were at their meals. But these assaults on his officers' freedoms were trivial compared to his unparalleled behaviour in placing all his executive officers under arrest for what can be characterized objectively as very minor (even insignificant) infractions of regulations.

Since all his officers wanted to see their captain court-martialled on their return to England, one wonders how close they may have come to attempting to remove him from command during the voyage on the grounds of mental instability. This, of course, would have been an extremely dangerous ploy, in that they would have risked charges of mutiny. Undoubtedly a critical factor here was the presence of a squad of Royal Marines on board, consisting of Sergeant Isaac Jeffreys, two other NCOs, and seven privates. On board any ship the Marines took their orders from the Captain; moreover, since Collinson's relatively benign treatment of his crew would also have extended to the Marines, they would have been inclined to be unusually loyal to him, rather than to the officers.

Collinson took it as a personal insult when the Admiralty refused to comply with his wish that his officers be court-martialled. But, for him, worse was to come.

When *Enterprise* reached England, a Select Committee of the House of Commons was sitting, charged with recommending awards that should be made for the discovery of the Northwest Passage. Collinson submitted a claim to this Committee, not for having discovered the Passage, but essentially for having sailed a substantial part of it, not previously navigated. The relevant section of Collinson's submission to the Committee reads as follows:

> **That**, entering from the West, [*Enterprise*] has reached the Longitude of 105°, where part of a door-frame, marked with the Queen's mark, was found, evidently belonging to one of the missing ships, and from which the existence of a passage by Peel Sound may be reasonably inferred.
>
> **Under** these circumstances, your Memorialist prays, that in the public acknowledgement to be given by the nation for the discovery of a North-West Passage, and for service in Arctic research, that the claim of the 'Enterprise' may be entertained; and that, while the honour of priority and discovery of the Prince of Wales Straits belongs to our consort, the consideration of having penetrated farther, and by her successful extrication from the ice, that the North coast of America has been opened, and already taken advantage of as a new field for the whale fishery, the Committee will be afforded a sufficient reason for not passing over the services of the 'Enterprise' on this occasion.
>
> **The** discovery of the Prince of Wales Strait by the 'Investigator' preceded the entry of that strait by the 'Enterprise' by ten months; but in the actual realization of the North-West Passage, namely, the crossing of Sir E. Parry's track on Melville Island, the traveling parties of the 'Investigator' preceded those of the 'Enterprise' by twenty days only. The shortness of this interval is not mentioned to detract in any way from the credit due to the great exertions of our consort, but to show that we were not wanting in the prosecution of the noble cause in which we were embarked.[21]

The Committee awarded £5,000 to Captain Robert M'Clure and a further £5,000 to the officers and men of HMS *Investigator*, despite the fact that in achieving the first transit of the Northwest Passage they had covered substantial parts of the entire distance on foot, across the ice, rather than by ship. Collinson, on the other hand, received what was effectively only an honourable mention.

In their report the committee members noted that they could not

refrain from expressing their high sense of the skill, judgement, and perseverance evinced by Captain Collinson in pushing his ship through Dolphin
and Union Straits to a point many degrees further eastward than has ever
been attained by any other vessel passing from the west along the northern
shores of America, and in successfully extricating her from the embarrass-
ments of so perilous a position.

They also feel it incumbent upon them to notice the determination of
this gallant officer to return to the eastward in search of his missing consort
previously to having communicated with Her Majesty's ship "Plover" and
from her obtained intelligence of Captain M'Clure's safety; nor can they
omit to mention the bold attempt made by him in the year 1850 to penetrate
to the northward into the heart of the Polar Sea, where he was stopped in
latitude 73½ by an impenetrable barrier of ice....

While Your Committee have not felt justified in recommending that the
principle of a pecuniary compensation should be carried beyond the case of
the commander, officers, and crew [McClure and company] who actually
achieved the objects sanctioned by an Act of Parliament, they cannot but
consider it their duty to suggest that the country at large would hail with
satisfaction any distinctions which might be conferred...upon the officers
whose names have been referred to Your Committee.... Your Committee
therefore venture to suggest that there are marks of honour and distinction
which, by brave and high-spirited men, would be valued even more highly
than that reward which your Committee have felt compelled to confine to
those within the spirit, if not the letter, of the legislative enactment which
originally offered it.[22]

Disillusioned, Collinson retired to Boldon to look after his aged parents, and never
sought a command in the Royal Navy again.[23] On his father's death in 1857, with
his mother and sister he moved to Ealing. He served as a Member of Council of the
Royal Geographical Society from 1857 onwards, later becoming its Vice President.
In 1858 the Society presented him with its Founders' Gold Medal for his work in
the Arctic. He also became a member of the Hakluyt Society, and edited one of its
volumes on the voyages of Martin Frobisher.[24] Long a member of the Royal United
Services Institution, he was elected a Member of its Council in 1858 and Vice-Presi-
dent in 1870, a position he retained until his death.

In 1861 he served on a committee of Army, Navy, and Colonial officers to report on the defences of the Canada/United States border from the Atlantic to Lake Superior; in this context he made a trip to North America where he focused on the defences on the St. Lawrence River and the Great Lakes. Contemporaneously with these various duties and offices, from 1858 he served as a "Younger Brother" at Trinity House, the corporation responsible for pilotage and for aids to navigation such as light-houses, buoys, and fog-horns around the British coasts. Elected an "Elder Brother" in 1862, he became Deputy Master (the working head of the establishment) in 1875 and held that position until 1883.[25]

Promoted Rear-Admiral in 1862 and Vice-Admiral in 1869, he attained the rank of Admiral in 1875. It should be noted, however, that these promotions were automatic with the death of more senior officers. In 1875, however, Collinson was also made a Knight Commander of the Bath in recognition of his early survey work and his contribution to Trinity House, as well as his arctic service. He thus received, if somewhat belatedly, one of the "marks of honour and distinction" that the Select Committee had recommended twenty years earlier.

Admiral Collinson died at his home in Ealing on 12 September 1883 and is buried at Perivale. Two other veterans of the Franklin search, Admiral Sir George Richards, who had commanded HMS *Assistance* in 1852–54, and Sir Leopold McClintock, who had discovered the fate of the Franklin expedition on King William Island in 1859, led the funeral cortège. Lady Franklin and her niece and companion, Sophia Cracroft, placed a wreath on his coffin.[26]

As his brother (and editor) has correctly noted with regard to the conflicts between Collinson and his officers, "No one…reading his journal, written during thevoyage, would suppose that any difficulty of the kind had occurred throughout it."[27] Undoubtedly the journal that Major-General T.B. Collinson consulted is that held at the National Maritime Museum at Greenwich; there are two versions of this journal, a draft copy and a fair copy. They are remarkable for the peculiarity on which he had put his finger: neither contains the slightest allusion to the problems on board HMS *Enterprise*. This is all the more remarkable given the emphasis on those problems in Collinson's Order Book, Night Order Book, Letter Book, and In-letter Book. Even a superficial perusal of these journals will reveal that they have been expurgated, that despite his brother's claim, neither of these versions of the journal was "written during the voyage." It is simply not credible that he would not have felt the need to unburden himself in the privacy of his journal. If the original of Collinson's original shipboard journal ever surfaces, it will undoubtedly show the man in his true colours.

As regards the officers who had suffered so much at his hands in the Arctic, Mr. Francis Skead shortly afterwards was made Navigating Lieutenant and was involved in the Cape of Good Hope survey. After retiring from the Navy, he became harbour master at Port Elizabeth, South Africa.[28] Lieutenant Phayre was one of the officers who, as Skead mentioned, was promoted almost immediately to Commander. Later he was made Captain, and by 1875 had retired from the Navy.[29] Lieutenant Jago was the other of the two officers who was promoted almost immediately, again to Commander.[30] He made Captain in 1866. And finally Lieutenant Parkes later rose to the rank of Commander, and had retired by 1875.[31] ●

ILLUSTRATIONS

Captain Richard Collinson in later life.

Southern beech (*Nothofagus*) forest as seen by Edward Adams
during a trip ashore at Bahía San Nicolas, Strait of Magellan, April 1850.
SPRI, Accession No. 83/11/9.

Waikiki Beach and Diamond Head, Oahu, June 1850.
SPRI, Accession No. 83/11/10.

Mikhailovski (now St. Michael, Alaska) where Lt. Barnard and Edward Adams
spent the winter of 1850–51.

SPRI, Accession No. 83/11/17.

Another of Adams's paintings of Mikhailovski.

SPRI, Accession No. 83/11/54.

Koyukuk Indians from the Lower Yukon.

SPRI, Accession No. 83/11/25.

Winter view of Deryabin (Nulato) where Lt. Barnard was killed.

SPRI, Accession No. 83/11/20.

Another of Adams's paintings (unfinished) of Deryabin (Nulato).

SPRI, Accession No. 83/11/53.

HMS *Enterprise* off Point Barrow, July 1851.

SPRI, Accession No. 83/11/?.

Largest of the Princess Royal Islands where M'Clure wintered in HMS *Investigator* in 1850–51,
showing the cairn he left on the summit, as seen by Edward Adams, August 1851.

SPRI, Accession No. 83/11/28.

An Inuk in a traditional dancing cap adorned with the beak of a loon, as sketched by Adams during the wintering at Winter Cove, Victoria Island, 1851–52.

SPRI, Accession No. 83/11/29.

An Inuit family who visited the ship at Winter Cove, Victoria Island;
the man is holding a leister or fish-spear.

SPRI, Accession No. 83/11/31.

HMS *Enterprise* in winter quarters, Winter Cove, Victoria Island, winter 1851–52.

SPRI, Accession No. 83/11/?.

HMS *Enterprise* in winter quarters, Camden Bay, Alaska, 1853–54.
SPRI, Accession No. 83/11/35.

Page 264

Top: Eider drakes: King Eider (*Somateria spectabilis*), left, and Common Eider (*S. mollissima*), right,
two of the species of ducks brought aboard by hunting parties during the various winterings.
SPRI, Accession No. 83/11/37.

Bottom: An arctic char (*Salvelinus alpinus*), the species Collinson's men caught in such large numbers
in Greiner Lake in the spring of 1853.
SPRI, Accession No. 83/11/39.

One of the Gwich'in who visited the ship at Camden Bay, July 1854.

SPRI, Accession No. 83/11/24.

NOTES

Preface

1 Great Britain. Parliament. 1855a. *Further papers relative to the recent Arctic expeditions in search of Sir John Franklin and the crews of H.M.S. "Erebus" and "Terror"* (London: Eyre and Spottiswoode), 903.

2 i.e. the officers.

3 Sharpe, P.R. 1854–55. Personal journal, H.M.S. Rattlesnake, vol. 2, 26 Feb.–23 December 1855, NMM SHP/4.

4 Collinson, R. 1889. *Journal of H.M.S. Enterprise, on the expedition in search of Sir John Franklin's ships by Behring Strait* (London: Sampson, Low, Marston, Searle and Rivington).

5 Collinson, R.L. 1850–55. Journal kept by Captain Richardson Collinson, RN, H.M.S. *Enterprise*, during the Franklin seach expedition in the Arctic, 1850–55, NMM CLS/20/1-3.

6 Collinson, R.L. 1850–55. Private journal kept by Richard Collinson, Captain of H.M.S. *Enterprise*, during the Franklin search expedition, 1850–55. NMM, CLS 21/1-2.

Chapter 1

1   Cyriax, R.J. 1939. *Sir John Franklin's last expedition: a chapter in the history of the Royal Navy* (London: Methuen).

2   Parry, W.E. 1821. *Journal of a voyage for the discovery of a North-West Passage from the Atlantic to the Pacific...* (London: John Murray).

3   Franklin, J. 1823. *Narrative of a journey to the shores of the Polar Sea, in the years 1819, 20, 21 and 22* (London: John Murray).

4   Franklin, J. 1828. *Narrative of a second expedition to the shores of the Polar Sea, in the years 1825, 1826, and 1827* (London: John Murray).

5   Ross, J. 1835. *Narrative of a second voyage in search of a North-West Passage, and of a residence in the Arctic regions during the years 1829, 1830, 1831, 1832, 1833* (London: A.W. Webster); Edinger, R. 2003. *Fury Beach. The four-year odyssey of Captain John Ross and the Victory* (New York: Berkley Books).

6   Simpson, T. 1843. *Narrative of the discoveries on the north coast of America; effected by the officers of the Hudson's Bay Company during the years 1836–39* (London: Richard Bentley); Barr, W., ed. 2002. *From Barrow to Boothia: The arctic journal of Chief Factor Peter Warren Dease 1836–1839* (Montreal and Kingston: McGill-Queen's University Press).

7   Cyriax, *Franklin's last expedition.*

8   Jones, A.G.E. 1969. Captain Robert Martin: a Peterhead whaling master in the 19th century, *Scottish Geographical Magazine* 85(3):196–202.

9   Richardson, J. 1851. *Arctic searching expedition: a journal of a boat-voyage through Rupert's Land and the Arctic Sea, in search of the discovery ships under command of Sir John Franklin* (London: Longman, Brown, Green and Longmans).

10 Rich, E.E. 1953. *John Rae's correspondence with the Hudson's Bay Company on arctic exploration 1844–1855* (London: Hudson Bay Record Society).

11 Rae, J. 1852. Recent explorations along the south and east coast of Victoria Land, *Royal Geographical Society Journal* 33:82–96.

12 Hooper, W.H. 1853. *Ten months among the tents of the Tuski, with incidents of an arctic boat expedition in search of Sir John Franklin...* (London: John Murray).

13 Seemann, B. 1853. *Narrative of the voyage of H.M.S. "Herald" during the years 1845–51, under the command of Captain Henry Kellett, R.N., C.B.*, 2 vols. (London: Reeve & Co).

14 Gilpin, J.D. 1850. Outline of the voyage of H.M.S. *Enterprise* and *Investigator* to Barrow Strait in search of Sir John Franklin, *Nautical Magazine* 19(1):8–9; 1(2):89–90; 19(3):160–70; 19(4):230.

15 Seemann, *Narrative of the voyage of H.M.S. "Herald".*

16 Hooper, *Ten months*; Pullen, H.F., ed. 1979. *The Pullen expedition in search of Sir John Franklin* (Toronto: Arctic History Press).

17 Osborn, S. 1852. *Stray leaves from an arctic journal; or, eighteen months in the polar regions, in search of Sir John Franklin's expedition, in the years 1850–51* (London: Longman, Brown, Green and Longmans).

18 Snow, W.P. 1851. *Voyage of the "Prince Albert" in search of Sir John Franklin; a narrative of every-day life in the Arctic seas* (London: Longman, Brown, Green and Longmans).

19 Dodge, E. 1973. *The polar Rosses: John and James Clark Ross and their explorations* (London: Faber & Faber); Ross, M.J. 1994. *Polar pioneers: John Ross and James Clark Ross* (Montreal and Kingston: McGill-Queen's University Press); Wilson, M.R. 1973. Sir John Ross's last expedition, in search of Sir John Franklin, *The Musk-Ox* 13:5–11.

20 Sutherland, P.C. 1852. *Journal of a voyage in Baffin's Bay and Barrow Straits, in the years 1850–51, performed by H.M. Ships "Lady Franklin" and "Sophia", under the command of Mr. William Penny, in search of the missing crews of H.M. Ships Erebus and Terror* (London: Longman, Brown, Green and Longmans).

21 Gill, H.B. & J. Young, eds. 1998. *Searching for the Franklin expedition: The arctic journal of Robert Randolph Carter* (Annapolis: Naval Institute Press); Kane. E.K. 1854. *The U.S. Grinnell expedition in search of Sir John Franklin: a personal narrative* (London: Sampson Low, Son & Co).

22 Collinson, T.B., ed. 1889. *Journal of H.M.S. Enterprise on the expedition in search of Sir John Franklin's ships by Behring Strait 1850–55 by Captain Richard Collinson, C.B., R.N., commander of the expedition* (London: Sampson Low, Marston, Searle and Rivington), 447–48.

23 F. Skead to R. Collinson, 28 August 1846, Collinson's Letter Book, KML.

24 R. Collinson to H. Stewart, 5 October 1846, Collinson's Letter Book, KML.

Chapter 2

1 T.B. Collinson, *Journal of H.M.S. Enterprise*.

2 R. Collinson to Secretary to the Admiralty, 18 December 1849, Collinson's Letter Book, KML.

3 Wilson, C. 1955. Footnotes to the Franklin search, Pt.I, Halkett's air boat, *The Beaver* 285(1): 46–48.

4 R. Collinson to Secretary of the Admiralty, 18 December 1849; 26 December 1849, Collinson's Letter Book, KML.

5   R. Collinson to Captain Horatio Austin, 18 December 1849, Collinson's Letter Book, KML.

6   R. Collinson to Comptroller General, 23 December 1849, Collinson's Letter Book, KML.

7   R. Collinson to Secretary to the Admiralty, 23 December 1849, Collinson's Letter Book, KML.

8   R. Collinson to Horatio Austin, 26 December 1849, Collinson's Letter Book, KML.

9   R. Collinson to Secretary to the Admiralty, 26 December 1849, Collinson's Letter Book, KML.

10 R. Collinson to Secretary to the Admiralty, 1 January 1850, Collinson's Letter Book, KML.

11 R. Collinson to Secretary to the Admiralty, January 1850, Collinson's Letter Book, KML.

12 R. Collinson to Secretary to the Admiralty (3 letters), January 1850, Collinson's Letter Book, KML.

13 Skead, F. 1850–52. Private journal, H.M. Ship Enterprise, 1850–/54, SPRI MS 1161.

14 G. Arbuthnott to R. Collinson, 7 August 1855, Collinson's Letter Book, KML.

15 Neatby, L.H., ed. 1967. *Frozen ships. The arctic diary of Johann Miertsching 1850–1854* (New York, St. Martin's Press), 5.

16 Cabo Virgenes, at the eastern entrance to the Strait of Magellan.

17 Hawaii.

18 Collinson, *Journal of H.M.S. Enterprise*, 24–28; Great Britain. Parliament. 1850. *Arctic expedition. Return to an order of the Honourable the House of Commons dated 5 February, etc.*, House of Commons. Sessional Papers, Accounts and Papers 1850, vol. 35, no. 107, p. 89–90.

19 Neatby, *Frozen ships*, 5–6.

20 Skead, Private Journal, 2.

21 Skead, Private Journal, 2.

22 Jones, A.G.E. 1958. Robert Shedden and the Nancy Dawson, *Mariner's Mirror* 44(2):137–39.

23 Collinson, *Journal of H.M.S. Enterprise*.

24 Great Britain. Parliament. 1851. *Arctic expeditions. Return to an address of the Honourable the House of Commons, dated 7 February 1851…Ordered by the House of Commons to be printed, 7 March 1851*, House of Commons Sessional Papers, Accounts and Papers, 1851, vol. 33, no. 97.

25 Collinson, *Journal of H.M.S. Enterprise*; Skead, Private journal.

26 Skead, Private journal, 6–7.

27 Cabo Froward is the southernmost point on the mainland of South America.

28 Skead, Private journal, 7.

29 Collinson, *Journal of H.M.S. Enterprise*; Skead, Private journal.

30 R. Collinson to Secretary to the Admiralty, 18 April 1850, Collinson's Letter Book, KML.

31 For this decision and further details on Johann Miertsching, and the role he played on board *Investigator* see Neatby, *Frozen ships*.

32 Skead, Private journal.

33 Skead, F. Annotations to his personal copy of: Collinson, *Journal of H.M.S. Enterprise*, 49. Skead's copy is held at SPRI.

34 Skead, Private journal, 8.

35 Monna Kaala according to Skead (Private journal, 11); Mauna Roa according to Collinson (*Journal of H.M.S. Enterprise*, 54).

36 13,500 feet according to Skead (Private journal).

37 Skead, Private journal.

38 A light anchor, usually used for warping.

39 Skead, Private journal, 49–50.

40 R. Collinson to Secretary to the Admiralty, 29 June 1850, Collinson's Letter Book, KML.

41 R. Collinson to Accountant General, 29 June 1850, Collinson's Letter Book, KML.

42 R. Collinson to General Miller, 10 March 1851, Collinson's Letter Book, KML.

43 R. Collinson to Rear-Admiral Hornby, 26 June 1850, Collinson's Letter Book, KML.

44 Great Britain. Parliament. 1851. *Arctic expeditions*, 45–50.

45 In the Chukchi Sea, on the coast of northwestern Alaska.

46 Great Britain. Parliament. 1851. *Arctic expeditions*, 10.

47 R. Collinson to Henry Kellett, 29 June 1850, Collinson's Letter Book, KML.

48 Seguam Strait, between the islands of Seguam and Amukta.

49 Collinson, *Journal of H.M.S. Enterprise*, 55.

50 Skead, Private journal, 13–14.

51 Skead, Private journal, 13.

52 Osborn, S., ed. 1856. *The discovery of the North-West Passage by H.M.S. "Investigator", Capt. R. M'Clure, 1850, 1851, 1852, 1853, 1854* (London: Longman, Brown, Green, Longmans & Roberts).

53 Skead, Private journal, 14.

Chapter 3

1 Great Britain. Parliament. 1850. *Arctic expedition. Return to an order of the Honourable the House of Commons dated 5 February 1850*, House of Commons, Sessional Papers, Accounts and Papers 1850, vol. 35, no. 107, p. 89.

2 Skead, Private journal, 16.

3 Collinson, *Journal of H.M.S. Enterprise*, 60. This was a large barrel, secured to the foremast, where a lookout was stationed to warn of ice hazards or to locate leads of open water, since the additional height made this a better vantage point than anywhere on deck.

4 Collinson, *Journal of H.M.S. Enterprise*, 63.

5 Skead, Private journal, 21.

6 Osborn, *The discovery of the North-West Passage*.

7 Skead, Private journal, 18.

8 Skead, Private journal, 19.

9 Skead, Private journal, 19.

10 Collinson, *Journal of H.M.S. Enterprise*, 63–64.

11 R. Collinson to G.A. Phayre, John Barnard, F. Skead, George Arbuthnot and John Atkinson, 21 August 1850, Collinson's In-letter Book, NMM CLS/41; Collinson, *Journal of H.M.S. Enterprise*, 65; Skead, Private journal, 63–64.

12 Skead, Private journal, 20–21.

13 Skead, Annotations, 64–65.

14 Skead, Private journal, 15–16.

15 Collinson, *Journal of H.M.S. Enterprise*, 67–68.

16 Skead, Private journal, 24–26.

17 R. Collinson to John Barrow Jr., 13 September 1850, Barrow Bequest, BL, Add. 35, 308.

18 Skead, Private journal, 29.

19 Collinson, *Journal of H.M.S. Enterprise*, 67.

20 Collinson, *Journal of H.M.S. Enterprise*, 67.

21 Osborn, *The discovery of the North-West Passage*, 92.

22 Oahu.

23 Great Britain. Parliament. 1851. *Arctic expeditions*, 12–13. See also Osborn, *The discovery of the North-West Passage*, 42–47.

24 Osborn, *The discovery of the North-West Passage*, 41.

25 Armstrong, A. 1857. *A personal narrative of the North-West Passage with numerous incidents of travel and adventure* (London: Hurst and Blackett); Neatby, *Frozen ships*, 37.

26 Armstrong, *Personal narrative*, 56–57.

27 Armstrong, *Personal narrative*, 57–8.

28 Skead, Private journal, 30; Skead, Annotations, 67.

29 Collinson, *Journal of H.M.S. Enterprise*, 70.

30 Collinson, *Journal of H.M.S. Enterprise*, 70.

31 Seemann, *Narrative of the voyage of H.M.S. "Herald"*.

32 Skead, Private journal, 31.

33 Seemann, *Narrative of the voyage of H.M.S. "Herald"*, 2:185.

34 Skead, Private journal, 31.

35 Skead, Private journal, 32.

36 Skead, Private journal, 33–34.

37 Skead, Private journal, 33.

38 Skead, Private journal, 34.

39 Bockstoce, J., ed. 1988. *The journal of Rochfort Maguire 1852–1854* (London: The Hakluyt Society).

40 Skead, Private journal, 34.

41 Collinson, *Journal of H.M.S. Enterprise*, 75.

42 Skead, Private journal, 35.

43 Skead, Private journal, 36.

45 Collinson, *Journal of H.M.S. Enterprise*, 76.

46 Skead, Private journal, 36.

47 Collinson, *Journal of H.M.S. Enterprise*, 76.

Chapter 4

1 Skead, Private journal, 36.

2 Richardson, *Arctic searching expedition*.

3 "Bosky" was the nickname bestowed by the British, this being a nineteenth-century euphemism for a drunk. His real name was Pavil Aklayuk, a half-breed native from Kodiak Island who had spent some time at the Russian American Company's post at Fort Ross on Bodega Bay, California, and hence spoke Spanish. He had previously

served as interpreter on board HMS *Herald* (Captain Henry Kellett) and HMS *Plover* (Captain Thomas Moore). Initially he had communicated with the British in Spanish, but by the time he joined Barnard's party at Mikhailovski, he must have acquired some command of English (Bockstoce, J. 1988. *Rochfort Maguire*, 18).

4 Collinson, *Journal or the H.M.S. Enterprise*, 81.

5 Skead, Private journal, 38.

6 Collinson, *Journal or the H.M.S. Enterprise*, 81.

7 Skead, Private journal, 38.

8 Adams, E. 1850–51. Journal kept ashore in and near St. Michael's, Alaska, SPRI, MS 1115, pp. 2–3.

9 Collinson, *Journal of the H.M.S. Enterprise*, 84.

10 Skead, Private journal, 39.

11 Skead, Private journal, 40.

12 Barometer.

13 Skead, Private journal, 40.

14 Skead, Private journal, 41.

15 Collinson, *Journal of the H.M.S. Enterprise*, 88.

16 Skead, Private journal, 42.

17 Born in what is now Lithuania in 1809 of a noble Baltic German family, Nikolay Yakovlevich Rozenberg was appointed Captain, 2nd Class and, simultaneously, Governor of Russian America on 25 January 1850. He asked to be relieved due to ill health late in 1851 or early 1852, soon after *Enterprise*'s visit; he died on 29 November 1857 and was buried in the Smolensk Orthodox cemetery. Pierce, R.A. 1990. *Russian America: a biographical dictionary* (Kingston ON and Fairbanks AK: The Limestone Press), 432–34.

18 Born in Reval, Estonia, in 1802, Mikhail Dmitriyevich Teben'kov was appointed Governor of Russian America on 24 April 1844 and took up residence in Sitka with his wife Mariya Alekseyevna. They left Sitka for the long voyage back to St. Petersburg on board *Atkha* on 22 November 1850. He retired from the Navy with the rank of Vice Admiral in 1860 and died on 3 April 1872. Pierce, *Russian America*, 500–04.

19 Skead, Private journal, 42–43.

20 Charles Dodd was born in Norwich, England in 1808. He first reached the Northwest Coast from England as second mate on board the Hudson's Bay Company ship *Beaver*. He took command of the ship in 1842 and remained her captain until 1852. Named Chief Factor in 1860, he was placed in charge of operations on the Northwest Coast. Taken seriously ill at Fort Simpson, also in 1860, he died at Victoria on 2 June 1860. Pierce, *Russian America*, 122.

21 In 1848. Pierce, *Russian America*, 502.

22 Skead, Private journal, 43–44.

23 Skead, Private journal, 44.

24 A spar used to stretch the foot of the foresail.

25 Skead, Private journal, 45.

26 Collinson, *Journal of the H.M.S. Enterprise*, 100.

27 Secured by means of a fid, a square bar of wood or iron with a wider shoulder at one end, that takes the weight of a topmast, the fid being driven through a square hole in the heel of the topmast and a similar hole in the head of the lower mast.

28 C.T. Jago to R. Collinson, 11 December 1850, Collinson's In-letter Book, NMM CLS/41.

29 R. Collinson, General Order, 9 December 1850, Collinson's Order Book, KML.

30 C.T. Jago to R. Collinson, 9 December 1850, Collinson's In-letter Book, NMM CLS/41.

31 A chain or wire cable running from the end of the bowsprit down to the ship's stem or cutwater, to take some of the strain on the bowsprit since the fore topmast was stayed to the bowsprit and exerted a strong upwards pull when the sails were full of wind.

32 R. Collinson to C.T. Jago, 11 December 1850, Collinson's Letter Book, KML.

33 C.T. Jago to R. Collinson, 11 December 1850, Collinson's In-letter Book, NMM CLS/41.

34 R. Collinson, Memo to ship's officers, 12 December 1850, Collinson's Order Book, KML.

35 At least two accurate chronometers, one keeping Greenwich time, the other local time (based on the time of local noon), were absolutely essential for determining the ship's longitude, i.e. the distance east or west of the 0° meridian passing through the Royal Observatory at Greenwich.

36 Skead, Private journal, 45–46.

37 Cape Agulhas, the southernmost tip of Africa.

38 Outward bulges in a ship's sides, designed to throw back waves, but also effective in throwing back ice floes if a ship were caught in a nip in pack ice.

39 Skead, Private journal, 46–47.

40 Warping involved moving the ship by securing a cable to a kedge anchor or small anchor that was then taken by boat in the direction in which it was planned to move the ship. The kedge anchor was then dropped to the seabed, and by hauling in on the cable by means of the capstan, the ship was moved in the desired direction.

41 Collinson, *Journal of the H.M.S. Enterprise*, 103.

42 Skead, Private journal, 49–50.

43 Skead, Private journal, 50–51.

44 R. Collinson, Memo to ship's officers, 17 January 1851, Collinson's Night Order Book, NMM CLS/37.

45 R. Collinson, Memo to ship's officers, 30 January 1851, Collinson's Night Order Book, NMM CLS/37.

46 R. Collinson, Memo to ship's officers, 31 January 1851, Collinson's Night Order Book, NMM CLS/37.

47 G.A. Phayre to R. Collinson, 1 February 1851, Collinson's In-letter Book, NMM CLS41.

48 F. Skead to R. Collinson, 1 February 1851, Collinson's In-letter Book, NMM CLS/41.

49 Dr. Alan Pearsall, former curator, National Maritime Museum, Greenwich, England, personal communication, January 2003.

50 G.A. Phayre to R. Collinson, 7 February 1851, Collinson's In-letter Book, NMM CLS/41.

51 Collinson, *Journal of the H.M.S. Enterprise*.

52 Kane, *The U.S. Grinnell expedition*.

53 Snow, *Voyage of the "Prince Albert"*.

54 Gilpin, Outline of the voyage.

55 Collinson, *Journal of the H.M.S. Enterprise*, 109.

56 R. Collinson to Naval Storekeeper, Hong Kong, 27 February–10 March 1851, Collinson's Letter Book, KML.

57 R. Collinson to Captain T. Massey, 20 March 1851, Collinson's Letter Book, KML.

58 Skead, Private journal, 54.

Chapter 5

1 Collinson, *Journal of the H.M.S. Enterprise*.

2 Skead, Annotations, 110.

3 F. Skead to R. Collinson, 1 April 1851, Collinson's In-letter Book, NMM CLS/41.

4 D.R. (deduced reckoning): estimating a ship's position by calculating courses and distances from the last known observed position.

5 Slops: clothing to be issued to the crew and charged against their pay.

6   R. Collinson to F. Skead, 19 April 1851, Collinson's Night Order Book, NMM CLS/37; 20 April 1851, Collinson's Letter Book, KML.

7   F. Skead to R. Collinson, 20 April 1851, Collinson's In-letter Book, NMM CLS/41.

8   Dr. Alan Pearsall, personal communication, January 2003.

9   Beechey, F.W. 1831. *Narrative of a voyage to the Pacific and Beering's Strait, to co-operate with the polar expeditions; performed in His Majesty's Ship Blossom...in the years 1825, 26, 27, 28,* 2 vols. (London: Henry Colburn & Richard Bentley).

10   Skead, Private journal, 57.

11   Beechey, *Narrative of a voyage to the Pacific,* 2:230.

12   Gough, B., ed. 1973. *To the Pacific and Arctic with Beechey. The journal of Lieutenant George Peard of H.M.S. 'Blossom' 1825–1828* (Cambridge: Cambridge University Press for the Hakluyt Society), 218.

13   Beechey, *Narrative of a voyage to the Pacific,* 2:231.

14   Skead, Private journal, 57.

15   Skead, Private journal,. 57–58.

16   Collinson, *Journal of the H.M.S. Enterprise,* 118.

17   *Journal of the H.M.S. Enterprise,* 119.

18   Skead, Private journal, 58–59.

19   Skead, Private journal, 62.

20   Collinson, *Journal of the H.M.S. Enterprise,* 121.

21   *Journal of the H.M.S. Enterprise,* 121.

22   *Journal of the H.M.S. Enterprise,* 125.

23   R. Collinson to Secretary to the Admiralty, July 1851, Collinson's Letter Book, KML.

24   Sharpe, Personal journal.

25   R. Collinson to F. Skead, 20 June 1851. Collinson's Night Order Book, NMM CLS/37.

26   Hooper, *Ten months.*

27   Skead, Private journal.

28   Pintle: a vertical metal pin on the leading edge of the rudder that fits into a gudgeon, or ring, fixed to the ship's stern, to allow the rudder to swing.

29   Skead, Private journal, 65.

30   Adams, Journal kept ashore.

31   Collinson, *Journal of the H.M.S. Enterprise,* 130n.11.

32   R. Collinson to Secretary to the Admiralty, July 1851, Collinson's Letter Book, KML.

33   Collinson, *Journal of the H.M.S. Enterprise,* 134.

34 Skead, *Annotations*, 134. By this remark Skead meant that he anticipated that they
    would have little success in rescuing any members of Franklin's expedition, due to their
    delay in getting into the Arctic.

35 Bockstoce, J.R. 1986. *Whales, ice, and men. The history of whaling in the Western Arctic*
    (Seattle and London: University of Washington Press)..

Chapter 6

1   Collinson, *Journal of the H.M.S. Enterprise.*

2   Bockstoce, *Rochfort Maguire.*

3   Skead, Private journal, 67.

4   Polynya: an area of open water among the sea ice.

5   Skead, Private journal, 67.

6   A whitish appearance on the underside of clouds, caused by reflection from sea ice,
    which may still be below the horizon.

7   Collinson, *Journal of the H.M.S. Enterprise*, 137.

8   Captain James Cook reached this point on his final voyage, in his ships *Resolution* and
    Discovery, on 17 August 1778, while searching for the Northwest Passage. But he was
    blocked by ice at this point and was forced to turn back. Cook, J. and J. King, 1785. *A
    voyage to the Pacific Ocean. Undertaken by the command of His Majesty, for making discoveries in
    the northern hemisphere...in the years 1776, 1777, 1778, 1779 and 1780,* 3 vols. (London:
    G. Nicol and T. Cadell).

9   Skead, Private journal, 69.

10 Boots made from sealskin or caribou skin; they were so well sewn that they were
    reasonably waterproof.

11 Skead, Private journal, 70.

12 Skead, Private journal, 70–71.

13 Skead, Private journal, 71.

14 Skead, Private journal, 71.

15 Historically, the residents of coastal towns and villages of Cornwall had the dubious
    reputation of assembling on the cliff tops when a ship was seen to be in danger of being
    wrecked and of looting the wreck as soon as possible after it struck. They were even
    accused of trying to lure ships ashore by displaying lights to confuse ships' officers as to
    their position.

16 Collinson, *Journal of the H.M.S. Enterprise*, 141–42.

17 Skead, Private journal, 73.

18 Skead, Private journal, 74–75. This was a well-founded fear on Skead's part. Numerous ships have suffered this fate in this area, probably the best known being Vilhjalmur Stefansson's *Karluk* of the Canadian Arctic Expedition; beset in the ice in this area in mid-August 1913, she drifted west and northwest and was ultimately crushed and sank north of Ostrov Geral'da and northeast of Ostrov Vrangelya on 11 January 1914. Of the 25 people on board, only 11 ultimately survived. Bartlett, R. and R.T. Hale. 1916. *Northward ho! The last voyage of the Karluk* (Boston: Small, Maynard and Co.).

19 Skead, Private journal, 75.

20 Collinson, *Journal of the H.M.S. Enterprise*.

21 Skead, Private journal, 77.

22 Skead, Private journal, 78.

23 Skead, Private journal, 79.

24 Skead, Private journal, 80.

25 Skead, Private journal, 81.

26 Skead, Private journal, 82.

27 Collinson, *Journal of the H.M.S. Enterprise*.

28 Skead, Private journal, 84–85.

29 Skead, Private journal, 85.

30 Skead, Private journal, 85.

31 Collinson, *Journal of the H.M.S. Enterprise*, 153.

32 Skead, Private journal, 86.

33 Skead, Private journal, 86–87.

34 Skead, Private journal, 89.

35 Studding sails (pronounced stunsails): additional sails, used only in fair weather, set outside the square sails by extending the yards with booms.

36 Skead, Private journal, 89–90.

37 Skead, Private journal, 91.

38 Skead, Private journal, 91.

39 Skead, Private journal, 91–92.

40 Skead, Private journal, 93.

41 Collinson, *Journal of the H.M.S. Enterprise*, 158.

42 Osborn, *The discovery of the North-west Passage*, 217.

43 Skead, Private journal, 93.

44 Skead, Private journal, 94.

45 Skead, Annotations, 160.

46 Skead, Private journal, 94–95.

Chapter 7

1 Collinson, *Journal of the H.M.S. Enterprise.*

2 Condon, R.G. 1996. *The Northern Copper Inuit: A history* (Toronto: University of Toronto Press), xv; Damas, D. 1984. Copper Eskimo. In: *Handbook of North American Indians, Vol. 5. Arctic* (Washington: Smithsonian Institution), 401, Table 1.

3 Rich, *John Rae's correspondence.*

4 Skead, Private journal, 96.

5 Skead, Private journal, 97–98.

6 Osborn, *The discovery of a North-west Passage.*

7 Skead, Private journal, 98.

8 Skead, Private journal, 99.

9 Skead, Private journal, 99.

10 Skead, Private journal, 98–99.

11 Skead, Private journal, 101.

12 Skead, Private journal, 101.

13 Skead, Annotations, 167.

14 R. Collinson to all officers, 27 September 1851, Collinson's Night Order Book, NMM CLS/37.

15 The Sylvester stove, produced by Mr. Sylvester, a London engineer, was effectively a central-heating system for the ship. A coal-fired stove, situated inside a large metal chamber open at the bottom, was located in the hold. Some of the air heated in this chamber escaped via a sliding brass register on the lower deck, while warm air was also led through flues along both sides of the ship, near the deck in the hold, feeding warm air to the officers' and the captain's cabins. The Royal Navy had made use of Mr. Sylvester's stoves on ships bound for the Arctic from at least as early as Captain William Parry's second expedition (1821–1823), and Parry has left a good description of how they functioned, in Parry, W.E. 1824. *Journal of a second voyage for the discovery of a North-West Passage from the Atlantic to the Pacific, performed in the years 1821–1822–1823, I His Majesty's Ships* Hecla *and* Fury (London: John Murray), v–vi.

16 Osborn, *Stray leaves*, 135.

17 Skead, Annotations, 170.

18 Collinson, *Journal of the H.M.S. Enterprise*, 170.

19 Collinson, *Journal of the H.M.S. Enterprise*, 171.

20 Collinson, *Journal of the H.M.S. Enterprise*, 172.

21 Collinson, *Journal of the H.M.S. Enterprise*, 173.

22 Stefansson, V. 1913. *My life with the Eskimo* (New York: Macmillan), 287.

23 Skead, Private journal.

24 Collinson, *Journal of the H.M.S. Enterprise*, 173.

25 Collinson, *Journal of the H.M.S. Enterprise*, 174.

26 Skead, Private journal, 104–05.

27 R. Collinson to all officers, 11 January 1852, Collinson's Night Order Book, NMM CLS/37.

28 C.T. Jago *et al.* to R. Collinson, 12 January 1852, Collinson's In-letter Book, NMM CLS/41.

29 R. Collinson to all officers, 10 March 1852, Collinson's Night Order Book, NMM CLS/37.

30 M.T. Parkes to R. Collinson, 11 March 1852, Collinson's In-letter Book, NMM CLS/41.

31 R. Collinson to F. Skead, 19 March 1852, Collinson's Night Order Book, NMM, CLS/37.

32 F. Skead to R. Collinson, 19 March 1852, Collinson's In-letter Book, NMM, CLS/41.

33 Collinson, *Journal of the H.M.S. Enterprise*, 178.

34 F. Skead to R. Collinson, 1 April 1852, Collinson's In-letter Book, NMM CLS/41.

35 R. Collinson to F. Skead, 2 April 1852, Collinson's Letter Book, KML.

36 F. Skead to R. Collinson, 6 April 1852, Collinson's In-letter Book, NMM, CLS/41.

37 Collinson, *Journal of the H.M.S. Enterprise*, 180.

38 R. Collinson to G.A. Phayre, 11 April 1852, Collinson's Letter Book, KML.

39 Collinson, *Journal of the H.M.S. Enterprise*, 183.

40 Collinson, *Journal of the H.M.S. Enterprise*, 188.

41 Collinson, *Journal of the H.M.S. Enterprise*, 198.

42 Collinson, *Journal of the H.M.S. Enterprise*, 200.

43 Collinson, *Journal of the H.M.S. Enterprise*, 201.

44 Planking on the ship's sides immediately above the waterline.

45 Fishing: strengthening a sprung, or damaged, mast or yard by lashing reinforcing pieces of wood on either side.

46 Collinson, *Journal of the H.M.S. Enterprise*, 187.

47 Collinson, *Journal of the H.M.S. Enterprise*, 205.

48 Condon, *The Northern Copper Inuit*, xv.

49 *Journal of the H.M.S. Enterprise*, 206.

50 *Journal of the H.M.S. Enterprise*, 207.

51 R. Collinson to E. Adams, 10 June 1852, Collinson's Night Order Book, NMM, CLS/37.

52 Collinson, *Journal of the H.M.S. Enterprise*, 211.

53 This was where Parry had wintered with *Hecla* and *Griper* in 1819–1820. At his wintering site was a very conspicuous boulder, Parry's Rock, where it could be anticipated that Franklin, or others of the search expeditions, might have left messages.

54 Osborn, *The discovery of the North-West Passage*.

55 Collinson, *Journal of the H.M.S. Enterprise*, 212.

56 Collinson, *Journal of the H.M.S. Enterprise*, 216.

Chapter 8

1 Log, H.M.S. *Enterprise*, 8 August 1852, KML.

2 Log, H.M.S. *Enterprise*, 14 August 1852.

3 Log, H.M.S. *Enterprise*, 25 August 1852; Collinson, *Journal of the H.M.S. Enterprise*.

4 At that time the North Magnetic Pole lay some 850 km due east of their position, and while Collinson and his officers were aware of this, the compasses were probably very sluggish.

5 Collinson, *Journal of the H.M.S. Enterprise*; Shingleton, R. Journal aboard H.M.S. *Enterprise*, cont'd, 1854–55, VMM Lar G665 1852 C6, 11 September 1952. Only the second volume of Shingleton's journal has survived, and hence it provides no information on the voyage prior to this date.

6 Shingleton, Journal aboard H.M.S. *Enterprise*, 12 September 1852.

7 Collinson, *Journal of the H.M.S. Enterprise*; Shingleton, Journal aboard H.M.S. *Enterprise*; Log, H.M.S. *Enterprise*, 13 September 1852.

8 Shingleton, Journal aboard H.M.S. *Enterprise*, 20 September 1852.

9 Collinson, *Journal of the H.M.S. Enterprise*, 237.

10 Shingleton, Journal aboard H.M.S. Enterprise, 23 September 1852.

11 The wind was thus offshore.

12 Shingleton, Journal aboard H.M.S. Enterprise, 24 September 1852.

13 A spare anchor about one third the size of the main anchors, but larger than a kedge anchor.

14 Log, H.M.S. *Enterprise*, 24 September 1852.

15 Collinson, *Journal of the H.M.S. Enterprise*, 239.

16 Shingleton, Journal aboard H.M.S. Enterprise, 26 September 1852.

17 Collinson, *Journal of the H.M.S. Enterprise*, 241.

18 Shingleton, Journal aboard H.M.S. Enterprise, 28 September 1852.

19 Collinson, *Journal of the H.M.S. Enterprise*, 241.

20 Log, H.M.S. *Enterprise*, 30 September 1852.

21 Shingleton, Journal aboard H.M.S. Enterprise, 3 October 1852.

22 Damas, Copper Eskimo, 401, Table 1.

23 R. Collinson to M.T. Parkes, 3 October 1852, Collinson's Night Order Book, NMM, CLS/37.

24 Collinson, *Journal of the H.M.S. Enterprise*.

25 R. Collinson to G.A. Phayre, 7 October 1852, Collinson's Night Order Book, NMM, CLS/37.

26 Gunner's mate.

27 G.A. Phayre to R. Collinson, 7 October 1852, Collinson's In-letter Book, NMM CLS/41.

28 R. Collinson to E. Adams, October 1852. Collinson's Night Order Book, NMM CLS/37.

29 Shingleton, Journal aboard H.M.S. Enterprise, 7 October 1852.

30 Collinson, *Journal of the H.M.S. Enterprise*, 244.

31 Shingleton, Journal aboard H.M.S. Enterprise, 10 October 152.

32 Journal aboard H.M.S. Enterprise, 15 October 1852.

33 Journal aboard H.M.S. Enterprise, 15 October 1852.

34 Journal aboard H.M.S. Enterprise, 29 October 1852.

35 Collinson, *Journal of the H.M.S. Enterprise*, 246–47.

Chapter 9

1 Shingleton, Journal aboard H.M.S. Enterprise, 5 November 1852. On 5 November 1606 Guy Fawkes, a Catholic, was intercepted in the cellars beneath the Houses of Parliament with over 20 barrels of gunpowder. In reprisal for the oppressive treatment of Roman Catholics in England, he intended detonating these explosives when King James I and his ministers were in the building above. Fawkes was tried and executed. Ever since then this date has been commemorated by British children by letting off fireworks and building and lighting bonfires on which effigies (guys) of Guy Fawkes are burned.

2 Shingleton, Journal aboard H.M.S. Enterprise, 11 November 1852.

3 Shingleton, Journal aboard H.M.S. Enterprise, 9 December 1852.

4 Shingleton, Journal aboard H.M.S. Enterprise, 10 December 1852.

5 Shingleton, Journal aboard H.M.S. Enterprise, 16 December 1852.

6 Shingleton, Journal aboard H.M.S. Enterprise, 22 December 1852.

7 Shingleton, Journal aboard H.M.S. Enterprise, 25 December 1852.

8 Shingleton, Journal aboard H.M.S. Enterprise, 26 December 1852.

9 Shingleton, Journal aboard H.M.S. Enterprise, 6 January 1853.

10 Shingleton, Journal aboard H.M.S. Enterprise, 7 January 1853.

11 Shingleton, Journal aboard H.M.S. Enterprise, 21 January 1853

12 Shingleton, Journal aboard H.M.S. Enterprise, 28 January 1853.

13 Shingleton, Journal aboard H.M.S. Enterprise, 11 February 1853.

14 Shingleton, Journal aboard H.M.S. Enterprise, 23 February 1853.

15 Shingleton, Journal aboard H.M.S. Enterprise, 4 March 1853.

16 Collinson, *Journal of the H.M.S. Enterprise*.

17 Shingleton, Journal aboard H.M.S. Enterprise, 21 March 1853.

18 Collinson, *Journal of the H.M.S. Enterprise*, 254.

19 Shingleton, Journal aboard H.M.S. Enterprise, 29 March 1853.

20 Collinson, *Journal of the H.M.S. Enterprise*.

21 McClintock, F.L. 1859. *The voyage of the "Fox" in the Arctic seas* (London: John Murray).

22 Rich, *John Rae's correspondence*.

23 Collinson, *Journal of the H.M.S. Enterprise*, 261.

24 Skead, Annotations, 261.

25 Skead, Annotations, 263.

26 R. Collinson to G.A. Phayre, 11 April 1853, Collinson's Night Order Book, NMM CLS/37.

27 Old rope.

28 Collinson, *Journal of the H.M.S. Enterprise*, 262.

29 Collinson, *Journal of the H.M.S. Enterprise*, 262.

30 Collinson, *Journal of the H.M.S. Enterprise*, 262–63.

31 McKenzie, W.G. 1975. The identity of Gateshead Island, *Polar Record* 17(110):547.

32 Collinson, *Journal of the H.M.S. Enterprise*, 264.

33 Rich, *John Rae's correspondence*, 199–200.

34 Collinson, *Journal of the H.M.S. Enterprise*, 265.

35 1 cable = 100 fathoms = 200 yards = 183 m.

36 Collinson, *Journal of the H.M.S. Enterprise*, 266.

37 Collinson, *Journal of the H.M.S. Enterprise*, 266.

38 Collinson, *Journal of the H.M.S. Enterprise*, 266.

39 Collinson, *Journal of the H.M.S. Enterprise*, 266.

40 Collinson, *Journal of the H.M.S. Enterprise*, 266.

41 Collinson, *Journal of the H.M.S. Enterprise*, 267.

42 Collinson, *Journal of the H.M.S. Enterprise*, 267.

43 Collinson, *Journal of the H.M.S. Enterprise*, 268.

44 Collinson, *Journal of the H.M.S. Enterprise*, 268.

45 McKenzie, The identity of Gateshead island.

46 Collinson, *Journal of the H.M.S. Enterprise*,. 271.

47 Collinson, *Journal of the H.M.S. Enterprise*, 273.

48 Shingleton, Journal aboard H.M.S. Enterprise, 26 April 1853.

49 Shingleton, Journal aboard H.M.S. Enterprise, 2 May 1853.

50 Shingleton, Journal aboard H.M.S. Enterprise, 6 May 1853.

51 Shingleton, Journal aboard H.M.S. Enterprise, 12 May 1853.

52 Shingleton, Journal aboard H.M.S. Enterprise, 13 May 1853.

53 R. Collinson, General Order, 2 June 1853, Collinson's Night Order Book, NMM, CLS/37.

54 R. Collinson, General Order, 4 June 1853, Collinson's Night Order Book, NMM, CLS/37.

55 Collinson, *Journal of the H.M.S. Enterprise*, 274.

56 Shingleton, Journal aboard H.M.S. Enterprise, 11 June 1853.

57 Shingleton, Journal aboard H.M.S. Enterprise, 15 June 1853.

58 Collinson, *Journal of the H.M.S. Enterprise*, 275.

59 Shingleton, Journal aboard H.M.S. Enterprise, 23 June 1853.

60 R. Collinson to F. Skead, 20 June 1853; 23 June 1853, Collinson's Night Order Book, NMM, CLS/37.

61 Shingleton, Journal aboard H.M.S. Enterprise, 29 June 1853.

62 Collinson, *Journal of the H.M.S. Enterprise*, 276.

63 Collinson, *Journal of the H.M.S. Enterprise*, 278.

64 Shingleton, Journal aboard H.M.S. Enterprise, 9 July 1853. Shingleton was mistaken, however. The stone weirs that were built on so many of the rivers to catch char as they ran back upstream from the sea in the late summer and fall were widespread throughout the North American Arctic and commonly produced hundreds of fish in a very short time.

65 G.A. Phayre to R. Collinson, 29 June 1853, Collinson's In-letter Book, NMM, CLS/41.

66 R. Collinson, General Order, 28 June 1853, Collinson's Night Order Book, NMM, CLS/37.

67 G.A. Phayre to R. Collinson, 4 July 1853, Collinson's In-letter Book, NMM, CLS/41.

68 R. Atkinson to R. Collinson, 4 July 1853, Collinson's In-letter Book, NMM, CLS/41.

69 R. Collinson, General Order, 4 July 1853, Collinson's Night Order Book, NMM, CLS/37.

70 R. Collinson, General Order, 4 July 1853, Collinson's Night Order Book, NMM, CLS/37.

71 Shingleton, Journal aboard H.M.S. Enterprise, 3 July 1853.

72 Shingleton, Journal aboard H.M.S. Enterprise, 23 July 1853.

73 Collinson, *Journal of the H.M.S. Enterprise*, 281.

74 Shingleton, Journal aboard H.M.S. Enterprise, 2 August 1853.

75 Shingleton, Journal aboard H.M.S. Enterprise, 7 August 1853.

76 Shingleton, Journal aboard H.M.S. Enterprise, 10 August 1853.

77 Skead, Annotations, 260.

78 Skead, Annotations, 300.

Chapter 10

1   Shingleton, Journal aboard H.M.S. Enterprise, 11 August.

2   Collinson, *Journal of the H.M.S. Enterprise*.

3   Shingleton, Journal aboard H.M.S. Enterprise, 16 August.

4   Shingleton, Journal aboard H.M.S. Enterprise, 16 August.

5   Shingleton, Journal aboard H.M.S. Enterprise, 17 August 1853.

6   Chains or chain-wales: wooden projections from the sides of square-rigged ships abreast of each mast, to which the shrouds, supporting the masts, are secured.

7   Log, H.M.S. *Enterprise*, 17 August 1853.

8   Shingleton, Journal aboard H.M.S. Enterprise, 19 August 1853.

9   Collinson, *Journal of the H.M.S. Enterprise*, 296.

10 Shingleton, Journal aboard H.M.S. Enterprise, 29 August.

11 But there is now another murre colony in the abandoned schoolhouse on Herschel Island (Bockstoce, personal communication, September 2006).

12 9–10 hundredweights, i.e. 1008–1120 lbs.

13 Shingleton, Journal aboard H.M.S. Enterprise, 31 August 1853.

14 Collinson, *Journal of the H.M.S. Enterprise*, 297.

15 Shingleton, Journal aboard H.M.S. Enterprise, 31 August 1853.

16 Mathews, W.H. and A.M. Bustin. 1984. Why do the Smoking Hills smoke? *Canadian Journal of Earth Sciences* 21(7):737–42.

17 Shingleton, Journal aboard H.M.S. Enterprise, 1 September 1853.

18 Shingleton, Journal aboard H.M.S. Enterprise, 2 September 1853.

19 Shingleton, Journal aboard H.M.S. Enterprise, 3 September 1853.

20 Shingleton, Journal aboard H.M.S. Enterprise, 7 September 1853.

21 Collinson, *Journal of the H.M.S. Enterprise*.

22 Shingleton, Journal aboard H.M.S. Enterprise, 8 September 1853.

23 Shingleton, Journal aboard H.M.S. Enterprise, 13 September 1853.

24 Shingleton, Journal aboard H.M.S. Enterprise, 18 September 1853.

Chapter 11

1   Shingleton, Journal aboard H.M.S. Enterprise, 30 September 1853.

2   Shingleton, Journal aboard H.M.S. Enterprise, 3 October 1853.

3   Distributaries: the channels into which a river splits to discharge the river's flow across the delta to the sea.

4   Collinson, *Journal of the H.M.S. Enterprise*, 307.

5   C.T. Jago to R. Collinson, 13 October, 1853. Collinson's In-letter Book, NMM CLS/41.

6   R. Collinson to C.T. Jago, 15 October 153, Collinson's Letter Book, KML.

7   C.T. Jago to R. Collinson, 17 October 1853. Collinson's In-letter Book, NMM CLS/41.

8   R. Anderson to R. Collinson, 16 October 1853. Collinson's In-letter Book, NMM CLS/41.

9   Shingleton, Journal aboard H.M.S. Enterprise, 16 October 1853.

10 Shingleton, Journal aboard H.M.S. Enterprise, 11 November 1853.

11 Shingleton, Journal aboard H.M.S. Enterprise, 22 November 1853.

12 Shingleton, Journal aboard H.M.S. Enterprise, 1 December 1853.

13 Shingleton, Journal aboard H.M.S. Enterprise, 16 December 1853.

14 Shingleton, Journal aboard H.M.S. Enterprise, 15 February 1854.

15 Shingleton, Journal aboard H.M.S. Enterprise, 15 February 1854.

16 Shingleton, Journal aboard H.M.S. Enterprise, 13 March 1854.

17 Shingleton, Journal aboard H.M.S. Enterprise, 24 March 1854.

18 Shingleton, Journal aboard H.M.S. Enterprise, 27 March 1854.

19 Shingleton, Journal aboard H.M.S. Enterprise, 14 March 1854.

20 Shingleton, Journal aboard H.M.S. Enterprise, 25 March 1854.

21 Collinson, *Journal of the H.M.S. Enterprise*, 312.

22 Collinson, *Journal of the H.M.S. Enterprise*, 314.

23 Shingleton, Journal aboard H.M.S. Enterprise, 30 May 1854.

24 Shingleton, Journal aboard H.M.S. Enterprise, 19 June 1854.

25 Shingleton, Journal aboard H.M.S. Enterprise, 25 June 1854.

26 Collinson, *Journal of the H.M.S. Enterprise*, 315.

27 R. Collinson to Secretary to the Admiralty, 30 June 1854, Collinson's Letter Book, KML.

28 Collinson, *Journal of the H.M.S. Enterprise*, 315.

29 Shingleton, Journal aboard H.M.S. Enterprise, 2 July 1854.

30 Shingleton, Journal aboard H.M.S. Enterprise, 2 July 1854.

31 Shingleton, Journal aboard H.M.S. Enterprise, 4 July 1854.

32 R. Collinson to John Barrow Jr., 4 July 1854, Barrow Bequest, BL ADD. 35,308, f. 20.

33 Collinson, *Journal of the H.M.S. Enterprise*, 317..

Chapter 12

1   Collinson, *Journal of the H.M.S. Enterprise*, 319; Shingleton, Journal aboard H.M.S. Enterprise, 15 July 1854.

2   Collinson, *Journal of the H.M.S. Enterprise*, 320.

3   Bockstoce, *The journal of Rochfort Maguire*, 367.

4   Collinson, *Journal of the H.M.S. Enterprise*, 320–21.

5   Shingleton, Journal aboard H.M.S. Enterprise, 20 July 1854.

6   Log, H.M.S. *Enterprise*, 21 July 1854.

7   Rodgers, N. 1982. *Articles of War: The statutes which governed our fighting navies, 1661, 1749 and 1886* (Havant, Hants.: Kenneth Mason), 22.

8   R. Collinson, General Order, 22 July 1854, Collinson's Night Order Book, NMM CLS/37.

9   F. Skead to R. Collinson, 23 July 1854, Collinson's In-letter Book, NMM CLS/41.

10 Collinson, *Journal of the H.M.S. Enterprise*, 322.

11 Osborn, *The discovery of a Northwest Passage*.

12 Barr, W., ed., 1992. *A Frenchman in search of Franklin. De Bray's arctic journal, 1852–1854* (Toronto: University of Toronto Press); McDougall, G.F. 1857. *The eventful voyage of H.M. discovery ship "Resolute" to the arctic regions in search of Sir John Franklin… 1852, 1853, 1854* (London: Longman, Brown, Green, Longmans & Roberts); Osborn, *The discovery of the North-West Passage*.

13 Log, H.M.S. *Enterprise*, 21 August 1854, KML.

14 Rodgers, *Articles of War*, 26–27.

15 Rodgers, *Articles of War*, 28.

16 R. Collinson, General Order, 22 July 1854, Collinson's Night Order Book, NMM CLS/37.

17 Collinson, *Journal of the H.M.S. Enterprise*, 331.

18 The stay that holds the jib-boom down against the pull exerted by the fore topgallant-mast stays.

19 Bockstoce, *The journal of Rochfort Maguire.*

20 Shingleton, Journal aboard H.M.S. Enterprise, 13 September 1854.

21 The combination of four alphabetical flags in the International Code of Signals assigned to each ship.

22 Shingleton, Journal aboard H.M.S. Enterprise, 3 November 1854.

23 *Illustrated London News.* 1854. Arrival of the Discovery Ship "Enterprise," Captain Collinson, at Hong-Kong, *Illustrated London News*, 30 December 1854, 687.

24 Arrival of the Arctic discovery ship Enterprise, *The Times*, 7 May 1855.

25 Shingleton, Journal aboard H.M.S. Enterprise, 17 November 1855.

26 Shingleton, Journal aboard H.M.S. Enterprise, 17 November 1855.

27 Collinson, *Journal of the H.M.S. Enterprise*, 336.

28 Shingleton, Journal aboard H.M.S. Enterprise, 24 November 1854.

29 Shingleton, Journal aboard H.M.S. Enterprise, 29 November 1854.

30 R. Collinson, General Order, 28 November 1854, Collinson's Night Order Book, NMM CLS/37.

31 E. Adams to R. Collinson, 28 November 1854, Collinson's In-letter Book, NMM CLS/41.

32 R. Collinson to E. Adams, November 1854, Collinson's Letter Book, KML.

33 E. Adams to R. Collinson, 30 November 1854, Collinson's In-letter Book, NMM CLS/41.

34 Collinson, *Journal of the H.M.S. Enterprise*, 337n.36.

35 R. Collinson, General Order, 19 December 1854, Collinson's Night Order Book, NMM CLS/37.

36 G.A. Phayre to R. Collinson, 19 December 1854, Collinson's In-letter Book. NMM CLS/41.

37 Shingleton, Journal aboard H.M.S. Enterprise, 26 December 1854.

38 Shingleton, Journal aboard H.M.S. Enterprise, 14 January 1855.

39 Collinson, *Journal of the H.M.S. Enterprise*, 338.

40 Shingleton, Journal aboard H.M.S. Enterprise, 16 January 1855.

41 Collinson, *Journal of the H.M.S. Enterprise*, 338.

42 Rich, John Rae's correspondence; Richards, R.L. 1985. Dr. John Rae (Whitby: Caedmon); McGoogan, K. 2001. *Fatal Passage: The Untold Story of John Rae, the Arctic Adventurer who Discovered the Fate of Franklin* (Toronto: Harper/Flamingo Canada).

43   Shingleton, Journal aboard H.M.S. Enterprise, 11 February 1855.

44   Shingleton, Journal aboard H.M.S. Enterprise, 25 February 1855.

45   Shingleton, Journal aboard H.M.S. Enterprise, 3 March 1855.

46   Shingleton, Journal aboard H.M.S. Enterprise, 4 March 1855.

Chapter 13

1   Barrow, J.M. [Note on articles brought home by Captain Collinson in June 1855],
     PRO ADM 1/5658, Yards.

2   W.M. Rice and C.S. Martin to W.M. Wigham, 2 July 1855. PRO, ADM 1/5658 Yards.

3   W.M. Rice and C.S. Martin to W.M. Wigham, 2 July 1855. PRO, ADM 1/5658 Yards.

4   Great Britain. Parliament. *Further papers*, 947.

5   Arrival of the Arctic discovery ship Enterprise, *The Times*, 7 May 1855.

6   *The Times*. 1855. Naval and military intelligence, *The Times*, 14 May 1855.

7   *Illustrated London News*. 1855. Naval and military intelligence, *Illustrated London News*,
     26 May 1855, 510.

8   For example: *The Times*. 1854a. The late arctic expedition, 18 October, 8; 1854b.
     The arctic voyagers, 20 October, 10.

9   Collinson, *Journal of the H.M.S. Enterprise*, 402.

10   Collinson, *Journal of the H.M.S. Enterprise*, 403.

11   Skead, Annotations, 403–04.

12   Amundsen, R. 1908. *The North West Passage; being the record of a voyage of exploration
     of the ship Gjøa 1903–07*, 2 vols. (London: Constable), 2:105.

13   Amundsen, *The North West Passage*, 121.

14   Neatby, L.H. 1970. *The search for Franklin* (Edmonton: M.G. Hurtig), 225–26.

15   Sharpe, Personal Journal.

16   Holland, C.A. 1982. Collinson, Sir Richard. In: *Dictionary of Canadian Biography, Vol. XI,
     1881–1890* (Toronto: University of Toronto Press), 19–201.

17   Berton, P. 1988. *The arctic grail. The quest for the North West Passage and he North Pole
     1818–1909* (Toronto: McClelland and Stewart), 295–96.

18   Berton, *The arctic grail*, 296.

19   See Ch. 2, p.22–23.

20   See p.207.

21 Collinson, R. 1855. Printed memotrandum to the Chairman of the Committee of the Honourable the House of Commons on the Arctic Expedition (Cameron Treleaven's Collection).

22 Great Britain. Parliament. 1855b. *Report of the Select Committee on Arctic Expedition; together with the proceedings of the Committee, minutes of evidence, and appendix. Ordered by the House of Commons to be printed, 20 July 1855.* House of Commons, Sessional Papers, Reports from committees, 1854–55, vol. 7. no. 409, p. vi–vii.

23 Collinson *Journal of the H.M.S. Enterprise*, 347.

24 Collinson, R., editor. 1867. *The three voyages of Martin Frobisher, in search of a passage to Cathaia and India by the north-west, A.D. 1576-8* (London: Hakluyt Society).

25 Holland, C. 1982. Collinson, Sir Richard. In: *Dictionary of Canadian Biography*, vol. XI, 1881 to 1890 (Toronto: University of Toronto Press).

26 Anonymous. 1883. Obituary: Vice-Admiral Sir Richard Collinson, KCB, *Royal Geographical Society Proceedings*, New Series 5:606-09.

27 Collinson, *Journal of the H.M.S. Enterprise*, 403.

28 Markham, C.R. 1875. *The Arctic Navy List; or, A century of Arctic & Antarctic officers 1773-1873* (London: Griffin & Co.) (repr. 1992. The Royal Naval Museum and Dallington, Portsmouth: The Naval & Military Press), 49.

29 Markham, *The Arctic Navy List*, 42.

30 Markham, *The Arctic Navy List*, 26.

31 Markham, *The Arctic Navy List*, 40.16 Holland, C. A. 1982. Collinson, Sir Richard. In: *Dictionary of Canadian Biography*, Vol. XI, 1881–1890. Toronto: University of Toronto Press, pp. 19–201.

17 Berton, P. 1988. *The arctic grail. The quest for the North West Passage and he North Pole 1818–1900.* Toronto: McClelland and Stewart, pp. 295–6.

18 Ibid, p. 296.

19 See Ch. 2, pp. 24–25.

20 See p. 207.

21 Collinson, R. 1855. Printed memotrandum to the Chairman of the Committee of the Honourable the House of Commons on the Arctic Expedition (Cameron Treleaven's Collection.

22 Great Britain. Parliament. 1855. *Report of the Select Committee on Arctic Expedition; together with the proceedings of the Committee, minutes of evidence, and appendix. Ordered by the House of Commons to be printed, 20 July 1855.* House of Commons. Sessional Papers, Reports from committees, 1854–55, vol. 7. no. 409, pp. vi–vii.

23 Collinson *Journal...*, p. 347.

24 Collinson, R., editor. 1867. *The three voyages of Martin Frobisher, in search of a passage to Cathaia and India by the north-west, A.D. 1576-8*. London: Hakluyt Society.

25 Holland, C. 1982. Collinson, Sir Richard. In: *Dictionary of Canadian Biography*, Vol. XI, 1881 to 1890. Toronto: University of Toronto Press.

26 Anonymous. 1883. Obituary: Vice-Admiral Sir Richard Collinson, KCB, *Royal Geographical Society Proceedings*, New Series 5: 606-9.

27 Collinson, *Journal...*,p. 403.

Markham, C.R. 1875. *The Arctic Navy List; or, A century of Arctic & Antarctic officers 1773-1873*. London: Griffin & Co. (reprint edition: Portsmouth: The Royal Naval Museum and Dallington: The Naval & Military Press), p. 49.

28 Ibid, p. 42.

29 Ibid, p. 26.

30 Ibid, p. 40.

ABBREVIATIONS OF NAMES
OF REPOSITORIES

BL: British Library, London.

KML: Karpeles Manuscript Library, Santa Barbara CA.

NMM: National Maritime Museum, Greenwich, London.

PRO: Public Record Office, Kew, London.

SPRI: Scott Polar Research Institute, Cambridge.

VMM: Vancouver Maritime Museum, Vancouver BC.

BIBLIOGRAPHY

Adams, E. 1850–51. Journal kept ashore in and near St. Michael's Alaska. SPRI, MS 1115.

Amundsen, R. 1908. *The North West Passage; being the record of a voyage of exploration of the ship Gjøa 1903–07*. London: Constable.

Anonymous. 1883. Obituary: Vice-Admiral Sir Richard Collinson, KCB. *Royal Geographical Society Proceedings*. New Series 5:606–09.

Armstrong, A. 1857. *A personal narrative of the discovery of the North-West Passage with numerous incidents of travel and adventure*. London: Hurst and Blackett.

Barr, W., trans. and ed. 1992. *A Frenchman in Search of Franklin. De Bray's arctic journal, 1852–1854*. Toronto: University of Toronto Press.

Barr, W., ed. 2002. *From Barrow to Boothia: The Arctic Journal of Chief Factor Peter Warren Dease 1836–1839*. Montreal and Kingston: McGill-Queen's University Press.

Barrow, J.M. 1855. [Note on articles brought home by Captain Collinson in June 1855] PRO ADM 1/5658, Yards.

Bartlett, R.A., and R.T. Hale. 1916. *Northward ho! The Last Voyage of the Karluk*. Boston: Small, Maynard and Co.

Beechey, F.W. 1831/1968. *Narrative of a voyage to the Pacific and Beering's Straits to co-operate with the polar expedition*. 2 vols. London: Henry Colburn & Richard Bentley. Repr. Amsterdam & New York: N. Israel & Da Capo Press.

Berton, P. 1988. *The Arctic Grail: The Quest for the North West Passage and the North Pole 1818–1909*. Toronto: McClelland and Stewart.

Bockstoce, J. 1986. *Whales, Ice, and Men: The History of Whaling in the Western Arctic.* Seattle and London: University of Washington Press.

———, ed. 1988. *The Journal of Rochfort Maguire 1852–1854.* London: The Hakluyt Society.

Collinson, R., ed. 1867. *The three voyages of Martin Frobisher, in search of a passage to Cathaia and India by the northwest, A.D. 1576–78.* London: Hakluyt Society.

———. 1889/1976. *Journal of H.M.S. Enterprise on the expedition in search of Sir John Franklin's ships by Behring Strait 1850–55.* London: Sampson Low, Marston, Searle and Rivington. Repr. New York: AMS Press.

Condon, R.G. 1996. *The Northern Copper Inuit: A History.* Toronto: University of Toronto Press.

Cook, J., and J. King. 1785. *A voyage to the Pacific Ocean: Undertaken by command of His Majesty, for making discoveries in the northern hemisphere... in the years 1776, 1777, 1778, 1779 and 1780.* 3 vols. London: G. Nicol and T. Cadell.

Cyriax, R.J. 1939. *Sir John Franklin's Last Expedition: A Chapter in the History of the Royal Navy.* London: Methuen.

Damas, D. 1984. Copper Eskimo. In *Handbook of North American Indians, Vol. 5. Arctic.* Ed. D. Damas. Washington DC: Smithsonian Institution.

Dodge, E. 1973. *The Polar Rosses: John and James Clark Ross and their Explorations.* London: Faber & Faber.

Edinger, R. 2003. *Fury Beach: The Four-year Odyssey of Captain John Ross and the* Victory. New York: Berkley Books.

Franklin, J. 1823. *Narrative of a journey to the shores of the polar sea, in the years 1819, 20, 21 and 22.* London: John Murray.

———. 1828. *Narrative of a second expedition to the shores of the polar sea, in the years 1825, 1826, and 1827.* London: John Murray.

Gill, H.B., & J. Young, eds. 1998. *Seaching for the Franklin Expedition: The Arctic Journal of Robert Randolph Carter.* Annapolis: Naval Institute Press.

Gilpin, J.D. 1850. Outline of the voyage of H.M.S. *Enterprise* and *Investigator* to Barrow Strait in search of Sir John Franklin. *Nautical Magazine* 19(1): 8–9; 19(2): 89–90; 19(3):160–170; 19(4): 230.

Gough, B., ed. 1973. *To the Pacific and Arctic with Beechey: The Journal of Lieutenant George Pead of H.M.S. 'Blossom' 1825–1828.* Cambridge: Cambridge University Press for the Hakluyt Society.

Great Britain. Parliament. 1850. *Arctic expedition. Return to an order of the Honourable the House of Commons dated 5 February 1850, etc.* House of Commons. Sessional Papers. Accounts and Papers 1850. vol. 35, no. 107, p. 89–90.

———. 1851. *Return to an address of the Honourable the House of Commons dated 7 February 1851… Ordered by the House of Commons to be printed, 7 March 1851*. House of Commons. Sessional Papers. Accounts and Papers, 1851. vol. 33, no. 97.

———. 1855a. *Further papers relative to the recent Arctic expeditions in search of Sir John Franklin and the crews of H.M.S. "Erebus" and "Terror."* London: Eyre and Spottiswoode.

———. 1855b. *Report of the Select Committee on Arctic Expedition; together with the proceedings of the Committee, minutes of evidence and appendix. Ordered by the House of Commons to be printed, 20 July 1855*. House of Commons. Sessional Papers. Accounts and Papers, 1854–55. vol. 7, no. 409.

Holland, C.A. 1982. "Collinson, Sir Richard." In *Dictionary of Canadian Biography, Vol. XI, 1881–1890*. Toronto: University of Toronto Press.

Hooper, W.H. 1853. *Ten months among the tents of the Tuski, with incidents of an arctic boat expedition in search of Sir John Franklin….* London: John Murray.

Illustrated London News. 1854. Arrival of the Discovery Ship 'Enterprise,' Captain Collinson, at Hong-Kong. *Illustrated London News*, 30 December 1854, 687.

———. 1855. Naval and military intelligence. *Illustrated London News*, 26 May 1855, 510.

Jones, A.G.E. 1958. Robert Shedden and the Nancy Dawson. *Mariner's Mirror* 44(2):137–39.

———. 1969. Captain Robert Martin: A Peterhead Whaling Master in the 19th Century. *Scottish Geographical Magazine* 85(3):196–202.

Kane, E.K. 1854. *The U.S. Grinnell expedition in search of Sir John Franklin: a personal narrative.* London: Sampson Low, Son & Co.

McClintock, F.L. 1859. *The voyage of the "Fox" in the Arctic seas.* London: John Murray.

McDougall, G.F. 1857. *The eventful voyage of H.M. discovery ship "Resolute" to the Arctic regions in search of Sir John Franklin…. 1852, 1853, 1854.* London: Longman, Brown, Green, Longmans & Roberts.

McGoogan, K. 2001. *Fatal Passage: The Untold Story of John Rae, the Arctic Adventurer who Discovered the Fate of Franklin.* Toronto: Harper/Flamingo Canada.

McKenzie, W.G. 1975. The identity of Gateshead Island. *Polar Record* 17(110):545–59.

Markham, C.R. 1875/1992. *The Arctic Navy List; or, A century of Arctic & Antarctic officers, 1773–1873.* London: Griffin & Co. Repr. The Royal Naval Museum and Dallington, Portsmouth: The Naval Military Press.

Mathews, W.H., and A.M. Bustin. 1984. Why do the Smoking Hills Smoke? *Canadian Journal of Earth Sciences* 21(7):737–42.

Neatby, L.H. 1967. *Frozen Ships. The Arctic Diary of Johann Miertsching 1850–1854.* Toronto: Macmillan.

———. 1970. *The Search for Franklin.* Edmonton: M.G. Hurtig.

Osborn, S. 1852. *Stray leaves from an arctic journal; or, eighteen months in the polar regions, in search of Sir John Franklin's expedition, in the years 185–51*. London: Longman, Brown, Green and Longmans.

————, ed. 1856. *The discovery of the North-West Passage by H.M.S. "Investigator", Capt. R. M'Clure, 1850, 1851, 1852, 1853, 1854*. London: Longman, Brown, Green, Longmans & Roberts.

Parry, W.E. 1821. *Journal of a voyage for the discovery of a North-West Passage from the Atlantic to the Pacific*. London: John Murray.

————. 1824. *Journal of a second voyage for the discovery of a North-West Passage from the Atlantic to the Pacific*. London: John Murray.

Pierce, R.A. 1990. *Russian America: A Biographical Dictionary* (Alaskan History, No. 33). Kingston ON and Fairbanks AK: The Limestone Press.

Pullen, H.F., ed. 1979. *The Pullen Expedition in Search of Sir John Franklin*. Toronto: Arctic History Press.

Rae, J. 1852. Recent explorations along the south and east coast of Victoria Land. *Royal Geographical Society Journal* 33:82–96.

Rice, W.M., and C.S. Martin. 1855. Letter to W.M. Wigham, 2 July 1855. PRO, ADM 1/5658 Yards.

Rich, E.E. 1953. *John Rae's Correspondence with the Hudson's Bay Company on Arctic Exploration 1844–1855*. London: Hudson Bay Record Society.

Richards, R.L. 1985. *Dr. John Rae*. Whitby, Yorkshire: Caedmon of Whitby.

Richardson, J. 1851. *Arctic searching expedition: a journal of a boat-voyage through Rupert's Land and the Arctic Sea, in search of the discovery ships under command of Sir John Franklin*. 2 vols. London: Longman, Brown, Green and Longmans.

Rodgers, N. 1982. *Articles of War: The Statutes which Governed our Fighting Navies, 1661, 1749 and 1886*. Havant, Hants.: Kenneth Mason.

Ross, J. 1835. *Narrative of a second voyage in search of a North-West Passage, and of a residence in the Arctic regions during the years 1829, 1830, 1831, 1832, 1833*. London: A.W. Webster.

Ross, M.J. 1994. *Polar Pioneers: John Ross and James Clark Ross*. Montreal & Kingston: McGill-Queen's University Press.

Seemann, B. 1853. *Narrative of the voyage of H.M.S. "Herald" during the years 1845–51, under the command of Captain Henry Kellett, R.N., C.B.* 2 vols. London: Reeve & Co.

Sharpe, P.R. 1854–55. Personal journal, H.M.S. Rattlesnake. Vol. 2. 26 Feb–23 December 1855. NMM SHP/4.

Shingleton, R. 1852–55. Journal aboard H.M.S. Enterprise, cont'd. 3 November 1854. VMM Lar G665 1852 C6.

Simpson, T. 1843. *Narrative of the discoveries on the north coast of America; effected by the officers of the Hudson's Bay Company during the years 1836–39.* London: Richard Bentley.

Skead, F. 1850–54. Private journal, H.M. Ship Enterprise. SPRI, MS 1161.

——— . n.d. Annotations to Skead's copy of Collinson, T.B., ed. 1889. *Journal of H.M.S. Enterprise on the expedition in search of Sir John Franklin's ships by Behring Strait 1850–55 by Captain Richard Collinson, C.B., R.N., commander of the expedition.* London: Sampson Low, Marston, Searle & Rivington. Held at SPRI.

Snow, W.P. 1851. *Voyage of the "Prince Albert" in search of Sir John Franklin; a narrative of every-day life in the Arctic seas.* London: Longman, Brown, Green & Longmans.

Stefansson, V. 1913. *My Life with the Eskimo.* New York: Macmillan.

Sutherland, P.C. 1852. *Journal of a voyage in Baffin's Bay and Barrow Straits, in the years 1850–51, performed by H.M. Ships "Lady Franklin" and "Sophia", under the command of Mr. William Penny, in search of the missing crews of H.M. Ships Erebus and Terror.* 2 vols. London: Longman, Brown, Green and Longmans.

The Times. 1854a. The late arctic expedition. *The Times,* 18 October 1854, 8.

——— . 1854b. The arctic voyagers. *The Times,* 20 October 1854, 10.

——— . 1855a. Arrival of the Arctic discovery ship Enterprise. *The Times,* 7 May 1855.

——— . 1855b. Naval and military intelligence. *The Times,* 14 May 1855.

Wilson, C. 1955. Footnotes to the Franklin Search. Pt. 1. Halkett's air boat. *The Beaver* 285(1): 46–48.

Wilson, M.R. 1973. Sir John Ross's Last Expedition, in Search of Sir John Franklin. *The Musk-Ox* 13:5–11.

INDEX